Lawyers

Lawyers

JACK BATTEN

MACMILLAN OF CANADA
A DIVISION OF GAGE PUBLISHING LIMITED
TORONTO, CANADA

Macmillan of Canada
A Division of Gage Publishing Limited

Printed in Canada

Canadian Cataloguing in Publication Data

Batten, Jack, 1932-
    Lawyers

ISBN 0-7715-9568-9

1. Law—Anecdotes, facetiae, satire, etc.
2. Lawyers—Canada. I. Title.

PN6268.L4B37   340'.02'07   C80-094368-6

For Bob Fulford
in gratitude and friendship

Contents

I WISH TO ACKNOWLEDGE WITH MY THANKS
THE INDISPENSABLE FINANCIAL ASSISTANCE
FROM THE CANADA COUNCIL AND
THE ONTARIO ARTS COUNCIL.

Lawyers

Prologue: My Legal Career

The first time I appeared in court as a lawyer, my client was up on a charge of indecent exposure. He was a short, fat young man and had a face that sent out waves of despair. The facts were simple. And damning. He'd had a few beers with his buddies after work and was driving home alone when he noticed a girl, also alone, walking on a dark residential street. He parked his car several yards ahead of her, stood on the sidewalk with his pants unzipped, and, as she drew near, asked, "Do you wanna?"

She didn't.

She ran home and told her father, who returned to the scene of the proposition. My short, fat, sad client had remained in place. His pants had remained unzipped. The father summoned the cops and they hustled my client to jail.

"I'm guilty," he told me when I turned up in the police cells the next day. His mother had retained me early that morning.

"Well, wait a minute," I said.

"No, no. I don't know what came over me. I deserve what I get."

"Maybe you won't get anything if you listen to me. I'll ask for a remand and work out strategy. That's what your mother's paying me for. We'll plead a blackout or something. Drunkenness. Temporary insanity."

1

"I'm so ashamed," he said, his eyes watering. "I undid my fly in front of that girl. I pulled out my...I mean, I exposed myself. I'm disgusting."

"Well, if you put it that way."

The case lasted five and a half minutes. A policeman recited the facts. I called the mother as a character witness, and she told the court her son was a good boy who stayed home most nights playing pinochle with his father. As far as she knew, he'd never unzipped himself except in the privacy of the family bathroom. The magistrate fined my client two hundred dollars, and the last I saw of him, his face a portrait of remorse, he was in the gentle clutches of a Salvation Army officer who felt spiritual guidance was in order. I didn't have the heart to send his mother a bill for my services.

That's how my legal career proceeded. It was not so much disastrous as unfortunate. I was called to the Ontario bar in 1959 and practised in a Toronto firm that was downtown, medium-sized, and—apart from such exceptional clients as the flasher—respectable. I handled mechanics'-liens actions and mortgage foreclosures, drew deeds and probated wills, collected unpaid accounts for a ready-mixed-concrete company, and put together articles of incorporation for small-business men. I did not distinguish myself and seemed headed for neither disbarment nor the annual list of Queen's Counsel published each New Year's Day morning in the *Globe and Mail*. Clearly something about the practice of law escaped me, and in September 1963 I left the profession to make my way in the world by writing magazine articles, newspaper features, and non-fiction books.

On November 26, 1977, I was back in the same courtroom where I'd appeared so ineffectually on behalf of the fat young man. This time I was a witness at a preliminary hearing and, once again, not in sparkling form. The accused person in the case was the stuff of headlines, Keith Richards, guitarist and founding member of the Rolling

Stones rock group. RCMP narcotics agents had arrested Richards at the Harbour Castle Hilton Hotel in Toronto and charged him with possession of heroin for the purposes of trafficking, an offence that's good for life imprisonment. Richards' lawyer, a leading member of the Canadian criminal bar named Austin Cooper, wanted to demonstrate to the judge that, while his client had been addicted to heroin, he was also gifted, famed, and wealthy and therefore had no financial need to traffic in the junk. Cooper asked me to provide the testimony about Richards' gifts, fame, and wealth.

I had the qualifications. For five ear-wrenching years in the late 1960s and early '70s, writing in the *Toronto Star* and later the *Globe and Mail*, I had reviewed the rock bands that passed through Toronto on concert tours and nightclub engagements. Cooper thought the combination of lawyer and rock reviewer, admittedly unique, would impress the judge. Maybe it did. My verbal dexterity as a witness undoubtedly didn't.

Cooper, on examination-in-chief: "How long have the Stones been productive and functioning as a group?"

Batten: "That's probably one of the most remarkable things about them and about Mr. Richards is that rock and roll is sort of a bit of fly-by-night business and as I observed in all those years of reviewing bands who got to be a sensation one week and then vanished the next week, but the Rolling Stones, unlike so many others, are still with us and still regarded as the very best today after sixteen, seventeen years."

The court reporter's transcript, as this passage indicates, made me sound approximately as articulate on the witness stand as the Watergate tapes showed Richard Nixon to be in the Oval Office. Still, Keith Richards' day in court had beneficial consequences for me as well as for him. He was eventually found guilty on a lesser offence of simple posses-

sion of heroin, and as punishment — a mere tap on the wrist
— he was directed to perform a benefit concert in aid of the
Canadian National Institute for the Blind, which was apparently the judge's favourite charity. Richards was grateful
to the court. So, in a different way, was I.

The Richards trial influenced me to rethink my outlook
on the legal profession. I admired Austin Cooper's conduct
in court. He pointed out to the judge in a low-key and
thorough closing argument that Richards had cured himself of his drug addiction. He had endured torment. Now
he was clean and whole. What need to punish him further?
Cooper was cool and resourceful and persuasive. He
suggested to me the sort of lawyer's style I'd once imagined
for myself. I had never set my ambitions on a career as
exclusively a courtroom advocate. I would have been an
all-round practitioner: a little criminal work, some dabbling
at the higher reaches of corporate negotiations, a few more
humble services along the lines of assisting old ladies to
redraw their wills and young couples to arrange their first
house purchase. It was simply Cooper's excellence that
stirred my original feelings about the law. After all, adding
up my time in law school, in articles, and in practice, I had
devoted nine years to the profession, and even though the
law and I had proved to be an incompatible pair, I found in
me a residue of admiration for people who, like Austin
Cooper, made successes of themselves at the bar.

But where had I, in those nine years, failed to find a
connection with the law and its practice? Why hadn't I
turned out to be a reasonable facsimile of Austin Cooper?
The questions fretted me for a couple of months after the
Richards trial until, partly out of exasperation but more
from an authentic sense of curiosity about a part of my own
past (the failed part, most people would judge), I called on
Cooper and asked him a few questions about the way he
earned his living.

"You could say I'm a hired gun," he said, looking not at all like one. He's a tall, balding, benignly handsome man in his early fifties and works in an office that has a nautical flavour — models of graceful old sailing ships on display, an ancient sea lantern in one corner. "I act for people who come in here asking to be defended. It doesn't matter who they are. If I got fussy about my clients, I'd be betraying the system, do you see? We go around in this country saying we operate under a democratic process, but then we're awfully ready to lean on people we don't like, people who might somehow have done wrong, people who are nothing more than unpopular. It's the criminal lawyers — bastards like us who have independence in our bones — who stand up and say, wait a minute, every man is supposed to be entitled to his day in court."

I hadn't expected a speech on civil liberties from Cooper. Maybe I should have. His record is heavy on worthy causes. He helped establish legal aid in Ontario, a government-funded system that allows the poor to be represented in court without charge by capable counsel. He was a leader among the furious band of Toronto lawyers who succeeded in fending off ninety per cent of Justice Minister Ron Basford's proposals in 1977 to widen the police's wiretap powers. He has defended murderers, child molesters, two Philadelphia Flyers hockey players charged with assaulting a Toronto player during a National League game at Maple Leaf Gardens, and a wealthy businessman who was mixed up in a lucrative scam with some members of the harbour commission in Hamilton, Ontario. But Cooper also helped send Karleton Armstrong to prison, and that, one would suppose, represented a contradiction in Cooper's record.

"Karleton Armstrong was the man who blew up a science building on the campus of the University of Wisconsin early one morning in 1970 as a protest against the Vietnam War," Cooper explained. "One thing Armstrong didn't know, there was a man working late in the building. He died. It was murder. Armstrong hid out in Toronto, and when he

5

got caught in 1975, the State of Wisconsin retained me to act for it in extradition hearings to get Armstrong back home for a murder trial.

"Well," Cooper hesitated for a moment, putting in balance a memory that was at once proud and painful, "you have to remember the hearing took place against the background of Vietnam and all its passions. People would stand up in the spectator section of the courtroom and shake their clenched fists. They oinked at me whenever I entered the court. 'Pig! Pig!' That's what greeted me every day. Armstrong's counsel called it a political trial and Armstrong himself screamed about injustice. The hippies and the yippies had their innings."

Cooper sat very erect in the chair behind his desk. "What Armstrong and his followers didn't understand was they were setting out to destroy justice in the name of justice. They told me I should only act for a client, the State of Wisconsin in this case, if I believed in its cause. They said otherwise I was nothing better than a hired gun. To them, that was some kind of evil epithet. But they were wrong. They didn't appreciate we have a structure in our society, the court system, where both sides of the question, of the *accusation*, are argued out. If we didn't have that system, believe me, society as we know it would collapse. And what's integral to everything is people like me, lawyers who can argue the best points for whichever side retains us. It's the hired-gun concept that makes the system work."

Thirty minutes later, thirty more minutes of illustrating his thesis by reference to other cases he's handled, Cooper was showing me to the elevator when he added, almost as an afterthought, something I'd already assumed.

"I'm blessed," he said. "I like my work. I believe in it."

My uncle Reg has reached the stage in *his* legal life when he doesn't bother articulating his feelings about the practice of law. He's seventy-four years old, small and grey and tireless, senior partner in the historic Toronto firm of McLaughlin, Soward, Morden and Bales, and another logi-

6

cal person to whom I took my gathering speculations about lawyers. Reg Soward arrives at the office by ten each morning and spends the rest of the day in a sort of tear. He talks on the phone standing up. He walks his signed letters down two long corridors to the firm's mail room. He needs a guide map to the files that teeter in nervous stacks on the desk, chairs, couch, and regions of the carpet in his spacious office. Uncle Reg would say he, too, loves the law, but he never pauses long enough to consider such emotional issues.

"I was called to the bar in the worst of all years, 1931," he told me one noon hour at his club, the Albany, on King Street East in Toronto. As we talked, Senator David Walker, Minister of Public Works in a Diefenbaker Cabinet, sat across the room from us, and Allan Lawrence, Joe Clark's Solicitor General, held forth in another corner. The Albany is commonly referred to as a Tory bastion.

"The depression was on," Uncle Reg continued, "and it hit lawyers as hard as anyone. Right after my call, I got married and left for my honeymoon on the assumption that the McLaughlin firm was paying me $1,800 a year. I came back to find they'd cut me to $1,500, all they could afford."

Uncle Reg used to spend two nights a week sitting in a small real-estate office, picking up crumbs. "Fifty cents for swearing an affidavit." And he became a joiner. "I enrolled in the Independent Order of Foresters, a fraternal lodge rather low on the scale of things. It wasn't my cup of tea, but I had to do it. Some of the people I met there are still my clients today."

Uncle Reg stuck with the McLaughlins through the decades, acquiring clientele and responsibilities, dealing mostly in real-estate work, mortgages, wills, and estates. He became the firm's senior partner in the late 1960s, and in later years he's spent much of his time calculating the technical details of the enormous loans on shopping plazas that the Sun Life Assurance Company grants to Cadillac Fairview Corporation, a mighty development conglomerate.

It's intricate and exacting work, checking the small print that, unattended to, might erupt in legal grief some years further on. Uncle Reg's career, it was clear to me, offered a lesson in thrift, hard work, and integrity, all the more worthy, I congratulated myself, because it came from a man whose genes I shared. But I waited for something more in our conversation, some sense of the satisfaction in the practice of law. It arrived in a casual anecdote.

"I had a phone call from a lawyer over in Hamilton this week," Uncle Reg said. "He's acting for a man's estate and he said the widow wanted to come to me for some advice. She was gonna follow whatever suggestion I gave her. All right, I said, but I couldn't see the point of travelling here when there are perfectly able lawyers in her own city. Well, it turned out the dead man had told his wife I was the only lawyer he'd ever encountered whom he considered trustworthy. It was true I'd had some correspondence with the man a long time ago. I remembered that. It lasted about two years and it had to do with the mortgage on his house. But the fact is I never set eyes on the man, never met him in the flesh in my life."

Uncle Reg gathered his briefcase from the side of the table, preparing to leave. "Clients like to know that a lawyer cares about them, and I guess the man from Hamilton found something of that in my ordinary letters about his mortgage."

On this final word, Uncle Reg set off at his customary bustle on the return walk to the office.

Ross McKay came next. I caught up with him, my old high-school classmate, as he was delivering his final pitch to the jury on behalf of an accused murderer in a trial at the Toronto Courthouse on University Avenue.

"Tony Genovese," Ross was saying, "is an outlaw and in some ways he walks to a different beat, but he's entitled to the same consideration as the rest of us, because if justice doesn't work for Tony Genovese, it won't work for the rest of us."

Genovese was no angel. He'd had a hand, usually with a gun in it, in thirty-five armed robberies across North America, and he spread the loot around on hotel suites and chauffeured limousines. The last time out, the case that brought Ross McKay into court as his defence counsel, Genovese was accused of organizing and driving the get-away car in a $46,000 robbery of a Hudson's Bay store in Toronto. One of Genovese's stick-up partners shot a clerk who got in the way. Genovese stood trial for murder, and before the case went to the jury the trial lasted seventy-six days, the longest in Canadian judicial history.

"Worst thing a case like this does," McKay said, "is wreak havoc with the rest of your practice."

Ross was the kid in our high-school class who was always being summoned to the principal's office. He was an intelligent student, but he couldn't resist trouble. Later, after law school, he was chosen to article with Arthur Martin, an honour since Martin reigned as the dean of Canadian criminal lawyers. Ross's own criminal practice started promisingly, but a private demon haunted him. He boozed away years and opportunities. By the early 1970s he had his act back together. He was in Alcoholics Anonymous and in his own one-man criminal office.

"The way he's been the last few years," another criminal lawyer told me, "Ross McKay is the best there is in any court on any day at cross-examination."

Cross-examination, I knew, was special. Professor John Henry Wigmore, author of the last word on the subject, a weighty tome called *Wigmore on Evidence*, described it as "beyond doubt the greatest legal engine ever invented for the discovery of truth".

Ross and I went out for a coffee to talk about his special craft. He had the same hip insouciance that I remembered from high school. He was always a jazz fan, always walked as if he were silently snapping his fingers to a tricky five-four rhythm, and he hadn't lost the style. His face, though, wore an attractively ravaged look. These days, Ross was type-cast for the kind of movie roles Robert Ryan used to play. He ordered coffee, lit up a slim black cigarillo, and offered a few maxims on the hard art of cross-examination.

"The key is to be in command as between yourself and the witness without making the jury think you're a bully," he began. "You operate on instinct and experience. When you're cross-examining one witness, you have to be thinking of what the witness two or three down the line is going to say. You're creating a mosaic, you follow me, when you cross-examine. If you hammer at one witness and destroy him but you let the others get off easy, then your mosaic is broken up. You want everything the witnesses say in answer to your questions to add up to a certain sum. Then, when you finally address the jury you can say, look, here's the total of all the answers. How can you convict my client on such small and uncertain evidence?"

Ross puffed on his cigarillo. "You learn plenty of techniques. On examination-in-chief—here's an example: a witness follows the crown's questions and gives his testimony in a certain order, ABCDE. Most lawyers, when they cross-examine, go down things in the same order, ABCDE. That's not smart. The witness is confident. He sees no surprises. So what I do, I usually start with D or E. It gets the witness off balance at the beginning, especially if D is his weakest point. It unsettles him for the rest of the cross-examination."

Ross was warming to the subject. He could write a Ph.D. on cross-examination. He took pleasure in his expertise. "Don't press insignificant matters of credibility. If a witness is out on his timing of some incident by ten minutes, don't pound hell out of him unless something important turns on it. Otherwise you lose the jury's sympathy. But *cops*! You get a real confrontation when you cross-examine cops. They aren't content to say what they saw and heard. They're like mini-prosecutors and they'll never admit a mistake. With them you goad a little. Very subtly. You go over times and places with them from a bunch of different angles. You ask to look at what they've written in their notebooks. Eventually they get mad. You've been calm all the time. The jury

10

hasn't seen any temper from you. No raising of the voice. But when the cop gets mad, you can feel the jury giving you a silent signal, okay, cut loose on this guy. So you stay on top of the cop till you've got the testimony you need."

It was exciting to absorb Ross's knowledge and flair. Listening to him, I was getting a handle at one remove on a basic part of one kind of lawyer's equipment. Yeah, I thought, *this* is how criminal lawyers function.

"I have a bit of a reputation in identification cases," Ross went on. "You know, leaving doubt in a jury's mind that the witness really saw the person he swears he saw. I defended a black guy once, charged with forging a cheque. I couldn't call him to the stand because he had a record for forgery. So I worked on the bank teller who was the main witness against my man. The teller started off by saying the man who brought the forged cheque into the bank, the guy the teller waited on, was a Negro.

" 'Well, what do you mean by Negro?' I asked. 'Describe him. Did he have thick lips?'

" 'Yes,' the teller said. 'Thick lips.'

" 'Was his nose fleshy, more fleshy than yours or mine?'

" 'Yes, it was fleshy, the nose.'

"All the questions I asked were designed to evoke the cliché of the Negro. But actually my guy had very fine features. He looked more white than Negro except for the colour of his skin.

" 'This man,' the teller finally said after I'd been questioning him for a while, 'the man who came into the bank, looked like Sammy Davis Jr.'

"That was perfect. Nobody is more of a cliché black man than Sammy Davis Jr. At the noon recess I send my guy and his father out to bring me back pictures of Sammy Davis. They collected four or five covers from record albums. But all of them had been doctored by the cover artist to make Davis look smooth and Caucasian just like my guy.

" 'Jesus,' I said. 'Get those albums out of sight before the jury sees them.'

"I couldn't use the pictures, but when it came time to

11

address the jury, I said, 'Does the accused man look like Sammy Davis Jr.? Isn't Sammy Davis — a wonderful entertainer by the way — isn't he the fellow with the thick nose, the one eye, the fat lips? But does that describe the man you see in the prisoner's dock? Isn't it just possible the bank teller, in all sincerity, thinks most Negroes look alike? Has he really made a positive identification of the accused?'

"My guy was acquitted."

Ross stubbed out the cigarillo and went back to the courthouse. The Genovese jury had deliberated for twenty-three hours over three days, and when they returned to the courtroom they found Ross's client guilty of second-degree murder. The judge put Genovese away for twenty years.

"Well, I think my cross-examinations may have raised a few doubts," Ross said. "Without them, the jury wouldn't have had to leave the box to make up its mind."

He lit another cigarillo, his constant companion, and left to straighten out the chaos of the rest of his practice.

Ross had given me one peek inside the profession. From him I picked up a few of the mechanics of a criminal lawyer's craft. From Uncle Reg I gathered lessons about a lawyer's scruples and satisfactions. Austin Cooper had illuminated a corner of the ethical world of lawyers.

"Poke around some more," Cooper had told me. "Maybe you'll find out what you missed when you were in the profession."

I was on my way. I'd talk to more lawyers. I'd record them in action. All sorts of lawyers. Litigation lawyers and corporate lawyers. Lawyers in arcane fields. Lawyers who practise in the country and lawyers who operate out of the top floors at First Canadian Place in Toronto. Lawyers on the Prairies. Lawyers in the Arctic. Lawyers, lawyers. I'd look them up and, most of all, I'd listen to their voices.

"Lawyers always talk about the law," the lawyer-narrator says in a 1977 American novel called *The Associates*. "It's as if the law is a script with too many lines, requiring constant rehearsal."

12

That was good enough for me. If story-telling goes with the territory, I was willing to listen. Maybe along the way I'd make the connection I failed to find years earlier with the law and its practice. Maybe I'd discover where the dream had vanished, the one that had cast me as an all-round practitioner.

First Adjournment

The Bell Arena in suburban Ottawa, Ed Ratushny's first stop on this late-December Sunday afternoon, stank of ammonia, frozen sweat, and stale popcorn. Ratushny didn't mind. He's used to the smell. He coaches the Johnson Controls hockey team through two or three games and at least one practice every week, and on this Sunday he had a laugher, 10-0 for Johnson Controls. Danny Ratushny, right defence and assistant captain, scored two goals. Danny is Ed's son. He's ten years old, and the Johnson team competes in one of Ottawa's atom leagues.

"Way to play, you guys," Ratushny told his kids in the dressing-room after the game. "Just like *les Canadiens*. Good positional hockey wins every time."

The team went into its chant.

"Go Controls!" the boys shouted, their soprano voices ricocheting off the walls of the tiny room.

Ratushny left and drove to a small, neighbourly Italian restaurant in downtown Ottawa. It was time to eat and to talk about a revolution in the Canadian judicial system that Ratushny took part in through the mid-1970s.

He's a solidly built, generous man in his late thirties, and he teaches law at the University of Ottawa. He grew up in Saskatchewan, the son of a small-town barber, and took his LL.B. at the University of Saskatchewan when Otto Lang was dean of the law school. Ratushny was teaching at the University of Windsor's law school in the summer of 1973 when Lang, by then a Member of Parliament and Minister of Justice, summoned him to Ottawa. For the next three and a half years, first under Lang and later under his successor, Ron Basford, Ratushny's title was Special Advisor to the Minister of Justice. His mandate was to scout the country for lawyers worthy to be appointed to the provincial supreme courts, the county courts, and the Supreme Court of Canada.

"Up till then we had a tradition in Canada since Confederation of strictly partisan political appointments," Ratushny said, talking through a meal of deep-fried zucchini, stuffed veal, and red wine. "The way it works is that the Minister of Justice recommends the people he thinks should fill vacancies on the bench and the Cabinet gives the final formal okay. Well, the Minister of Justice used to be at the mercy of his Cabinet colleagues. Maybe there'd be a vacancy on the New Brunswick Court of Appeal. So the Minister of Justice would ask someone in the Cabinet from New Brunswick to suggest a good lawyer in the province to fill the job. Chances were the New Brunswick minister wasn't a lawyer himself and the only lawyer he knew was someone who'd raised a lot of money for his last campaign. This guy might have spent his whole career handling nothing more demanding than real-estate transactions, and yet, through all the wrong political circumstances, he'd end up on the provincial court of appeal."

The beginning of change came during Pierre Trudeau's brief tenure as Minister of Justice. He submitted prospective appointees' names to the Canadian Bar Association for critiques. John Turner, when the justice portfolio fell to him, moved a step further by phoning around the country to canvas opinion before he named a man or woman to the bench. Otto Lang represented the definitive breakthrough. He hired Ratushny and brought a system, non-political and scrupulous, to the appointment process.

15

"We used to get names at the ministry," Ratushny said. "Lawyers and judges would write us suggesting people to fill vacancies on different courts. We'd have lawyers putting their own names forward. Not many shrinking violets in the legal profession. Once we got sixty-eight letters recommending one guy to an opening. He didn't get the job, by the way. And we'd also have names of people we liked ourselves.

"I'd take all these names and start travelling. Go into each province. I talked to the chief justice, to other judges, the head of the law society and the bar association, the leading counsel in every city and town. I'd get the local scene down cold. I'd have one sheet of paper for each name I started out with and I wrote down all the comments, good and bad, that my contacts gave me. If the negatives began to pile up for a guy—'Heavy drinker', 'Reprimanded by chief justice', 'Never been in a courtroom'—I put his sheet of paper at the bottom of my stack. The guys with the favourable comments rose to the top. My short list."

Then he took the sheets back to Ottawa.

"The sheets were in my handwriting, and the only people who saw them were Otto and me. He'd ask me questions, maybe send me out for more information, and when he'd decided on a name he'd go to the Cabinet and tell them who he was appointing and why. Sometimes that'd raise a terrific stink because another Cabinet minister might have promised the job to a crony back home. But Otto was stubborn. He once said that in those Cabinet discussions of his appointments 'we have hair all over the place, anybody's hair.' It was high priority with him to upgrade the judiciary. Otto fought. With Ron Basford, later, it was slightly different. Ron was such a political animal that he'd get into more of the give and take. Compromise on one appointment. Make a deal on another. But Otto was more single-minded. He didn't give a damn what the other ministers thought. His attitude paid off."

Ratushny ticked off the appointments of the Lang-

Basford period, lawyers who matured as strong judges. Fred Kaufman and Jean Beetz of the Quebec Court of Appeal. Exactly one-half of the fourteen judges on the Ontario Court of Appeal. David Griffiths at the trial level of the Ontario Supreme Court. Chief Justice Bill McGillivray of the Alberta Appeal Court. Calvin Tallis on the Supreme Court of the Northwest Territories. Several County Court judges, Ed Houston in Ottawa, Carl Zalev in Windsor. Many more. Two of the appointees, Beetz and Willard Estey from the Ontario Appeal Court, eventually rose higher, to the Supreme Court of Canada.

"There were problems," Ratushny went on. "Otto and Ron both wanted to put more women on the bench, but we couldn't find them. In the age range for judicial appointments, around forty to fifty-five, there were very few women who had much courtroom experience. And so many of them kept turning us down. Four women in Toronto alone told us no. Couldn't figure it out. But we had our successes. Bertha Wilson on the Ontario Court of Appeal, the first woman ever appointed to an appellate court in Canada. She hadn't done court work as a lawyer, but at Osler, Hoskin and Harcourt in Toronto she supervised research for the litigation partners. She's a scholar, which is what you need in an appeal-court judge. Appeal-court life is monastic. It's all about reading and concentration. Whenever I came across a lawyer who was smart but restless, I'd mark him or her down for the trial-court level. Not for appeal. Not for the monastery."

Life-style was another problem.

"A man has to give up his old way of living when he goes to the bench. His salary drops from $200,000 to $60,000. His world suddenly becomes smaller. The judicial role is restrained. It's cut off. One judge told me, 'The most difficult thing about this job is that the phone never rings any more.' It's a tough transition. And another thing that's essential is to find guys who aren't burned out. We can't have judges who look at the bench as a place to retire to."

After dinner, Ratushny drove back to his house. Guests had arrived, mostly lawyers. Frank Muldoon, chairman of the Canada Law Reform Commission. Pete Johnson, assistant legislative counsel at the Ministry of Justice. A few others. Ratushny's wife Lynn, bright, blonde, and good-looking, is a lawyer, too, practising general law with a downtown Ottawa firm. Talk got around to the Supreme Court of Canada. There was a consensus of opinion. Chief Justice Bora Laskin hadn't brought enough leadership to the court. Some polite resentment had lingered among other judges over Laskin's elevation from puisne judge, one of the eight ordinary judges below the chief justice, to the chief's job ahead of Mr. Justice Ronald Martland, who outranked Laskin on the court in seniority. And Laskin's personality contributed to the court's lack of direction. He was brilliant and independent. He dissented often in the court's judgments, and the result was a split in many important decisions, sometimes four judges voting one way, three another, and the remaining two taking a middle course. The divisions left the lower courts floundering in a search for precedent and guidance from above.

"The best court in the country today," someone said at the party, "is the Ontario Court of Appeal."

It's a court heavy on mid-1970s appointments. Arthur Martin, perhaps the country's most successful criminal lawyer in his time. Charles Dubin, another distinguished counsel. Chief Justice William Howland, who came, paradoxically enough, from a corporate-law background. John Morden, named to the bench when he was a mere thirty-eight.

"So many brains on that court," Ratushny said. "So much hard work."

Ratushny poured himself a final beer when the guests had left and spoke of the need in the country for strong courts like the Ontario Court of Appeal.

"For a lot of people, ordinary citizens I mean," he said, "the most important day of their life may take place in a courtroom. Something decisive is going to happen to them in there. So it doesn't matter what the court is—county, supreme, appeal—if the judge is inattentive or lazy or incompetent or impatient, then the process is unfair to the people who are counting on it. People have to know they've had a hearing. Otherwise the system isn't worth a damn."

CHAPTER ONE

Lawyer for the Oppressed

This is what Martin Wunder's clients see when they face him across the desk in his office on the tenth floor of the Canada Trust Building in Windsor, Ontario. First, Martin Wunder's large and commanding head. Features bigger than lifesize. A high, balding dome circled in curly black hair. Large spectacles, a thick bramble of moustache, a sixty-watt smile that is never turned off. A Terry-Thomas gap in his front teeth and a strong jaw. And through the windows beyond Wunder's shoulders, a panoramic view of the Detroit River and the city of Detroit skyline dominated by the new Renaissance Center, five massive towers of glass and steel. Breath-taking.

This is what Martin Wunder sees from his side of the desk. The halt, the lame, and the blind. Kids with brain damage. Men whose legs are held together by metal pins stuck through the femurs. Young women who need cosmetic surgery to clean away the scars on their faces and psychiatric counselling to wipe away the misery in their heads. Heart-breaking.

Martin Wunder is a plaintiffs' lawyer. He acts for men, women, and children who have been hurt and maimed. He sues the people whose negligence wreaked the damage. He goes after careless car drivers and their insurance companies. He negotiates settlements and wins judgments in court. He coaxes compensation for his clients. He's good, maybe the most effective at his specialty in the country. He keeps 182 or 183 active files in balance at any given working moment.

"The right number for top efficiency would be 175," he says, "but an extra case comes along and I can't say no. I have a natural identification with the injured and the oppressed. People who live well, scions and bank presidents, them I don't act for. I act for people who have to go out on an icy night to drive their kid to a hockey game. Somebody crashes into them and they get hurt or their kid gets hurt. Those people, them, they're my clients."

To handle the 182 or 183 files, all those oppressed plaintiffs, Wunder runs an office that's part IBM and part cavalry charge, an unlikely combination of humming efficiency and emotional attack. He has one other lawyer on staff, Bill Coleman, a junior whom he took on in 1978 after twenty-one years as a one-man band. He has five secretaries who send up a steady whirr of typing. And he has Theresa Ducharme. Theresa is a woman of unselfconscious beauty, dark and slender, with a sweet generosity about her that invites people in. "My secret weapon," Wunder says of Theresa. She started as his secretary in 1970, nineteen years old, and now she works out of her own large corner office. She trains the secretaries. She manages the operation. She interviews potential clients before they get to Wunder. Is the injury genuine? Is the client on the level? Is the case full of holes? Theresa finds out.

"People tell her details they'd never think to tell any other investigator," Wunder says.

Something else he leans heavily on is medical literature. "I have to be tuned in to the medical community," he says. "How else am I supposed to know what the hell it is doctors are talking about when they say my client needs a myelogram or he's suffering from some functional overlay?" The shelves in Wunder's office library hold almost as many medical texts as case-law reports, and its walls are decorated

21

with four large medical charts showing veins and bones and muscles, the spinal nerves and the nervous system, all in intimidating Technicolor. For balance, the wall opposite the charts is hung with a framed reproduction of a Renoir nude in sensuous pinks.

Against another wall sits a videotape machine, a Wunder innovation in the world of civil litigation. The machine plays a series of taped Wunder talks—one for his clients, another for witnesses, a third for employees, and so on— that advise the viewers what they may expect in the course of a lawsuit. The tapes are in colour, about forty minutes long, and boast the professionalism of a network production. The witness tape shows Wunder sitting at ease in his study, looking into the camera, unblinking, and talking in a style that's relaxed, confidential, and enlightening. It's Wunder as everybody's favourite high-school teacher. "My client has a good case," he says to the viewers. "I want to help you express yourself accurately and gracefully." He proceeds to offer guidance on the clothes witnesses should wear to court, the manners they must observe around the courthouse, the style in which they ought to testify. "Don't be exact with numbers. Be relative when you are testifying about time and speed and distance. Talk in terms of over the limit rather than saying 32.9 miles per hour. No one can be so specific about such details." The tape, low-key and straight-arrow, has the persuasiveness of a pep talk.

"The tapes save me the 250 hours a year I'd ordinarily have to be talking to the people," Wunder says. "Besides, after you've had to advise witnesses in person a thousand times, you lose your concentration. People find the tapes are more real than actually listening to me speaking to them live in my office. They watch the tape and then I spend maybe twenty more minutes with them explaining the specifics of the individual case they're on. As far as the machine goes, there are only two other counsel I know of in Canada who use it, friends of mine that I persuaded to give the tapes a whirl. They're unique, those tapes."

Which is as accurate an adjective as any, unique, to describe Wunder. For proof, observe him during one typical three-hour burst of action in his office on an afternoon in late autumn. He shot off dictation to each of the five secretaries, took phone calls in relays, held swift conferences with Bill Chapman, and summoned Theresa to brief him on clients and to hunt down lost files; and he dealt with the grief or gratitude of five particular clients.

Mr. Horvath

A Middle European in his early fifties, Mr. Horvath had a powerful build and a voice, high-pitched and beseeching, that belonged to a different body. He arrived at the office to approve a settlement that Wunder had negotiated. Two years earlier, Mr. Horvath's ribs had been crushed in a car accident. He missed eight weeks from his job as a die-maker. The ribs healed, leaving behind no discomfort and no need for further medical treatment. It was settlement time.

"You'll get a cheque for $8,100, Mr. Horvath," Wunder said, handing him a typed form that listed sums and statistics. "My fee is $3,500. The other side paid $1,500 of that. You understand all this? The bit of money you got on your own medical insurance is deducted, too. See that? Leaves you with $8,100 all to yourself. Are you happy?"

"Please," Mr. Horvath said. "Not much."

"You want to go to court?"

"Yes."

"You won't get any more money from a court case."

"Please, I don't want to upset you."

"You can't upset me."

"I have friend at factory," Mr. Horvath said, clasping and unclasping his thick hands. "He was in accident out on 401 highway, not hurt as bad as me, and he gets $15,000."

"Listen, Mr. Horvath," Wunder said. "Let me tell you about a client I had. Joe, just think of him as Joe. I got $10,000 for Joe, and a couple of months later, a guy comes

23

into my office and says, 'Mr. Wunder, I've been broken up in a car accident and I want you to get me $20,000 like Joe says you got for him.' Mr. Horvath, people lie about these things. That's number one. Number two is that in your case I've driven the lawyer on the other side to the limit. He won't let his client pay you any more. You were badly injured, sure, but you're a strong man and well-motivated and you got better. You can't have it both ways. I've held out for every dime I can get you."

Mr. Horvath sat silent, working on the thick hands.

"Okay, Mr. Horvath," Wunder said. "Take as long as you need to make up your mind. A couple of days. Or go into my library down the hall and give these figures a lot of thought."

Mr. Horvath left for the library and returned in fifteen minutes.

"I want to go to court," he said.

"Mr. Horvath," Wunder said, "a court would give you no more than $8,000 and probably less. Either way, you subtract court costs and you end up with not as much money as I've got you. In all conscience I say this, Mr. Horvath, I wouldn't be giving you the best service I can give you if I let you go to court. You'll have to retain another lawyer."

"Please, I would look foolish," Mr. Horvath said. "Other lawyer laugh at me."

"Laugh at you? How come?"

"Because you're the best."

"What can I say?"

For a few seconds, Mr. Horvath fell silent again.

"Please," he said at last, "I take $8,000."

The Mangans

None of the three Mangans was over twenty-one. Mr. Mangan had rosy cheeks and a wispy moustache. Mrs. Mangan wore her hair down to her waist. The baby boy, two years old, playing on a blanket spread across Wunder's office floor, was deaf and retarded. His growth had been slowed down. He couldn't unclench his left fist.

"He's a content baby, though," Mrs. Mangan said.

Two years earlier, when the baby was six weeks old, he had been sitting on his mother's lap in the passenger's seat of a car driven by Mrs. Mangan's brother. The brother reached over to turn on the car radio and the car ran into a station-wagon. The baby was the only casualty. Wunder had issued a writ against Mrs. Mangan's brother.

"I asked you down here to review a couple of developments," Wunder said. "The lawyers for the brother's insurance company are counter-claiming for contribution and indemnity against you, Mr. Mangan, and the baby. They're saying you were negligent. Nothing to get excited about. Just part of the jockeying. They say you were negligent, Mr. Mangan, for letting the baby go in the car in a way he wasn't properly cared for. Don't worry. We know the baby wasn't negligent. Ridiculous. You either, Mr. Mangan. The other lawyers are just touching all the bases."

Mr. Mangan fingered his wispy moustache and stared at Wunder.

"The other thing, I've issued what I call a back-up writ. I issued the writ against your brother, Mrs. Mangan, and had it served. Okay, I've also issued a back-up writ against the two hospitals that looked at the baby, against the ambulance service that went to the scene of the accident, and against the Children's Aid Society. I've issued the writ, but I haven't served it. Maybe I never will. Probably not. You know why I issued it?"

Both Mangans shook their heads.

"Because I'm paranoid. If you're bright, you're paranoid. If you see things that escape others, then every once in a while you're going to imagine things that won't happen. I imagine in your case that maybe the other side will say, hey, we're partly liable but so are all these other people, the hospitals, the ambulance service, and, hey, Wunder hasn't sued them. I don't want that to happen. I want to be in a position to claim against everybody who's possibly remotely liable. I use back-up writs in all kinds of cases. My little security blanket."

The Mangans nodded.

"Anything new with you then?"

"The chiropractor," Mrs. Mangan said.

"What? What chiropractor?" Wunder said.

"It was our idea," Mrs. Mangan said. "We've been taking the baby to him. Anything to help. That's what we thought anyway. You think it's not right?"

"Tell you what to do," Wunder said. "Go out and find a medical doctor who says it's a good idea for the baby to see a chiropractor. Get him to put it in a letter to me. The problem is—are you with me?—the other side'll say the chiropractor made the baby worse."

The Mangans nodded.

"That's a nice baby," Wunder said. "We'll get him compensation. If he has to go through life deaf, better he should be deaf with regular money coming in than with nothing to show for his deafness."

Mr. Robinson

When the phone call from Mrs. Robinson came through, Wunder had Theresa's report on Mr. Robinson in front of him. The report, in large, exact, vertical handwriting, covered four pages of yellow foolscap paper. Theresa had interviewed Mr. Robinson in the hospital a few days after his left leg had been amputated above the knee. He'd been standing on a sidewalk when a car bounced over the curb and pinned him to a post. Mr. Robinson, a black man, was eighty-one, but Theresa's notes said he wasn't your average octogenarian. He had thirteen children by his first marriage. His second wife was forty-nine. "I can't keep up with that man," the second Mrs. Robinson told Theresa. Theresa wrote it down on the yellow foolscap. Mr. Robinson tended to the housekeeping and cooked the meals. He made his wife's lunch and delivered it to her at work each noon hour. He went fishing twice a week and hunting a few times a month. He rode the buses every day, varying his routes for sightseeing pleasure. He greeted the mornings in peppy spirits and he had no plans to slow down. Theresa made a note of everything.

"This is borderline," Wunder said to Theresa before he talked on the phone. "We got to be selective. You know the rules."

"We only take cases that are, one, meritorious and, two, substantial," Theresa answered, speaking by rote.

"An eighty-one-year-old guy who's unemployed? He's got no life expectancy, no loss of wages. How can I get him any money?"

"Because he's such a sweet old gentleman."

"Mrs. Robinson," Wunder said into the phone, waving Theresa out of the office. "I'm sorry your husband has had this terrible accident. I tell you what I'm going to do. I'm . . . going to get him compensation. Yeah. But, listen, I'm not a gangster, but I need $500."

"Uh-huh."

"I'm going to be a very expensive guy to the person who ran into your husband. But I have to start off in the right direction, you follow me? I need the police report of the accident. I need to send out my investigator. He'll take pictures of the accident scene. He'll look at the motor vehicle. Like that. I tell every client the same thing, $500 is my go-ahead."

"Uh-huh."

"Listen, Mrs. Robinson, is $500 hard for you? Am I reading you that way?"

"Well, Mr. Wunder, people told me I should go to you, but I haven't got no $500 in the house, not right now."

"Tell you what, I'm breaking my inflexible rule. You bring in $200 right away and then pay the office $100 at the end of each of the next three months. Agreed?"

"Uh-huh."

"You need me, Mrs. Robinson."

"Uh-huh."

"You've got two years to sue the man that hit your husband, Mrs. Robinson. After that, the law says you're out of business. Don't wait until the Tuesday before the two years are up and then come and see me. I won't take your case. I'll turn you away from my door, Mrs. Robinson."

"Gimme an appointment for day after tomorrow."

"Uh-huh."

The Osbourne Family

Wunder asked a psychiatrist to examine Susan Osbourne, and the psychiatrist reported back that Susan was often suicidal.

"How much has the woman got to take?" Wunder said to Theresa. "Twenty-eight years old and she's afflicted with double vision. Can't judge depth and sees two of everything. Gone through a personality change. She's most of the time dull and lethargic. Now suicidal? She's got a claim that's worth $75,000 to her minimum. Deserves more like $125,000."

It had been an automobile accident two years earlier, and Susan was the victim. Her husband Tony looked after her when she left the hospital, but her depressions and erratic flights wore down his stamina, and Susan moved to her parents' home. It was the parents—a well-dressed couple, polite, concerned, upper-middle-class—who accompanied Susan to the appointment with Wunder, one of several over the previous couple of years.

"Susan, you look good," Wunder said.

"I'm stupid," Susan said in a voice too loud for the office. Everything about her had a slightly exaggerated quality, the thick glasses, the flamboyant hand gestures.

"I can't concentrate," she said. "I'm no good at the things I used to be good at. It's like I'm back where I was when I was a child."

"Look at it this way," Wunder said. "You're at step number

one. You're facing up to the things you have to beat. You're not avoiding your hassles. Susan, I admire you for what you just said. That takes guts."

Susan had no answer.

"All right, Mr. and Mrs. Osbourne," Wunder went on. "I got you in so you can consider the possibility of a claim under the Family Law Reform Act. This is something fairly new, a piece of legislation the Ontario government passed, and it's still giving us a lot of trouble. Basically, it means people have a claim for looking after the victim of an accident. Tony's got a claim under this Act, and I've already had him write me out a long list of all the things that were entailed in him caring for Susan. Now, I'm not sure what the parents in Susan's situation, you people, can claim where the Family Law Reform Act is concerned. How are the judges going to feel about it? How much money are they likely to award under it? Nobody knows at this stage. There haven't been any court decisions to give us an accurate picture. That's the way this kind of law works. I'm not saying it's a crap-shoot. I'm saying I got to cover all the options, and I want you people to be ready to help me on this. Think about it. Consider what you've invested of yourselves in helping Susan through this tough time."

"People have to treat me like a kid," Susan said.

"Susan, understand me, everybody has problems," Wunder said. "I feel bad because I don't have a full head of hair and because my marriage is over and I don't live with all my family any more. You feel bad because you had a dreadful car accident. But, okay, everybody has to build on what they got. You'll start again. You'll find yourself a job. Something new. Listen, talk about jobs, I had a dozen of them in between the time I left university and started law school. Two years of wandering in the wilderness. With you, maybe it'll take ten jobs before you find the right line of business. But, Susan, it'll work for you."

Susan allowed herself a hint of smile.

"I know the thing you need, Susan," Wunder said. "You

need to talk to someone. Let it all hang out. Why not me? You come in here without your parents some afternoon at five o'clock, and we'll talk. The twenty-second? Look, I'm writing it in my appointment book, the twenty-second at five o'clock, Susan Osbourne. No charge. This is on the house. You come in here and we'll shoot the breeze for as long as you can stand me. Okay?"

"I'd like that," Susan said in a voice that was no longer too loud for the office.

Wendy
"I got $60,000 out of them, Wendy," Wunder said. "You can walk away with $43,500 of it."

"I can't *believe* it," the girl said.

"You're surprised?"

"So *much*."

Wendy used to be a beauty queen and she could still qualify, now that her mouth has been rebuilt. Five years earlier, when she was a teenager, her boyfriend ran a red light and crashed into another car. Wendy took it in the mouth. She endured hundreds of hours of painful dental surgery, root-canal work, capping, bridge-building. For five years Wunder negotiated with the lawyers for the boyfriend's insurers. The negotiations paid off, and Wendy—slim, pretty, glasses stuck high in her glossy dark hair, dressed in a smart tan suit and high-heeled sandals—had come to hear about the settlement.

"You know I almost didn't take your case, Wendy," Wunder said. "When your dad came in here five years ago, he was so mad at your boyfriend, he wanted blood. I stay away from cases where I think I can never satisfy the client. Good thing I changed my mind, Wendy. Remember what the defence was offering at the beginning? Twelve thousand."

"I thought we'd have a trial."

"We almost did. Two months ago. The other side begged off at the last minute and asked for an adjournment. I was already in court that morning. I had my medical witnesses

30

prepped and then the defence lawyer asks for the adjournment. The judge didn't like it, not with me set to roll. He ordered them to pay $1,500 and costs just for the adjournment. That's when the other side started to talk settlement seriously."

"All that money."

"Wendy, my statistical rate of settlement is so high it's scandalous. That's because I'm prepared for trial all along. Most lawyers hear that a trial is to go on and they turn into crazy men the night before, running around looking up the law, screaming at their witnesses. But from the start, I'm making notes on what the other side is after, what I need, what the law is on every point. By trial date my case has no holes. So when the defence is talking settlement and I tell them their offer stinks and I'll take my chances in court, they know I'm not bluffing. I never bluff."

"Sixty thousand dollars, my *gawd*!"

"Okay, Wendy, break it down. The expenses come out of the sixty thousand. Some of it's my fee. The other guys paid $6,000 of that. It's all here on paper. Here, look, there's an extra $5,000 built-in that I talked out of them."

"Extra?"

"Listen, Wendy, the reality is this, dentists' devices don't last forever. In twenty years you're going to have to go through another reconstruction job. It'll cost you twenty grand anyway. All right, you follow me, take the extra $5,000 I got you, invest it so it'll earn $15,000 over twenty years, which gives you a total of twenty grand for the new mouth job. Nice? Am I right? Would another lawyer look after you like that?"

"Sixty *thousand*!"

"One thing, Wendy, if you accept the settlement, I don't want you to be saying to yourself in a couple of years, 'You chump, why did you let Martin Wunder sell you down the river?' Remember, you've only got one of these cases, I've got hundreds. Go out to the phone in the library and talk the settlement over with your father."

Wendy was gone five minutes.

"Dad says I'm a big girl now," she told Wunder. "I'll take what you got."

"The cheque'll be ready for you in two weeks," Wunder said. "You never had so much money in your life, so don't dissipate the fruits of my labour and the pain of your ordeal."

"I've been to Florida lots, but I've never gone to Vegas."

"Goodbye, Wendy."

Wunder chose Joe Muer's Restaurant for dinner. It's fifteen minutes from his office, through the tunnel to Detroit and up the wide highway past the Renaissance Center. Joe Muer's, fifty years old and a Detroit institution, specializes in seafood and is a favourite of Wunder's. He keeps his pleasures to a manageable few. He likes ice cream and is in love with the California coast. Two or three times a year he heads west and roams the Pacific shore from Monterey to La Costa. Beer is a sometime pleasure for him. He never smokes. He runs five miles most mornings of the week. He likes to talk and he likes the law.

"I'm the guy who's at his desk Sunday afternoons and New Year's Eve," he says. "For me, the line between work and play is erased."

At Joe Muer's, Wunder ordered a Bock beer, Manhattan clam chowder, and Dover sole. When the waiter had placed the beer in front of him, he launched into his conversation, swift and funny, a random, free-form mix of autobiography, one-liners, aphorisms, and salty observations on life around the courtrooms of Canada.

"My father was a happy truck driver. He didn't want anything more out of life. He believed in the golden rule and he used to have it printed up with examples of what it meant all over the house. He wanted me to be a 'consultant'. I never knew what he meant. I'm not sure he did either. But in a couple of ways, both my parents got me ready for the law. They made me take elocution lessons. I used to troop from church group to church group reciting my little pieces. And I had to compose my own dictionary. Five nights a week I came in with a new word. Looked it up, pronounced it, gave my parents its meaning, and wrote it in my book. But I couldn't figure out a future for myself. I was jealous of the guy who always knew what he wanted in life. I graduated from arts at the University of Western Ontario and took a bunch of dead-end jobs. It was my mother who came up with the idea of law school. I enrolled at Osgoode Hall, and after two months it fit me like a glove."

Wunder spooned into his clam chowder.

"The part I like about law is the confrontation. I'm a confrontation-seeker. I have such a good time doing it. You go up against somebody on the other side, the defence lawyer, a witness, anybody, and you say to yourself, what's going to motivate this guy? There's a one-word answer. Fear. It's like those comedy records, 'The Two-Thousand-Year-Old Man'. Mel Brooks plays a man who's two thousand years old, and the interviewer, that's Carl Reiner, is asking Brooks how things were years ago when the two-thousand-year-old man was young. 'What was the principal method of transportation in those days?' Reiner asks, and Brooks answers, 'Fear!'

"One place where it all comes together, the fear and the confrontation, is at an examination for discovery. That's a pre-trial proceeding where each side is allowed to examine the other side's people under oath and it's all taken down by a reporter. It's one on one, you against the other lawyer, and there's no judge at a discovery to save the young lawyer or the inexperienced lawyer or the inept lawyer. You can get killed in discovery and that can have terrible consequences for your client because so many cases are settled on the basis of what happens at discovery, what strengths and weaknesses show up in each side's case. Discovery is where you try to impress the other guy. Make him see how big your case really can be. I use all kinds of tactics. Defence lawyers—this is an example—like to have their clients examined first at discovery and they'll examine the plaintiff's people second. So they're busy being courteous and saying, 'Won't you go ahead with your examination, Mr. Wunder?' Sure I will. I want to examine first thing in the morning. That's when I'm sharpest. Let the courteous guys wait till it's close to lunch-time. They're getting hungry, a little tired, maybe cranky. They're not sharp. They miss things. They give me an edge."

The Dover sole arrived.

"Settlement is an art. I'm not kidding. When I'm negotiating a settlement, I refer myself to earlier cases where courts have dealt with injuries of the same nature as my client's. But I don't bother with the cases where the injuries were *worse* than my guy's. I don't do that because it puts a lid on what I can get. The defendant's lawyer looks at the case and says, 'Come on, Martin, this guy was hurt more seriously than your plaintiff and he got $25,000. We'll give you $15,000. Maybe less.' So I look for cases where the damages were the same or not as bad. Then I got scope to negotiate without a limit for my client."

Wunder reflected on the toughest type of injury to handle.

"Whiplash is hard. Very common but it's difficult to prove or disprove the injury. One approach I take, I tell my clients to save all their drug bills. In one whiplash case, a woman, the bills showed she took 3,500 pills over a period of two years. There wasn't a tiddle of evidence she was faking the whiplash, so she must have needed the medication. We went to court and I was able to use a line to the judge I'd been saving for years. 'What you have before you in this plaintiff,' I said, 'is either the real thing or the biggest fraud in the world, a woman so gifted as an actress that she should have won the last two Academy Awards.' The judge gave her $13,500 for the whiplash."

Wunder ordered chocolate ice cream. With chocolate sauce.

"The plaintiff's lawyer has all the work in injury cases. He's the guy who has to prove the probability of everything, the probable cause of the damages, the extent of the injuries. All the defendant's lawyer has to do is remember to bring his briefcase to court. But court, you know, it's a funny place. What happens is that you've been working in your office at an incredible pace, handling twenty or thirty cases every day, and then a trial comes along and all of a sudden everything moves at a crawl. In the office you make decisions so fast you haven't got time to think about them. In court you examine everything in minute detail. When you consider it, court is an anachronism. All that minutiae. If I didn't take along a book or something else to read, I'd go crazy."

Wunder licked the last of his chocolate sauce.

Orville and Yvonne Teno, Diane's parents, stopped by Wunder's office after dinner. It was a routine appointment to sign a couple of documents and pick up a cheque. The Tenos had been calling on Wunder since July of 1969. Their daughter's claim, reported in the case-books as *Teno* v. *Arnold*, represented one of Wunder's masterpieces. It wasn't merely the money. The largest award granted by an Ontario court to an injury victim before the Teno case was $250,000; Mr. Justice Donald Keith at the trial of *Teno* v. *Arnold* gave Diane Teno $950,000. But, beyond the money, the case allowed Wunder to put on display his entire courtroom repertoire of innovations and improvisations. He was daring in the Teno case, impeccably prepared, relentless, and passionately involved. He even took his videotape machine to court.

"I would be remiss," Mr. Justice Keith wrote in his judgment, "if I failed to acknowledge the assistance that I received from Diane's counsel in the presentation of the evidence in a most imaginative and I believe unique way in trials to date in Canada."

The case reached back for its beginnings to shortly after one o'clock on the afternoon of Dominion Day, July 1,

1969. It was a balmy day, sunshine all around, and the Teno kids were playing on the front lawn of their home on Academy Drive in Windsor. Academy Drive is leafy and residential. It runs north and south, and the two lanes for traffic, each eighteen feet wide, are divided by a twenty-two-foot boulevard. The Teno house stands on the east side of the street, and it was on the far curb of the west side of Academy, just past one o'clock, that Stuart Galloway, nineteen years old, pulled over in his ice-cream truck, its bells tinkling their tinny song of invitation.

Yvonne Teno was on the telephone when the kids came through the door asking for money to buy ice cream. Diane, four years and seven months old, ran out of the house with a dime. Her older brother Paul, one month short of seven years, had thirty cents. They crossed the east section of the street and hesitated on the boulevard when Stuart Galloway, who had spotted a moving car on his side of the street that the kids hadn't noticed, shouted to them to wait until the road was clear. They waited, then crossed to the serving window on the curb side of the truck. Diane bought a tiger-stripe cone. Paul stepped up for his turn, and Diane turned away from the window to dash back home.

Brian Arnold said later he didn't see Diane until she appeared a few feet, too few feet, in front of the car he was driving. It was his dad's car. Brian, who was eighteen and lived a few blocks away in the neighbourhood, was cruising south on the west side of Academy. He saw the ice-cream truck from the rear and saw the signs on the back of the truck. "Good Humor Ice Cream". "Watch Out For Children". He didn't see Diane until a second or two before he struck her. He said he was driving twenty or twenty-five miles per hour at the time.

Diane's injuries were cruel.

"She is one of the most disabled children I have ever seen," Dr. John Pritchard wrote three years later. Dr. Pritchard was the head of neurology and electroencephalography at the Hospital for Sick Children in Toronto. He had seen a lifetime of disabled children.

The accident left Diane's speech slow and slurred. She had an uncontrollable tremor in her right arm. She used to sit on it, "to keep it quiet," she said. Her left hand was clumsy. She could make marks on paper by holding a pencil in the palm and scribbling. There was spastic paralysis in her left arm. Her left leg had a spastic gait and she could walk only with a mighty effort. But, by an awful irony, she came out of the accident healthy in almost all other ways. Her life expectancy was 66.9 years. She could read and think and laugh and dream. It was the rest of life that was denied to her. She couldn't care for herself, not even put on her own clothes or tend to the most routine chores around a house. She would need perpetual care.

When the Tenos retained Wunder a week after the accident, he saw two formidable tasks. One had to do with damages. He must recover enough money to give Diane a chance at living as fully as her handicaps allowed. The other task centred on liability. He had no doubt that he could pin negligence on the driver and the owner of the car, Brian Arnold and his father. But Wunder had a larger notion. He would sue the ice-cream vendor, J. B. Jackson Limited. He'd go after the people who drew Diane into danger. He'd shoot for the big money.

"People thought I was crazy suing the ice-cream guys," Wunder says. "Even the judge at the trial told me in chambers before we started that he didn't see liability against them. He held differently later. The thing was there'd never been a case in Canada where anybody set out to attribute liability at common law to people in the position of ice-cream vendors. I had to establish a precedent that they were negligent because by the nature of their operation they enticed Diane into the street and then didn't exercise enough care for her safety once they got her where they wanted her."

Wunder turned himself into a whirlwind of research. He discovered that the boroughs of North York and Etobicoke in Metropolitan Toronto had passed by-laws banning ice-cream trucks from their streets. He went behind the by-laws and examined the material on which the borough councils had based their votes. In North York he found that police had logged forty-five accidents involving Good Humor trucks. In Etobicoke's files he uncovered an eight-page letter from the president of an ice-cream company listing safety measures that its trucks and drivers observed. Many of the precautions, Wunder satisfied himself, weren't part of the Windsor company's routine. Wunder pressed on. He corresponded with eighty American municipalities to search out their attitudes and by-laws on Good Humor trucks. He photographed the ice-cream truck that served Diane in the spot on Academy Drive where it had parked. A sign along the side of the truck read "Wait on curb. I will come to you." But the photograph revealed that over-hanging tree branches blocked out the last half of the warning. Wunder was weaving a web of liability around J. B. Jackson Limited.

And he struck pay dirt with Mr. John R. Jackson.

"A very honourable gentleman," Wunder says. "He'd once been the vice-president and general manager of the ice-cream company, and he admitted the whole purpose of the business, the only way those companies could make a dollar, was to get kids flocking into the street. He gave us details. I remember just before he testified for us at the trial I picked him up at the Windsor Airport, and in the car, I was driving and I had a secretary writing down my questions to Jackson in blue and his answers in red. There was only one thing he said in the car that we couldn't get him to repeat in the witness stand. He told me, 'The ice-cream trucks are designed to get a Pavlovian response from the children.' He wouldn't say 'Pavlovian' in court, but he said everything else."

Preparation for the trial stretched over five years, and for Wunder it was mostly uphill.

"A battle," he says. "It was one of those cases where a lawyer was afraid to smile at another lawyer during discovery for fear it would be construed as an admission of some fact. The defence lawyers wouldn't even admit that the Good Humor truck was set up to appeal to children. So I called an officer of the vendor into discovery. 'Tiger-stripe?' I asked. 'Tutti-frutti? These are supposed to be for adults?' I got my point on the record."

Wunder was especially proud of his craftsmanship in drawing the statement of claim, the pleadings that set out the basis of the plaintiff's case.

"The way I drew them," he says, "they were wide enough to cover more than one of the ice-cream vendor's insurers. I brought in the motor-vehicle insurer and the general-liability insurer. They were in agony over which one of them should carry the load. Those pleadings, once I'd drawn them, they never had to be amended a single time over the seven or eight more years it took to finish the case. I got them right the first time."

Wunder had only one doubt about the Teno case. Should he bear the burden of such an unprecedented argument all alone at trial? Or should he ring in another counsel to share the argument?

"This was four years after I got the case," he says. "I suffered over the decision. Really sweated it. I was jealous, not of the money but of the responsibility. I wanted it all to myself. But I realized I needed help. The liability was supposed to be the glamorous part of the case. Setting new law and everything. But I decided to get someone else to handle the liability and I'd argue the damages, which weren't as glamorous but still meant I had to develop a lot of new law on compensation for injuries."

Wunder could have chosen from among many litigation lawyers. Eight hundred of them to be precise. That's the membership of the Advocates' Society, an organization founded in 1965 by John Robinette and other prominent counsel and restricted in membership to lawyers who prac-tise in court. The society carries on an industrious program of educational updating in litigation matters, in main-taining links with the bench, in making representations on civil-liberties issues to elected officials. Its members like to huddle at intimate luncheons in Campbell House, a lovely Georgian home built in 1833 in Toronto by Chief Justice Sir William Campbell of the Upper Canada Queen's Bench and rescued from the wrecker's hammer by the society, which spent $900,000 on restoring it and moving it to a new location directly across the street from the courts of Osgoode Hall. The society, it's clear, is reserved for the elite of the litigation bar.

Wunder is a member and a past director, and he chose another member, a man who would be elected the society's president in 1979, to join him in the Teno case. Wunder's choice was Earl Cherniak from the London, Ontario, firm of Lerner and Associates. Some lawyers rate Cherniak among the three or four most gifted courtroom technicians in Canada. But Wunder had a reason apart from Cherniak's talent for inviting him into *Teno* v. *Arnold*. Wunder and Cherniak are first cousins, pals since boyhood days in southwestern Ontario. And they're look-alikes—both medium height, dark, balding, full of laughs and energy, a twin pair of firecrackers.

"Oh my God," an adjuster from Allstate Insurance, the company that held coverage on the Arnold car, said when he arrived in court for the Teno trial, "there's *two* of them!"

With Cherniak on liability, Wunder turned his exclusive concentration to damages. Diane was spastic on one side, hemiplegic on the other. Wunder made himself an expert on both conditions. He had Diane examined at regular intervals over a five-year period by arrays of medical specialists. He accumulated rows of files, notes, letters, and memoranda that documented Diane's disabilities, her health, her prospects for the future.

Wunder wasn't satisfied. Some element was missing, something that would get across to the court more graphically than medical records and doctors' testimony the horror of Diane's injuries and the need she faced to have someone care for her over the rest of her 66.9 years. Wunder turned to his videotape machine.

On August 31, 1973, he took a camera crew from a Windsor television station into the Teno house to shoot ninety minutes of film. Diane sat beside her mother on a sofa, and with Wunder's voice on the sound-track instructing and guiding and questioning, the little girl proceeded to demonstrate to the camera the hard truths of her everyday life.

The film is heart-breaking. As it begins, Diane, all spunk and smiles and effort, radiates no sense of suffering or discouragement. She wants only to please the camera. She shows off her success at running the zipper down the front of her red jumper. It takes several seconds to make her shaking left hand grasp the zipper and tug it down. But her smile says she's satisfied with the feat. It takes longer, almost a minute, to run the zipper back up. Wunder asks her to brush her teeth. Diane seizes the toothpaste tube in her right hand, the one that trembles frantically, and forces the hand between her knees. The knees close on hand and tube. The tube's almost steady now. Diane aims her left hand, not quite so mutinous as the right, for the top of the tube. The hand quivers around the top, finally seizes it and twists it off. She begins to squeeze the toothpaste on to her brush. It comes out messily, threatening the clean jumper. Her mother moves gently to her rescue.

"Yes," Mrs. Teno says in answer to Wunder's question, "I do the actual brushing of Diane's teeth."

Diane carries on, conscientious about trying every small job around the house, every piece of grooming and self-help. But she's not quite able to finish any one of them, not without her mother's calm aid. The film runs on, and as it nears the end of the ninety minutes, Wunder asks Diane to show to the camera the things she's worst at and the things she's best at. For Diane, it's a door that holds the most frustration. She can't open a door. The camera records her

41

as she tugs desperately at the knob. It refuses to turn for her. The door stays shut, and the message of the few seconds of film is that, unless someone else's hand turns the knob, Diane will never know what's on the other side of the door.

Then she faces directly into the camera to show her favourite accomplishment. She waves her left arm at the unseen audience. She waves vigorously, joyfully. She likes waving. It's easy for someone with a spastic arm to wave.

Diane is smiling, but the camera lingers on her a second too long, and in the film's last frames the waving stops, Diane's smile retreats, and for a moment all that's left on the screen is a final glimpse of her despair.

"We ran the film in court," Wunder says. "One of the defence counsel—he was seeing it for the first time— started to weep."

At nine o'clock on the morning of Wednesday, June 7, 1974, Wunder and Cherniak took the film, witnesses, stacks of records, and their arguments to the Windsor Courthouse to begin the trial before Mr. Justice Keith. In a real sense the trial came as an anticlimax, its result almost inevitable. The work that signalled the verdict had been done over the previous five years. So elaborate and exhaustive was the preparation by Wunder and Cherniak that the trial took a mere five and a half days to complete, a miraculously short duration for a case that demanded a grasp of sophisticated medical concepts and a leap to trail-blazing legal conclusions.

"A week before the trial," Wunder says, "we took a couple of rooms at the Sheraton Four Seasons Hotel in Toronto and paraded our witnesses through there for two days. All the doctors. We went over their testimony, decided on the sequence of evidence, tidied up on the law. For two days we holed up in there."

Wunder and Cherniak had their presentation nailed down tight.

"It helped that we took the defence by surprise on damages," Wunder says. "They didn't emphasize damages to the extent that we did. The defence lawyers were so busy concentrating on liability that they didn't call a single piece of evidence on damages. The plaintiff's case, I have to say, was complete."

To Mr. Justice Keith it was also persuasive. He took much of the summer to write his decision, but when he issued it on September 27, it squared in almost every particular with the Wunder-Cherniak arguments. The judge had no trouble finding liability against Brian Arnold and his father, the driver and the owner of the car that struck Diane. Under the Highway Traffic Act, when a car is involved in loss or damage on a road, the onus is on the driver of the car to show that the loss or damage didn't result from his negligence. In Mr. Justice Keith's view, Brian Arnold, knowing that children would be gathered around the ice-cream truck, failed to keep a proper lookout or reduce his speed. He didn't discharge the onus that the Highway Traffic Act placed on him. The Arnolds, father and son, owner and driver, were liable.

So, Mr. Justice Keith held, were the owner, J. B. Jackson Limited, and the driver, Stuart Galloway, of the ice-cream truck. The judge had made the leap in liability that Wunder and Cherniak had asked of him. Yes, he wrote, the Good Humor company had lured Diane into a dangerous situation. Yes, it had ignored the peril it placed her in. A four-year-old on the road! Stuart Galloway knew of the potential threats. Hadn't he warned Diane and her brother minutes before the accident to stay on the boulevard until another car passed by? The company that owned the truck, the Jackson company, knew too of the hazards its business created. Had it trained young Galloway in safety measures? A nineteen-year-old boy who'd been on the job, driving the truck and peddling tiger-stripe cones, for only six weeks? Had it instructed him to leave the truck and escort small

43

children across the streets? Had it hired a second person to ride the truck as a safety guide? No. The answer to all the questions was no.

John Jackson, Mr. Justice Keith wrote, gave "honest but damning testimony that the exigencies of the business, i.e., to make a profit, overrode safety factors."

The judge didn't mind making new case law in Canada. The ice-cream vendor was liable.

When it came to the amount the defendants should pay to Diane, Mr. Justice Keith hesitated: "Setting a dollar figure by way of compensation for personal injuries must be one of the most inexact sciences known to man, rather in the category of economic or weather forecasting." Then he plunged on. Diane, he wrote, "must not be denied the opportunity of developing her life as much as possible for lack of money." He wanted her to be able to travel, read, go to the theatre—to lead an independent life in a house or apartment of her own. He recognized her need for a constant companion who would offer the care that her parents were giving her as a child. And he reasoned that she'd need an income of about $27,000 a year to cover all necessities and hopes. He divided the award to Diane into two categories, non-pecuniary loss and pecuniary loss. The first covered Diane's pain and suffering and disability. The second took in future care and loss of future income, the money that Diane would need in the years ahead and the money she might have earned if the accident had never crippled her.

For the non-pecuniary loss, Mr. Justice Keith gave Diane $200,000.

For pecuniary loss: $750,000.

Total judgment against all defendants: $950,000.

"It took balls to hand down such a big award," Wunder says. "There's a lot of him, that one judge, in the Teno case."

The defendants, as expected, appealed Mr. Justice Keith's decision to the Ontario Court of Appeal and later to the Supreme Court of Canada. Both courts left his findings on liability basically intact. It was over the amount of damages that they wrangled. Inflation, interest rates, and income taxes were the items that presented the dilemma for the appeal courts.

The mathematics was tricky. In arriving at the size of the capital fund to produce future income for Diane and to replace her lost wages — the $750,000 fund — Mr. Justice Keith had to consider the interest that the fund would earn. He had to arrive at a discount rate to be applied in calculating the present value of the annual amounts necessary to provide Diane's future care. And he had to build inflation into the award. How to solve the knotty problems?

At the time, 1974, interest rates were escalating from 5 per cent to 8 per cent, and further. The defence lawyers contended, not surprisingly, that Mr. Justice Keith should base his calculations on a high interest rate, 9 per cent, and thereby reduce the amount of the capital award by a few hundred thousand dollars. Wunder, also not surprisingly, took the opposite tack and argued that it made more sense to ignore current market-place rates, about 8 per cent, and go with a low 5 per cent and a high capital award. That way, Diane's protection would be financially secure. Mr. Justice Keith took the Wunder route: 5 per cent and $750,000.

The Ontario Court of Appeal supported the trial calculations — with one exception. In a judgment written by Mr. Justice Thomas Zuber, who coincidentally had practised in Windsor, the Appeal Court went along with Mr. Justice Keith in his award of $200,000 for non-pecuniary loss and agreed with him that a 5-per-cent discount rate for the pecuniary loss made sound sense. But, the court went on, Mr. Justice Keith had added in one-third to the sum allowed for future care to cover the taxes which Diane would have to begin paying on her income from the fund when she turned twenty-one. Too much for taxes, the court held, and it reduced the award for pecuniary loss from $750,000 to $675,000, for a total, including the $200,000 non-pecuniary loss, of $875,000.

Then came the Supreme Court of Canada. And trouble.

In late June, 1977, the court decided to hear appeals on consecutive days of three damage actions, Diane's and two from western Canada that involved young men whose injuries in accidents had left them quadriplegics.

"When Earl and I heard that was the way it was going to be for us, three damage cases at once," Wunder says, "we decided right away we'd have our case heard last. We figured we were the best counsel, so we'd bat clean-up. We'd be in a position to make the greatest contribution."

Wunder's plan headed for disaster on the first day of the appeals when a lawyer in one of the western cases took too long presenting his argument. The nine judges grew restless, then impatient, then angry. Four days went by, an eternity, before the court reached *Teno* v. *Arnold*.

"My lords," Wunder began his statement on the damages issue, "we started with a little girl who was young and healthy and whole..."

"Just a moment, Mr. Wunder," Mr. Justice Wilfred Judson interrupted. "Don't say *that* again."

It wasn't Wunder's style to avoid emotion. "I'm not an appellate-court lawyer," he says. "It's too far removed from the hue and cry of the streets. When I'm talking in court I want everyone to hear the sound of the car brakes, feel the impact of the accident, sense the suffering. I wasn't going to be able to do that in the Supreme Court. In fact, it was clear to Earl and me that it was a situation of how fast we could stand up, say our piece, and sit down."

Wunder and Cherniak went home dreading bad news from the Supreme Court. They got it. Mr. Justice Wishart Spence wrote the court's decision, and he began by reducing the award for Diane's non-pecuniary loss from $200,000 to $100,000. It was done, he wrote, for reasons of "uniformity". The non-pecuniary awards in the two quadriplegic cases were set at the lower figure. So must Diane's be.

"Unrealistic in terms of today's prices," Wunder says.

Then Mr. Justice Spence proceeded to dismantle Mr.

Justice Keith's calculations for pecuniary loss. The judge announced that he was going outside the argument presented to him in court and taking judicial notice of the writings in 1973 of Dr. Deutsch of the Economic Council of Canada, who projected long-term inflation of 3.5 per cent. Take the present investment rate of 10.5 per cent, Mr. Justice Spence held, and subtract 3.5 per cent for inflation, thus arriving at a discount rate of 7 per cent for the Teno award. Since the rate was 2 per cent higher than Mr. Justice Keith's 5 per cent, the capital fund must be reduced. What amount seemed appropriate to Mr. Justice Spence? $440,000. Total amount for pecuniary and non-pecuniary loss: $540,000.

Wunder was floored. The amount of the award still ran high enough to protect Diane against most of her future's perils. But the Supreme Court's judgment left plenty of room for quarrel in law and in life.

"For starters," Wunder says, "bringing in Deutsch the way they did, the court was going outside the trial record. If I'd tried that, they would have torn my gown to shreds. You just don't take such liberties. The whole point, I guess, is that the Supreme Court of Canada only hears a case like ours every six months. They aren't used to this kind of issue. They're accustomed to a diet of constitutional cases, heavyweight stuff like that. They're far removed from what goes on in the world outside their court and their books."

Wunder wasn't alone in his distress over the Supreme Court's decision in the Teno case. The Ontario Court of Appeal gathered in a private meeting to consider ways to get around the senior court's judgment when future damage cases wound their way through the appeal process. The ceiling of $100,000 placed on non-pecuniary loss was far from realistic, and the calculations that reduced the Teno award for pecuniary loss didn't square with the everyday world. The Ontario Court of Appeal decided it was unhappy. It would look for ways to circle around the precedents the higher court had laid down in *Teno* v. *Arnold*.

"That case was a breakthrough in damages," Wunder says, "and one day Mr. Justice Keith's decision at trial is going to be vindicated."

At the evening appointment in Wunder's office, Orville and Yvonne Teno settled into the chairs across from Wunder as naturally as they would in their own living-room. They'd put in many hours since July 1969 in those chairs. Both were big people, strong-bodied, comfortable-looking, a husband and wife who'd carried the burden of their disabled daughter without complaint. They signed the documents Wunder placed in front of them. They thanked him for the cheque, a payment from one of the defendants' insurance companies. They made small talk.

"We're looking at a new house," Mr. Teno said.

"Something that'll have a bigger bedroom for Diane," Mrs. Teno said. "And a bathroom with equipment to make it easier for her."

"How is she these days?" Wunder asked. "Haven't seen her for a while. How's Diane anyway?"

"A young lady now," Mr. Teno said. "She's a teenager. Grown up almost."

"She's a doll, that one," Mrs. Teno said. "Just a doll."

"Well, you know," Wunder said, "you folks have done great by her from the start."

Orville Teno didn't miss a beat.

"So have you," he said to Wunder.

Second Adjournment

As Peter Steinmetz tells the story, it was Kelly Jay's T-shirt that tipped off the other partners in Cassels, Brock to precisely the sort of clientele that Steinmetz was bringing into the firm. Cassels, Brock — three dozen lawyers on the eighth and ninth floors at 165 University Avenue in Toronto — is Establishment. In Steinmetz's words, the partners include "a lot of the horsy set". Thus, Kelly Jay came as a shock on the winter morning a few years ago when he stepped off the elevator on the ninth floor and told Ruth, the receptionist, he had an appointment with Steinmetz. Ruth is fiftyish and permanently well-groomed. She rang Steinmetz's secretary. And she asked Kelly Jay, in her engaging mid-Atlantic accent, would he care to remove his coat and please take a seat?

"Well, you have to understand that Kelly Jay *looms*," Steinmetz says, relishing the story just enough. "He's such a big guy, way over six feet. He's got a couple of hundred pounds of gut. And that coat of his, a fur coat, it puts twenty animals on his back. Anyway, he peeled off the coat and stood there, very unconcerned, wearing his T-shirt with that incredible inscription blazing out at the world."

What did the inscription read?

" 'Fuck you'."

Ruth couldn't help noticing.

"She was so stunned I think she disconnected six phone

49

calls," Steinmetz says. "A little later a discreet memo made the circuit from the senior partners pointing out the standards expected around here. Really, though, Cassels, Brock gives me plenty of support in the work I do. They bend the rules of decorum. They let me come to the office in a sweater. They don't mind that I act for people like Kelly Jay."

Kelly Jay is a rock musician, and Steinmetz is one of about twenty-five lawyers in Toronto who practise "entertainment law". He acts for rock bands, record companies, and song composers, for the Good Brothers, Patsy Gallant, and the Canadian Brass. He is the envy of many young lawyers who are itching to push into his field. Some 150 students took the course in entertainment law at Osgoode Hall in the 1978-79 school year; not more than eight of them, according to the course lecturer, Bill Hinkson, who is himself an entertainment specialist, have cracked a small corner of the business. Those lawyers, like Steinmetz and Hinkson, who are full-time entertainment practitioners began building their clientele in the early 1970s, the years when the Canadian pop-music industry was at last asserting itself as a multi-million-dollar operation. They started early and hung in late.

"The legal stuff I do is easy," Steinmetz explained one April morning in his corner office at Cassels, Brock. "It's the business-affairs aspect that's tough. Suppose I'm acting for a band in arranging a contract with a record company. Well, whether the contract calls for the band to get a 5-per-cent royalty on the sale of each album or a 12-per-cent royalty is a very key issue. It means money for my client and I've got to do a job on the negotiation. But it isn't a legal problem. It's a business deal. The line blurs. Entertainment is different country from other kinds of law."

The décor in Steinmetz's office underlined the difference. Two gold records, signifying sales of 50,000 albums by two Steinmetz rock-band clients, Klaatu and Triumph,

hung in frames on the walls. Stereo speakers and a turn-
table sat behind him — the better to play his clients' music.
And the most eye-catching items on his desk were a copy of
Billboard Magazine and the jacket for a new Patsy Gallant
album.

"You have to like the music — most lawyers don't care for
rock — and you have to develop real empathy with your
clientele," Steinmetz went on, talking in a voice so low that it
rarely rose above a hush. Steinmetz is in his mid-thirties and
has a laid-back quality about him. He wears aviator glasses
and Roots boots. He's got a thousand records at home and
two teen-aged sons on whom he likes to test his clients'
products. One son's a drummer and the other a pianist –
guitarist – viola-player. Empathy with rock musicians
wouldn't present a problem for Steinmetz.

He ticked off some of the services he renders for his
clients. Drawing contracts on their behalf with record companies, with management companies, and with the publishing companies that, in exchange for a piece of the action,
undertake to promote a song into a hit. Thrashing out
royalty arrangements. Protecting the various financial
rights of a song-writer: performing rights (these arise out of
the number of times a song is performed in bars, at concerts, over Muzak, on the radio, in such commercial estab-
lishments as skating-rinks and dentists' offices), mechanical
rights (song performances on records and tapes), and syn-
chronization rights (in plays, TV shows, and movies).

"There's a legal foundation in all of this," Steinmetz said.
"It's copyright. An entertainment lawyer has to know the
Copyright Act cold. But even that doesn't get him much
past second base, because the Act is ambiguous. Out of date.
The people who drew it years ago didn't know what a
mechanical right to a song entailed, and the Act doesn't
begin to address itself to the way the music industry functions today. All these grey areas. To compensate, a lawyer
has to learn to wheel in the market-place."

51

He offered an example.

"I go to a record company for a client," he said, picking the Patsy Gallant album jacket and flipping it in his hands. "The company says that they'll pay my performer a royalty rate of 10 per cent. The 10 per cent is based on a figure for the number of albums sold minus sales tax and minus packaging costs. There's the rub, packaging costs. What they are is the cost of pressing the album in the plant and making the jacket and the sleeve that goes inside it. The record itself costs about forty-two cents, the jacket usually twenty cents, and the sleeve maybe half a cent. Meaning the whole item is ready to go to the retailer for something in the neighbourhood of seventy cents.

"Okay, but the company usually deducts eighty or ninety cents per album for packaging costs. That's off the top before anybody starts calculating royalties. It's the company's little hedge. I know this. The company knows I know it. So what I do for my client is negotiate better packaging deductions. Get the company down closer to its actual costs.

"I wouldn't try it for a new artist. Better he should have the record in the stores and make his name no matter what he sacrifices financially. But for an established artist, for Patsy" — he waved the Gallant album in his hand — "I'll say to the company, you leave in your big packaging deduction, your ninety cents, for the first 25,000 albums you sell, but after that I want the packaging deduction to drop off and I want the royalty to escalate from 10 per cent to 12 per cent."

Steinmetz dropped the jacket on his desk. "You have to understand the realities of the business to work out that kind of deal. Ninety-nine per cent of lawyers wouldn't even recognize that the record companies were taking their clients to the cleaners."

Steinmetz clearly has the smarts when it comes to entertainment law. He takes a leading role in the Canadian Bar Association's Media and Communications Section, and his speech at the CBC's continuing legal-education program in April 1978 titled "The Exploitation of Musical Copyright" is considered the last word on the subject. But to Steinmetz, smarts aren't enough.

"The music industry's a people industry, corny as that sounds," he said in his office. "Unless you bleed a little with your clients, you're not going to make it in this kind of law."

Then he told the sad saga of A Foot In Cold Water.

"Not a bad band at all. Four nice young Canadian guys who worked the bar circuit, dances, small concerts, paying their dues until they made it. They had a dream and they were determined. Then, out of the blue, Elektra Records in New York City got hot on them. Pure chance. Two women at Elektra — one was the director of promotion and the other was director of artists and repertoire — caught the band on a TV show and invited us down to New York to talk contract.

"Well, that was *it*. Elektra was a prestige label in those days. This was around 1974. Elektra had class. I mean, you went into the Paramount Record offices and a jukebox was blasting in the reception area. And at Atlantic, everything was off the wall. Atlantic was frantic. But at Elektra the scene was subdued and subtle and tasteful. It came from Jac Holtzman, who was Elektra's president. He had more class than anybody in the business. Capital C.

"Anyway, before we flew to New York I put a lot of time into drawing a deal memo. It was six pages, very carefully worded. I put in a personality sketch of the guys in the band. Talked of their aims in the business. I set out a range of royalties we'd like as opposed to just one specific rate. I showed we were serious and organized. I included the guys' social security numbers. Elektra wasn't dealing with a Mickey Mouse Canadian lawyer.

"So in New York Holtzman sat us around a table in his boardroom and ordered in a lovely lunch. The band was there and me and Holtzman and the two women who were so hot on us and a guy named Nussbaum who was Elektra's counsel. We ate and we talked about the Canadian economy, about politics, about the record industry.

" 'Let's just get to know one another.' Holtzman said, 'because fundamentally the deal is set. It's very refreshing to receive a deal memo out front like the one we got from Mr. Steinmetz. We want A Foot In Cold Water to record for Elektra.'

"The band went home and put a hell of an effort into cutting the first album. Brought in a special outside producer, guy named John Anthony, who produced the first album for Queen which was a big hit. Spared nothing. The band saw the dream coming true. Finished the recording session and mixing and delivered the master record to Elektra in New York for pressing, distribution, promotion, the whole trip.

"But, all of a sudden, disaster. Jac Holtzman was promoted to be vice-president of Warner Brothers, which owned Elektra. A new Elektra president came in. David Geffen. He was an intense guy, driven, but he was having a relationship with Cher. He was her lover in between Sonny Bono and Greg Allman, and he was never in the office. Other things happened. Elektra's headquarters moved from New York to Los Angeles. The two women who liked our band were let go. There was nobody left at the company who knew us. I spent hours on the phone, but Geffen wouldn't return my calls. Overnight the atmosphere became totally negative.

"The band's album came out. Oh yeah, Elektra *released* it. But to them it was just another piece of product. No hype, no promotion, no effort. They wrote it off. No other explanation for what they did to our people.

"Well, the band hung together for two more years. But the dream had gone up in smoke. A Foot In Cold Water fell apart. The guys were disillusioned. Three of them got out of music altogether. You could weep for them.

"I felt bewildered, all the work for nothing," Steinmetz said. "And I was only the lawyer."

CHAPTER TWO

The Country Lawyer

Paul Ross is a loving man. In the mornings, he wakes up his thirteen-year-old daughter with hugs and kisses. When he reads *Babar* to his five-year-old son, he turns on different voices for all the characters, W. C. Fields inflections for Cornelius, a quaver for the old lady, sensible tones for Babar. And he tells his wife she's beautiful in a way that makes you think her beauty is a fresh daily delight to him.

All of which—his openness and generous spirit—may explain why Paul Ross chose to practise law in the town of Clinton. Population: 3,200. Atmosphere: tranquil. Clinton is in Huron County in the far southwest reaches of Ontario. The surrounding countryside is given over to prosperous farming—dairy products, poultry, some beef—while Clinton itself functions mostly as a service centre for the area. The hospital is in Clinton. The Board of Education operates from the town. It's got an Ontario Provincial Police detachment, a library, three taverns, a factory that makes parts for pianos, and not much else. Local citizens tend to amble when they're out on the street, and the wise men of town—the editor of the weekly *News–Record*, the fellow who runs the IGA, and a few others—get together for a slow cup of coffee twice a day at Bartliff's Restaurant and Bakery. Clinton, all things considered, is a place where there's time to sniff the flowers. That's what brought Paul Ross to town.

"Things aren't angry like they are in a city law practice," he says. "This part of the world's got so much geographical room that you don't have people disputing for their own personal space. The larger spaces absorb all the aggressions."

Ross knows about the city. He grew up in Toronto and practised law there for several years. But on visits to Huron, he was seduced by the county's peace. He struck a deal with Beecher Menzies, the lawyer with the longest service in Clinton, and in January 1976, when Ross was thirty-eight years old, he entered into a new partnership. Menzies, Ross, 49 Albert Street, directly across the road from Bartliff's.

Ross and Menzies make a vivid contrast. Ross, the big-city boy, has wavy red hair, freckles, cord suits, and too much energy to suppress. He may be the fastest walker in the county. Menzies is large and amiable. He's a three-piece-grey-suit lawyer and has the kind of Old Ontario face, hearty and shrewd, that wouldn't look out of place in a portrait of the Family Compact. He grew up in Clinton, the son of the United Church minister, and returned from law school in 1955 to buy the town practice from a lawyer who was moving up to the bench. Menzies knows the territory.

"Beecher," Ross says, "has practised here long enough that he has the history of practically every piece of Huron property off by heart. When he's got a real-estate deal, he doesn't need to check the title. It's in his head."

There's a third lawyer in Clinton, Gerald Hiltz, a young man who started up a practice about a year before Ross came to town. Hiltz is meticulous, a worrier, and on real-estate deals with Beecher Menzies he'll submit detailed lists of requisitions, asking Menzies to clear up genuine or feared flaws on the property titles. Menzies ignores Hiltz's letter until Hiltz, a few blocks down Albert Street, telephones in exasperation.

"Don't you ever open your mail?" Hiltz asks.

"Aw, Gerry, the title's as good as gold," Menzies says.

"But my *requisitions*!"

"Gerry, do you want to close the deal or don't you?" Menzies says.

"That's *it*," Ross says. "When I hear Beecher talk like that, that attitude, I know why I'm here. None of the tension about a simple real-estate deal that I used to feel in the city."

"Tension? Over real estate?" Menzies says just before he strolls across the street for coffee with the other wise men at Bartliff's.

By mid-morning, the late October day had come up shiny and clear, and Ross decided to hit the road. It's a now-and-again habit of his to steal a few hours away from the office in the middle of the day and mosey through the back lanes of Huron County.

He checked the files stacked on both sides of his desk. Any emergency about to erupt? Not likely. There was the employment contract he was drawing for the new manager of the Little Inn over in Bayfield. There was the farmer east of Clinton who was getting an unfair deal from the Workmen's Compensation Board. There was the Draper Brothers and Reid purchase, a group of local men who were buying the old Heintzman piano factory. And there were the family-law cases, a specialty that Ross was developing in Huron, arranging adoptions, launching custody actions, drawing separation agreements.

"This one I call my Caspar Milquetoast file," he said, lifting a bulky folder with two hands. "My client is a simple farmer, a guy with manure on his boots, and he's married to a woman who's got a university education. She gives him a hard time until one day he snaps and walks out and ends up in this office. It's the first time in twenty years of marriage he's struck back against the wife. Only trouble is she's sitting on the farm and he's out in the cold. The farm is a $350,000 operation, but it isn't worth a penny unless somebody's running it, which nobody is with my guy off the property. I move fast. I get a court order. It puts my guy back on the farm. It gives the wife $50,000 to clear off. She does. He stops being Caspar Milquetoast. He's running his farm and nobody's hassling him. The wife's at some institution of higher education working on a Master's and hanging out with people who don't have manure on their boots. Happy ending."

Ross surveyed the stack of files. "I might've laughed at this stuff when I was a lawyer in the city. Maybe I'd have called it small potatoes. But now it makes me feel good. The Caspar Milquetoast, I'm really proud of that one."

Five minutes later, Ross's brown Chevette was on a two-lane highway running north out of Clinton through farmland that rolled just enough to take away the threat of boredom. Ross had a comment for each farm, each clump of woods, each grocery-store-and-gas-pump village. On the back roads of Huron County, he was part tour guide, part social historian, Baedeker crossed with Vance Packard.

"The farmhouse over there," he said, "all that old grey stone, it's lovely, you know, but inside the people've destroyed it. The idea of fine décor out here is a lot of flocked wallpaper over every surface. You look at the design they choose, and if you saw it on a Rorschach test, you'd say it was a row of naked female pelvises."

He pulled onto the shoulder of the road opposite a farm that smacked of money. The chicken-houses, long barracks two storeys high, showed fresh paint. The grass around them was clipped to the tidiness of a golf-course fairway, and men moved across the property in strides that said they were on profitable business.

"Know what the farmhouse on this place has?" Ross said. "Great big swimming-pool. Indoors. Some of the farms in the county are worth a million bucks. It's a matter of quotas, which is something country lawyers have to bone up on. Every farm comes with its own quota. Take milk. The federal government subsidizes dairy farmers, and it sets a big over-all quota of how much milk is going to be produced in the entire country in any given year. Then it parcels out

58

the quotas to the provincial governments and the provincial governments parcel them out to individual farmers. If a farmer gets a big quota, he's laughing. He can earn a lot of money. But if he goes over his quota and produces too much milk, he gets penalized. And the whole thing is complicated by the fact that there are different kinds of quotas. You have to understand all this intricate stuff—they don't teach it in law school—to be able to handle the job when a farm sale comes into the office because we're talking here about a pretty large legal fee."

Ross drove on down the highway.

"I didn't know anything about the economics of farming when I moved to Huron," he said. "So for six weeks I used to get up early and help a farmer milk his cows and listen to him talk before I went in to the office. Every morning I stood behind cows and watched their tails flick in my face. Cows' tails, one thing I learned about farming, are soaked in cows' piss."

Ross took his sweet time. He turned down dirt roads, stopped to check out properties that had for-sale signs posted on them, steered into a farmer's front yard to buy two pumpkins and a couple of Spy apples, price: $1.75. Everywhere he drove, the land had the feel of thrift. Huron had been settled a century and a half earlier by people who were hard-working, tight-fisted, and low church—Scotch Presbyterians, Congregationalists, and Methodists from the north of England. The Dutch came later, an even more conservative and strict people. They worship at the Dutch Reformed Church and send the kids to their own Clinton District Christian School where there's little truck with the evils of modern ways and plenty of emphasis on fundamental values. Huron County has no room for slackers.

"Things aren't *entirely* moral out here," Ross said. "Farmers' sons are still known to sneak into the barn and have relations with sheep."

Ross drove up a steep hill into Goderich. It's the largest

59

town in the county, almost 8,000 people, the headquarters for Huron's municipal government and courts. It's a town that might have been put together on order for a Walt Disney movie. It is pretty and miniature and ideal. It has a town square and a district where the best houses look down a steep hill to the Maitland River and to Lake Huron beyond it, and everyone who comes to town remarks on its magnificent sunsets. Goderich, by and large, stands still. John Galt and Tiger Dunlop, two early Ontario go-getters, had great hopes for the town when they organized it in the first part of the nineteenth century. But since then, Goderich has been content to get by on its salt business, a couple of foundries that manufacture agricultural equipment, the municipal government offices, and the tourists who crowd in during the warm months. The sunsets really are magnificent, and that's almost enough for everyone in Goderich.

"The *London Free Press* stopped carrying its Goderich section the other day," Ross said. "It's the biggest daily newspaper in the area. Runs weekly reports from all the more important communities around here. Now it's dropped Goderich. Maybe it's trying to tell us something."

For lunch, Ross decided on the Albion Hotel in Bayfield, a few miles south of Goderich. Bayfield bustles in the summer and empties in the fall. It's a village of cottages and small shops and restaurants and marinas on Lake Huron, and summer people, many of them Americans from Michigan, just naturally take to it. The Albion stays in business through the slack season and on this day the fat and friendly waitress said the special at $3.50 was trout fresh out of the lake. She'd cleaned it herself that morning. Anything for you, Mr. Ross, she said. Ross had acted for her in a custody action.

"A lawyer's fee," Ross said, discussing the nitty-gritty of his profession over the trout and a beer. "What the fee depends on is not the time a lawyer puts into a file, not the amount of work he has to do on it, not the result he gets for his client. It's none of those things. The truth is—this came to me since I moved down here—a lawyer's fee really depends on the standard of living he decides he wants to maintain. He charges his clients whatever amount is going to give him and his family the right-sized house, the proper number of cars, enough holidays in Florida. Like that."

He asked the waitress if there was another piece of fish, just a tiny piece more. There was.

"Okay," he went on, "what does my theory about fees mean to me personally? It means I can afford to charge less and earn less than I could in the big city. We don't have any fancy restaurants in Huron, no sixty-dollar lunches with clients. We don't need big cars and a different suit for every day of the week. And recreation? It's mostly outdoors. It's mostly free. A lawyer like me, handling an ordinary practice, can earn $30,000 to $40,000 a year, ball-park figures, and stay happy. That sounds like peanuts by Toronto standards, but in terms of life-style it goes as far as the salary of the downtown lawyer who hustles his ass off for one hundred grand a year."

Ross finished his lunch and walked across the hall to the Albion's bar, where the waitress was washing glasses. He asked her about the aftermath of the custody action. She took a long fifteen minutes to relive the episode in her life and to analyse her emotions. Ross folded his coat on a stool, leaned on the bar, and listened until she wound to the end of her story.

"Glad you're happy," Ross said.

The fat and friendly waitress smiled a lovely smile.

Back in the Chevette, Ross steered through a series of sharply curved dirt roads that led past the basin for the Bayfield Yacht Club to a beach edging on Lake Huron. Enormous brown waves broke against a pier that reached out from the beach. On the pier, a single Canada Goose hopped in the spray from the waves. He was alone and he

61

was baffled. Where had the other geese flown to? Where were his friends?

"Oh my God, that's terrible!" Ross said, his voice loud in the small car. "He looks so little. He's so vulnerable. That's the most pathetic thing I've ever seen."

At that moment, the way Ross spoke of the Canada Goose and its predicament, he might have been as concerned for it as he was for any of his clients, for Caspar Milquetoast, for the fat and friendly waitress.

"Maybe," he said, "there's time out here to be concerned for all kinds of strange things."

When the subject of the Truscott case surfaced, as it inevitably had to, it was at the lawyers' luncheon table in the Bedford Hotel. The Bedford fronts on Goderich's town square across the street from the courthouse, and each noon the grey-haired waitresses in the pink uniforms hold the dining-room's best table for any of the county's lawyers and judges — there are about thirty of them in all — who happen to be in the neighbourhood. A dozen usually show up, and conversation over the fried-egg sandwiches and coffee and the occasional beer centres on lawyerly gossip, lightweight stuff. But this day somebody mentioned Steven Truscott, the boy who was convicted of murder in the courthouse across the square.

He was fourteen at the time, and the victim of the crime, Lynne Harper, was twelve. She was raped, then strangled with her blouse, one June evening in 1959 in a woods near the old RCAF base at Clinton. Truscott was sentenced to be hanged. His age, and Lynne Harper's, made the case a sensation around the world. So did the prospect of the rope for a fourteen-year-old. Truscott's sentence was commuted to life imprisonment. He served ten years and was paroled, but the sensation lingered on.

Truscott insisted he was innocent. The locals had railroaded him. "It would be hard to match the bigotry, hate, and vindictiveness of the citizens of Huron County," he wrote in a book published in the fall of 1979. "I considered the people of Goderich and Clinton little better than a lynch mob."

At lunch this day, talk started off as usual. MacEwan Egener who practises in Goderich reminisced about the famous curling party that members of the bar threw a few years back at the arena up in Walkerton. There was as much drinking as curling, and when time came to adjourn for more celebrations at the County Court judge's house six miles down highway number four in Hanover, the legal profession had a transportation crisis on its hands. Who was sober enough to steer a car in traffic? Somebody influential phoned the OPP.

"The police used their cruisers to block off all the side roads," MacEwan Egener said, big smile in place. "Allowed no cars into the area. By the time our bunch set off from the curling rink, that highway was as clear as Main Street at four in the morning."

Alan Mill, a partner from a firm in Wingham, brought up the aging lawyer from over east of the county who got himself disbarred for a violation of the Mann Act in the United States. It seemed the aging lawyer liked to invite young girls to accompany him on visits to horse shows in Pennsylvania and Ohio and New York State. Somehow the visits invariably ended with hanky-panky in motel rooms. One of the young girls blew the whistle on the elderly solicitor, and he lost his right to practise when he was convicted of taking female persons across state lines for immoral purposes.

"Unfair," Alan Mill added jokingly. "Doing that sort of thing with young girls at his age, two or three times a night I understand, they shouldn't have disbarred him. They should have awarded him a Q.C. on the spot."

Then somebody got around to Steven Truscott.

"Any place you go outside the county," Beecher Menzies

said, "they hear you're from Clinton and they say, ah, the Truscott case, as if you're personally responsible for some notorious miscarriage of justice."

"That's so," Dan Murphy from Goderich said.

"The boy had a million dollars' worth of counsel," Bill Cochrane said, the judge of the Provincial Court. "Frank Donnelly at the trial here in town, John O'Driscoll on the appeal, Arthur Martin when the case was heard all over again in '66 by the Supreme Court in Ottawa. All three of those men got appointed to the Ontario High Court later on. Counsel like them, if there was a chance the boy was innocent, they'd have persuaded the courts he was."

"Hmmm," Dan Murphy murmured.

"The thing the Truscott people got wrong," Beecher Menzies said, "was making Glenn Hays out to be a monster. Glenn was a fair and decent crown attorney, that's the truth. If he went hard in prosecuting Truscott, well, it was his job to do so."

Dan Murphy nodded.

"They called Glenn bloodthirsty," Menzies said.

Murphy nodded again, and everyone considered Menzies' words.

"By a great coincidence," Murphy started in, "I arrived in Goderich to start practising on the day before the Truscott case began. I stayed out at the Donnelly cottage, lovely weather, too, end of the summer, y'know, and every morning, Mr. Donnelly, Frank, would get up, shave in cold water, and drive down to the courthouse. I went with him and never missed a day of the trial. Wonderful drama. Frank didn't put the boy on the stand, but when he was finished with his cross-examinations, there was something wrong with the crown's case. There were little pieces of timing that were out—the times when witnesses saw the boy, when the girl must have died, when the boy arrived back at his home. Didn't fit together. To my mind, Frank Donnelly raised a reasonable doubt that that boy murdered that girl."

Murphy took a sip of coffee and wiped his mouth with a paper napkin.

"Nine juries out of ten," he said, "nine out of ten would've acquitted Truscott. But he had one piece of bad luck."

Murphy took a slow look around the table.

"He got the tenth jury."

Judge Bill Cochrane's desk was bare except for his cheque-book. Middle-of-the-road pop music filled the office from a walnut-finished radio-and-stereo set. The wall-to-wall broadloom muffled outside noises, and when the judge was finished with his desk work—signing a few personal cheques—a book waited, Peter Newman's *The Bronfman Dynasty*, hardcover edition. It was 2:30 p.m. on a Thursday and, as usual, there was no afternoon business for the Provincial Court (Criminal) in the County of Huron.

"I've been two years in this job," Judge Cochrane said, "and for seventeen years before that I was the county's crown attorney. In all that time I've handled five murders, two bank robberies, and three rapes. That's all the big crime Huron's known."

The judge sat erect in his chair, a fastidious man, silver hair brushed back, silver moustache clipped to a fine line, grey suit fresh and creaseless, his manner old-world and courtly.

"It's easily explained about the lack of crime," he said. "We have no ethnic groups. No large centres of population. No place for a criminal to hang out. There were 50,000 people in the county twenty years ago and there are 50,000 today. The place never changes, not for the worse anyway."

Besides, the judge went on, Huron's native criminals, the few who turn up, tend to be short on the wiles of big-city crooks.

"Bob Smith decided to rob the bank over in Brucefield," the judge said. "This is a few years ago when I was the crown. Brucefield looked a good bet. Just a village. Bank only visits one day a week, Thursdays, to take care of the farmers. Good volume, though. Well, Bob cut the barrel off his dad's shotgun, got himself a balaclava to cover his face, and drove up to the bank on the Thursday after New Year's Day. His being short of funds over the holiday season was what prompted the adventure in the first place. Bob drove up to the bank in his old black-and-yellow car with the broken door on the driver's side wired shut and he came out with nine thousand dollars.

"He got across the back road as far as Seaforth, six or seven miles, and ran out of gas. Bad planning on Bob's part. But he pushed the old black-and-yellow car to a service station, bought gas out of his loot, stayed to chat awhile with the attendant, and went on up to Kitchener, another sixty miles. That's where he ran into his pal who owned a brand-new Camaro. Trouble was the brand-new Camaro had been repossessed by the dealer back in Exeter, which happens to be just south of where Bob had done his robbery. Didn't matter. The two lads drove to Exeter, Bob peeled off some more bills, and the friend let him drive the Camaro on his getaway to the States.

"No doubt from the start who the guilty party was. Bob had the only old black-and-yellow car with the driver's door wired shut that anyone around here could recall. The OPP knew Bob pretty well anyway. They'd turned him down when he applied to join the force. But it was Bob who sealed the case himself. He took a holiday in the Caribbean and dropped a line back to his friend the Camaro owner arranging to meet up with him in Nashville, Tennessee, at the Grand Ole Opry. Bob signed the letter, 'Your friendly bank robber'.

"FBI were waiting for Bob when he walked into the Opry and they shipped him up to us. Bob received five years. It wasn't a difficult case to prosecute. Not many are in Huron."

Judge Cochrane excused himself to sign another cheque.

66

Heather Ross is Paul Ross's second wife. She's the mother of five-year-old Quinn, a tornado of a kid, and stepmother to thirteen-year-old Tagen, a blonde who would drive Humbert Humbert to distraction. Before Heather married Paul, she worked at interesting jobs in Toronto, at the CBC radio program *This Country In The Morning* and at *The Canadian Magazine*. Before that, she grew up in the interior of British Columbia, and in 1970, when she was twenty, she was elected Miss Kelowna. Her loveliness isn't the standard stuff of beauty queens. It is surprisingly English. She is small and porcelain. Her nose is Audrey Hepburn and her dark eyes never blink. She radiates serenity.

She is also tough-minded. That made it no accident when she involved herself in the Great Huron County Book-Banning Fuss of 1978. It began when Lloyd Barth, a retired high-school teacher from Blyth, objected to three novels that the Huron Board of Education permitted as optional reading for grade thirteen students at the county's five high schools. The Catholic Women's League of Knightsbridge took up Barth's cause, and Renaissance Canada, an evangelistic pressure group from just outside Toronto, parachuted in its support. They asked that the board protect Huron's adolescents from the three books — Salinger's *Catcher in the Rye*, Steinbeck's *Of Mice and Men*, and Margaret Lawrence's *The Diviners* — and the board listened.

"Just by chance," Heather explained one morning as she baked a coffee cake in her kitchen, "I heard on a Friday late in the spring that the board was going to rule on the books the following Monday. That's how things happen out here. Very quietly. Well, I phoned some people and we got the board to postpone its decision and started writing a brief to show the anti-banning position. It wasn't a situation where the whole county was excited. There was a small group against the books, a small group in favour, and a big majority that didn't care. That's also how things happen out here."

67

Heather's friend Alice emerged as chief spokesperson for the pro-books faction, Alice Munro, the author and winner of two Governor General's Awards for her stories about small-town people. She grew up in Wingham in the north of the county and now, at almost fifty, lives in Clinton. Her days are marked by privacy and old-fashioned good manners. She stays at home, "looking at the wall, with nobody to notice," she says, waiting for the stories to come. When she feels it's time for a luncheon with Heather, she communicates a week in advance by polite note.

"In this kind of society," she has said of southwestern Ontario, "everyone has a different idea of who you are, so you learn to keep quiet and preserve yourself with the least possible trouble."

Still, Munro made herself visible on behalf of Heather's cause. She gave interviews to Toronto newspapers and TV stations, and she took a seat on the platform in the Clinton High School gym for a meeting organized by the Writers' Union of Canada to explain the anti-banning position. Five hundred citizens turned out. One man brought a Bible and told the gathering it was the only book that a high-school student needed to be taught. A couple of others led prayers for the county's soul. Alice Munro tried to talk of literature. It was an awkward gathering and, not long afterwards, Munro got a new unlisted phone number at home.

The Board of Education allowed time at a meeting one summer night for representations on the books issue. Heather intended to read her group's brief. But, attacked by nerves, she turned to her husband the lawyer, the man trained to persuade.

"Maybe I saw it as part of my role in the community to speak my piece," Ross says. "When Beecher set up practice here, he joined the Lions Club. I go down to the Board of Education and defend books that my neighbours think are dirty."

His appearance before the board wasn't encouraging.

"Oh, they *listened*," Ross says. "But the chairman had

already bragged that he hadn't read any of the books and didn't intend to. He could make up his mind on the basis of the excerpts that Renaissance Canada passed around."

On August 21, 1978, the board announced its decision. *Catcher in the Rye* and *Of Mice and Men* passed, but *The Diviners*, winner of the 1975 Governor General's Award for fiction, was struck from the Huron County high-school curriculum.

"Loss of respectability is important to middle-class people," Alice Munro said afterwards. "Maybe they shouldn't be educated out of it. Some of the values they hold are working very well for them. There's a great deal of comfort in a rooted permanent society where everybody knows what's expected of them."

Heather found that the books fuss caused her to take a deeper look at her life in the country and her place as a country lawyer's wife.

"I'm not sure that many of the lawyers around here would admit it," she says, "but their wives are very important to their practice, more important than city lawyers' wives by far. Meg, for example, Beecher's wife, Meg is a dynamo. She's a substitute teacher at the high school and does work at the hospital. She makes contacts all over the place. She's the one who asks people from out in the country over to their house for dinner, people that it would never occur to Beecher to entertain. Really, in an indirect way, Meg recruits clients for Beecher and helps keep them steady clients."

Heather is content with a lower profile and a more independent role. For a couple of years she ran the Arbor, a gift shop in Clinton. Now she looks after the kids, cooks, reads, thinks about getting back to the painting she used to do.

"I like the country very much," she says. "But there are two things I miss about life in the city. One is being able to tear off on the spur of the moment to a movie or to a good cheap little restaurant. You can't do that in Huron."

And the second thing she misses?

"Friends, the kind of friends where so much is understood between you without having to express it. Out here, I find that I always have to explain myself."

Late one night, Paul Ross poured a Scotch on the rocks. He put a record on the stereo set, a Mozart concerto for flute and orchestra, and pulled his chair close to the low fire in the grate in his living-room.

"The lawyers out here are good," he began. "Beecher is what you'd call the pillar of the legal community, and Donnelly and Murphy — that's Dan Murphy and Jimmy Donnelly, the son of the guy who defended Truscott — are such excellent counsel that they've got a lock on the litigation work in Huron *and* they get retained by firms to act in cases outside the county."

He sipped at his Scotch.

"Dan Murphy. There's one of my favourites. He's a lot of what Huron County's all about. He's a gregarious guy. He likes his white wine. He laughs all the time. He lives in one of those big houses in Goderich that look over the Maitland River. He's also a Catholic. He's got seven kids. He doesn't want any school to tell them they can read *The Diviners*. That's the mix you get in the man, smart and straight, a little outrageous, and very, very conservative. People in the county speak that language, and Donnelly and Murphy do terrific business."

Ross poured just an ounce more Scotch into his glass. He isn't a naturally generous drinker.

"It's not easy for an outside lawyer to break into a community like Clinton. It's an eggshell situation at first. You walk softly. I had some work for a real-estate agent in town, and through absolutely nobody's fault the deal fell through. I said him, 'Well, you win some and you lose some.' He didn't like that. Hasn't brought me any business since I made the crack. You wait a while before you enjoy the privilege of kidding around about money in Huron."

Ross turned over the Mozart.

70

"The first time I got myself involved in the town came when the Minister of Health down at Queen's Park said the provincial government was closing the Clinton hospital. That really struck at the heart of the community. They never move as a group here, they're individuals, but the hospital issue brought them together. The Minister, Frank Miller, came to town to make a speech about the reason the province had to close the hospital. Try and smooth things over. The people threw snowballs at him. That's how mad they were and how united. Well, I was a little reluctant to get into the situation, being new in town and everything, but I knew I had a feel for what should be done. At one point in my life I took eight months out of law and worked as a speech-writer for Cabinet ministers in Bill Davis's government. Anyway, I got in touch with people I'd met at Queen's Park and I figured out the lawyers to talk in Toronto. In the end, our side went to court and argued that the provincial government didn't have the power under the Hospitals Act to shut the Clinton hospital. The court looked at the Act and agreed. The hospital stayed open. It still is. That felt good."

Another ounce of Scotch, another small log on the fire.

"Almost everything feels good to me these days. No matter what else the practice of law *is* in the country, what it *isn't* is a battle. In Toronto, you look good to a client by making somebody else look not good. That doesn't have to happen in Clinton."

A sip of Scotch.

"Out here—this is one of the bottom lines for me about a country practice—you don't have to destroy the lawyer on the other side."

The Mozart concerto floated away on a soft flurry of high notes.

Third Adjournment

"Here's a cute one," Shelly Altman was saying one summer morning in his office on the twenty-fourth floor of the Eaton Centre in Toronto. "My guy is Dennis Tanner, he's about twenty-five years old, and he's got a long record for small stuff. Breaking and entering. Theft over $200. Parole violations. He's done a bit of time. On this particular case I got coming up for him this afternoon, he's charged with theft over and possession over. It's all about a Corvette. A bunch of guys stole it off a parking lot and drove it around over in Cabbagetown. The cops got one witness, a kid, acquaintance of my guy's, who gave them a statement saying my guy was at the wheel of the Corvette. But at the preliminary hearing, the crown asks the kid about his statement to the cops, and he says, what statement? I can't even read, he says. So now I'm going to trial in County Court and I don't know where we stand with this kid. What'll he testify? Is his first statement any good? I'm gonna speak to the cops beforehand, speak to the crown, and maybe we can work something out. Maybe they know they don't have a strong case. Maybe they don't want my guy bad enough. Maybe I can walk him."

Shelly Altman is a high-volume criminal lawyer. He handles in the neighbourhood of 225 cases a year. Much of what he does is legal-aid work, acting for con men and hookers and thieves and bandits who are too down-and-out to afford one of the prominent names of the criminal bar. Altman's cases don't often make headlines, not in the manner of, say, Eddie Greenspan, the Toronto counsel whose defences in two murder trials, the Christine Demeter case (reported in the book *By Persons Unknown*) and the Bruce Lorenz case, elevated him to the status of media star. Altman spends more days in court than Greenspan. He's in there *every* day. "I love court," he says. "The more hours I'm in there, the better I function." So he fights it out in the pits, in Provincial Court and County Court, defending men and women, losers, who represent to most respectable citizens the dregs of society.

Altman's career is marked by contradictions. His clients are homely and smelly, scabby and toothless, dressed in T-shirts and last year's jeans. Altman, in his mid-thirties, is almost beautiful. He has luminous dark eyes, a face of timeless good looks, compact build, and faultless taste in clothes. His clients, anxious or arrogant, seem resistant to sympathy. Altman is boundlessly patient with them, even kind, generous with his reassurances and his explanations of their predicaments.

"Ninety-nine per cent of my people come from really awful backgrounds," he said in his office. "They get in trouble. Why shouldn't they? The whole world has been dumping on them from the day they were born. They commit criminal acts, and when they do, it's out of strength. Maybe it's strength from booze or drugs, whatever, it's temporary. Then they're in court and they're operating out of weakness. But they have rights."

Altman lit up a cigarette. He's a chain-smoker. He's forever forgetting his own packages, leaving them in restaurants and courtrooms, and bumming a cigarette from anybody handy, a cop, crown attorney, one of his own low-life clients.

"For most of them I'm the only link they have out of their rotten culture," he went on. "In court they don't know what's happening. They don't recognize the niceties of the process. They don't realize I'm trying to make the crown prove they're guilty beyond a reasonable doubt. All they know — and this is visually, from the action they see in the courtroom — is whether I'm fighting for them. That's why I never let the crown have the last word. If the crown makes an argument, I make a counter-argument. I might know the crown in going to win the point, but the client doesn't know it. All he sees is that I'm on my feet. I'm fighting for him. A lot of the time, the results, whether a guy is sentenced to jail, don't mean as much to the client as the fact that *somebody* has fought for him. When I go to court, I never give up."

Altman rode the elevator from his office to the ground floor and cut through the glitter of Eaton Centre in the direction of the courts in the nearby Old City Hall.

"With lawyers, criminal law is kind of a game," he said as he walked. "We play it above board. We won't lie. The cops are the same way. Most of the time, anyway. Once, though, I was defending a guy who's a regular client, always in trouble. This time, he went into the Warwick Hotel and bought a briefcase full of cassettes for five bucks from some rounder he met in there. He came out and walked into a cop on the street. He's charged with possession of stolen property. I figure he's cooked but maybe I'll have a go at the complainant, the person who owned the cassettes before they were stolen from him by the guy who sold them to my guy in the Warwick. But the complainant turns out to be a *priest*. No way I can work on his credibility. We come up to the trial, and the crown asks me what I'm gonna do. Oh hell, I say, let's have a trial. The crown says, well, listen Shelly, why not make a deal? He wants me to plead my guy guilty and he'll recommend a suspended sentence, which is not bad considering the length of my guy's previous record. But I say I don't think so. The case is called, and the crown gets up and tells the judge he's offering no evidence. Case dismissed. The story behind it is the priest couldn't positively identify the cassettes as being his. It's a game."

Altman entered Courtroom 42 in Old City Hall. It was a room with a formal atmosphere, poorly lit and smelling faintly of musk. Altman was present for the second day of a preliminary hearing on charges against his client of theft and forgery. The client was waiting for him at the back of the courtroom, a dark, solid, swarthy woman in her early thirties. She was an immigrant, Greek, and the police version of the charges was that she had stolen the bank-book of a co-worker—both were waitresses in the dining-room at a University of Toronto college—and forged the co-worker's name on a withdrawal slip at her bank to clean out her account of $1,298.68.

"My girl's going to get committed for trial on all the charges," Altman said, waiting for court to resume. "But I always like to stir things around at the preliminary hearing. This is the stage where the judge rules whether there's enough evidence for a trial to proceed in a higher court, and it gives me the best shot I have to find out what the crown's got in the way of a case. Besides, on these charges against my girl, I want to ask the crown's hand-writing analyst a few questions."

As part of its case, the police had requested Altman's client, before her arrest, to write out her name a couple of dozen times. An expert from the Centre of Forensic Sciences had compared the specimen signatures with the forged signature on the bank withdrawal slip and declared all to have been written by the same hand.

When the analyst took the stand, a small, grey, precise man, Altman approached him in a conversational manner. It was as if two craftsmen, mutually respectful of one another, were enjoying a professional chat. Altman positioned himself close to the witness stand to review the sheet of specimen signatures and asked questions in a low, almost inaudible voice for about ten minutes. When he'd finished with the expert, he seemed satisfied.

"All right, gentlemen," the judge, a brisk, athletic man, said to Altman and the crown attorney after a couple of other witnesses had testified. "There'll be a committal for trial against the accused on all counts."

Altman arranged for bail to be continued for his client, spoke a few comforting words to her, and moved into the corridor.

"I like what I got from the hand-writing guy," he said. "At first he said he'd just picked out points in my girl's specimen signatures 'at random' and found points of likeness with the forged signature in the size proportion of the writing, the slant, the connections between letters, all that stuff. He said he selected them *at random*. But after I questioned him awhile, he switched from 'at random' and started using another word. 'Similarities'. I wondered if he really had gone through the signatures *at random*, or whether he was going through them unconsciously *looking* for similarities. It makes a difference to the case against my girl. I'm gonna get my own hand-writing expert and see what he says."

Altman made stops at two more courtrooms in the Old City Hall. One was to attend a bail hearing for a client charged with rape. The client, a pot-bellied, dull-faced man in his thirties, was let out on a $500 surety with the conditions that he have no contact with the complainant and reside with his mother. ("I don't know why they bother with that last one," Altman said. "His mother's a wino and my guy's got everything from ulcers to high blood pressure to a drinking problem.") The second stop was to consolidate nine cheque-kiting charges against another Altman client into three charges on the guarantee that the client would plead guilty to the three. ("Yesterday morning, Sunday, I took the sergeant in charge of the case to breakfast and we worked out the deal.") The crown attorney agreed to the arrangement, and the judge told Altman's client, a young man with a pock-marked face and sleek black hair, to report back in a month for sentencing.

"I never intended to be a lawyer," Altman said over lunch at a restaurant in the Eaton Centre. "I thought lawyers were wishy-washy. But I went to see *Judgment at Nuremberg*, the movie, and figured international law might be interesting. Lead to the diplomatic corps maybe. I enrolled at Osgoode and found out that international law isn't Maxmilian Schell in *Judgment at Nuremberg*.

"But I got involved in a couple of interesting deals at Osgoode. In first year I worked for the Toronto Bail Project. That meant interviewing people in jail to see if someone could go bail for them. Then, in between first and second years, I worked up at the institution in Penetang where they keep the criminally insane. My job was to go through the files of people who'd been declared unfit to stand trial and find out where they stood in the system. I sat in on group-therapy sessions up there, too, and that was all very enlightening for a kid like me who'd come from a nice, closed little Toronto Jewish community. Up until then, I didn't know much about the outside world.

"Still, by third year of Osgoode I was ready to quit. One of the professors, a lovely man who took a real interest in his students, asked me what kind of law I'd even consider practising. Criminal, I said, and this teacher immediately got in touch with Harvey Salem on my behalf. Harvey is one of the nicest, wisest men in the world, a criminal lawyer, and he asked me one question on the telephone.

" 'Do you want to be an observer,' he said, 'or a participant?'

" 'Participant,' I said.

" 'Come on down,' he said, and I've been practising criminal law ever since that phone call."

Altman took a cigarette from his pack, paused to ask a waiter for a light as he left the restaurant, and headed towards the courthouse on University Avenue to sort out the Dennis Tanner case.

77

"Some defence lawyers won't talk to the crown or the cops," he said on the way. "I talk to them all the time. Maybe I'll get something out of them. They've got all those resources I don't have. Why not ride with them? Anyway, if you don't talk to them, you'll never find out whether really, deep down, they think they haven't got much of a case against your guy. Maybe they're just waiting for you to *ask* them to throw the thing out."

Altman rode the courthouse escalator to the lawyers' lounge, a large room on the second floor filled with heavy armchairs and chesterfields where lawyers, crown attorneys, and policemen sit out the wait between cases. Altman spotted the two detectives on the Tanner case and brought them a couple of coffees from a serving table in the centre of the lounge. One detective was beefy and had red hair and large red freckles on the backs of his folded hands. The other was a cool customer in tinted glasses and a dark three-piece suit. Neither seemed pleased to be joined by Altman.

The lack of warmth in the detectives' welcome didn't ruffle Altman. He handed round the coffees, made chit-chat, and quickly drew flickers of interest out of the two men. Altman's a natural and habitual story-teller.

"I had this kid who was always into something," he said. "Breaking and entering, theft over, almost every petty crime in the book. But each time he came to court, I'd walk him or the charge'd be withdrawn or he'd draw probation. Never went inside. This final time, though, he broke into a tire store and ran out with a Michelin under each arm straight into a police officer. I told the kid he'd get three to six months anyway. But at the trial, by some kind of ridiculous miracle the judge gave him probation again. When I explained this to the kid, he was mad as hell. 'What do you mean probation? It can't be. I had a party last night. Everybody said goodbye to me because I was finally going in. I was gonna do time. I was gonna be a man. I can't go back

78

and face my friends now. This is terrible.' And I never again saw the kid as a client."

The two detectives laughed and Altman swooped in on the Tanner case.

"What you're faced with here is a previous inconsistent statement, right?" he said, smooth and earnest. "The kid who's your witness—how old is he anyway? Eighteen? Nineteen?—he said he saw my guy at the wheel. But then he gets up in court at the preliminary and says, no, my guy wasn't at the wheel. My guy was in the passenger seat, and the passenger seat isn't good enough to get him on possession of the stolen vehicle. There are cases that say that."

The detectives nodded.

"I don't think the kid's first statement is going to stand up. Especially when he says he can't read."

"Another thing," the beefy detective said, "we lost track of the kid. He's got a subpoena but we're not sure where he is exactly."

"Yeah?" Altman said.

"If the kid doesn't show up today, it's game over anyway," the cool detective said.

"Well, you know if your witness isn't in court," Altman said, "I'm going to rant and rave at the judge to get the case thrown out."

"Sure," the beefy detective said.

"Where's the crown on the case?" Altman asked. "He around here today?"

"Right over there," the cool detective said, nodding at a big man with a full head of salt-and-pepper hair sitting across the room.

"Oh yeah, Steve's got it," Altman said, looking around. "Why don't you go over and talk to him about it? I'm sure you're in trouble on the previous inconsistent. Maybe Steve won't want to waste his time."

The two detectives moved to the crown attorney's chair while Altman waited with his coffee and cigarette. The conference had lasted no more than three or four minutes when the crown attorney called across to Altman.

"Okay, Shelly, forget it," he said. "That's it. No case."

Altman smiled at the two detectives and left the lounge.

"Plea bargining isn't the right word for that," he said. "It's plea *negotiation*."

Outside one of the courtrooms, Altman found Dennis Tanner. He was big and muscular and wore a light blue T-shirt that revealed an array of tattoos on his arms. "Carol" was remembered and "Debbie" and "Karen". Tanner's apparent autobiography was also noted: "Born to raise hell" ran across one bicep.

"You can go home, Dennis," Altman said to him.

"I'm walked?" Tanner answered without a change in his expression.

"Stay clean," Altman said. "Just for a change. Just for me."

Tanner looked as if Altman were speaking to him in a foreign language.

Altman made his way down the courthouse corridor. As he opened an outside door, a handsome, sturdy young woman came through from the other direction.

"Why, *hello*," Altman said, brightening.

The woman gave him a frosty glance and kept walking.

"She's a cop," Altman said. "She was an undercover agent on a case where there was a pimp she wanted to nail so bad. I acted for the guy and found a bunch of holes in the case. He got off."

Altman smiled, an almost seraphic smile.

"It's a game," he said. "But seriously played."

CHAPTER THREE

The Crown

Shortly after seven p.m. on Monday, July 2, a soft and balmy evening, Kathleen Wels set out for her evening run from the family house at 5 Hillscourt Avenue on the north fringes of Whitby, Ontario. She wore a T-shirt, shorts, and running shoes. She was sixteen and she moved like a natural athlete. She was blonde, pretty, five feet six, and she possessed a figure that might one day be statuesque. At her school, Anderson Collegiate, she had won awards for running and played on the school basketball team. She earned an 87-per-cent average on her previous year's work and was developing into a promising painter. She was an active kid. She liked to move. She ran in the evenings, not from a sense of duty, but for fun and fitness.

Her usual route started from home, a one-storey red-brick house set in a comfortable outdoor clutter of garden tools, sports equipment, and family utensils, then took her east down Hillscourt. To the west, Highway 12 is busy with north and south traffic. To the east, Hillscourt gives way a few hundred yards along the road to an unpaved section, eventually dwindling to a path that leads past heavy brush into the edge of a cornfield. The corn was growing high as Kathleen jogged by it. She hit Garden Street, not really a road but more a pair of dirt ruts meandering north and south. There are no houses in that immediate section of

81

Garden, and it makes a popular spot for teenagers to park for night-time talk and sex. Civilization is just around the corner—houses are further north and south on Garden—but psychologically, the small piece of suburban wilderness has the feel of isolation. Kathleen didn't mind the loneliness. It felt good. She was in familiar territory.

But this evening, July 2, something was different. A stranger had invaded her stretch of Garden Street. Kathleen jogged around the corner of the cornfield and saw him. He had a bicycle and he looked harmless, but somewhere in the back of his head—could Kathleen sense it?—he carried violence. He spoke to Kathleen. She wanted to keep jogging, didn't want to lose the rhythm of her run. He came closer to her. He put his bike aside. He was still talking. She tried to ignore him. Things were moving too swiftly for Kathleen. The stranger gave off an atmosphere of anger. He struck at Kathleen with his fist. She turned around, heading back along the route she'd come. The stranger chased her. He caught her. She pushed him off with her arms. The two, Kathleen and the stranger, struggled across the grass by the side of Garden Street, flattening it and churning it up in chunks of earth. It was all so mindlessly sudden. The stranger punched Kathleen to the ground. He was too strong, too furious, too maddened. He kicked her once, twice...He kicked her ten times. He ran a few yards away and picked up an old cedar fence-post that lay in the grass and beat Kathleen with it in the head and upper body. He beat her until she was dead. He dropped the fence-post and kicked her three or four more times.

He stopped. Kathleen lay on her back at his feet. There was no sound except the stranger's heavy breathing. He leaned over Kathleen and slowly pulled down her running-shorts and her underpants. He pulled them far enough to expose her pubic hair to the evening air and to his gaze. It satisfied him. Or perhaps it terrified him. He walked away. He stopped at a puddle of rain water in Garden Street and washed Kathleen's blood from his North

Star running shoes. The stranger got back on his bike and rode north on the ruts of Garden, back to his home not more than a half-mile away.

By nine o'clock, Carl Wels had grown worried about his daughter. He worked at the Firestone store in Whitby, a nice man, modest, content that he and his wife Rita were raising a family of three good kids. He sent Derek, a year younger than Kathleen, to look for his sister. Derek rode east on Hillscourt on the family motorbike. He got as far as the cornfield when the bike conked out and he pushed it home. If he'd carried on another 150 feet, he would have found his sister's body. Carl Wels found it, after two more hours of searching, at 11:19 that night.

"Her head was beaten in," he said later. "I picked her up, but I knew she was dead. Her body was very cold. She must have been dead a couple of hours."

Detective-Sergeant Doug Aird came out from Oshawa, a few miles east of Whitby, to take charge of the murder investigation. He's a big man with a hefty paunch, a bottomless sense of calm that might be associated with an older police officer — Aird's about forty — and an unremitting patience for detailed work. He put together a special squad of eight men to concentrate on the Wels case. He directed policemen to examine the ground around the murder scene on their hands and knees looking for signs of the murderer's identity. He interviewed people in the nearby houses. He comforted the Wels family.

"That picture is etched in my mind," Carl Wels said. "Every time I try to close my eyes, I see her. She wasn't a pretty sight."

Aird was also meticulous in funnelling information about the Wels case into the crown attorney's office. Whitby, a town of slightly more than 30,000, is in the Regional Municipality of Durham. The Region lies a few miles east of Toronto and has a population of some 250,000 citizens. The crown attorney for Durham, working out of offices in the courthouse that is situated three-quarters of a mile

directly south of the spot on Garden Street where Kathleen
Wels was murdered, is named Ted Howell.

Ted Howell is in almost every respect a perfect servant of
the crown. He is an admirably correct man. There is no
stuffiness in his make-up but he sends out the message that
he values propriety and turns off at bad manners. He
conducts himself according to such old verities, and for all
the years he has worked in the Durham crown attorney's
office, since July 1, 1966, he's used them as his personal
guides in court when he prosecutes men and women
accused of crimes.

"It comes from something Howard Cosell says, the sports
announcer," Howell explains. "I don't especially care for
Cosell, but I like his expression 'Tell it like it is.' That's what
a crown can do. 'Tell it like it is.' If you have a guy in court
and he's done something against the law, but he isn't really a
bad person, well, a crown attorney can do something about
him. Give him a break if you figure he deserves it. Ask the
court for a light sentence or a suspended sentence. Put in a
good word for him. On the other hand, suppose you have a
guy who likes to throw his weight around. With him, a
genuinely rotten character, you can ask for a long sentence
that'll show him and others like him they can't push people
around and get away with it."

It pleases Howell, too, that he finds a clinching rightness
in his work. He considers concepts like rigged cases and
police brutality to be, in this day and age, so much nonsense.
The system of criminal justice works, as far as Howell reads
the situation, and the fair play and honest work begin at the
level of the cop in the patrol car and the detective on the
desk in the police station.

"I have the wonderful feeling all the time that the crown is
on the *right* side," Howell says. "The police are so sophisticated these days that they won't lay a charge unless they're
sure there's no reasonable doubt in the case. The crown has
it easier than the defence in that respect. We go to court

84

because we want to, because the police have brought us a case that needs to be prosecuted. The defence goes in because he has to. And we have more options too, go hard or easy on the accused depending on what's right. The defence can only try for an acquittal or for a light sentence, and neither one of those may be in his client's long-run best interests."

Howell's route to the crown attorney's office began, bizarrely, with a fictional defence lawyer. "Perry Mason," he says. "I'm not proud of the origins. But from the time I started reading Erle Stanley Gardner as a kid, around grade seven, I wanted to be a courtroom lawyer." Howell grew up in a small western-Ontario town. He won a public-speaking award in high school, and an essay he wrote about Canada's role in the U.N. took him on an all-expenses-paid weekend to Ottawa, where he proudly shook hands with Prime Minister Louis St. Laurent. Howell was a diligent student and he was headed for law.

After his call to the bar in 1960, he opened a practice on his own in Toronto as a defence counsel. It was interesting enough work, well-paying, but something about it began to pall on Howell.

"I was dissatisfied," he says, "and I couldn't put my finger on the reason. At about this time—I'd been in defence for six years—a friend in the Attorney General's office tipped me off that the government didn't think it had enough lawyers who could think on their feet. They were over-loaded with guys who only functioned from behind desks. They needed good crowns. I went away on a Caribbean cruise, and by the time I got back, something in me wanted a crown's job so much it ached. I took a position that was open as assistant crown in Whitby, and it was the smartest move of my life."

Howell is dark-haired, a spick-and-span dresser, more youthful-looking than his mid-forties would indicate. He has a wife and two sons. He's a cagey businessman, and his salary—in the $45,000 neighbourhood—and his outside investments have brought him a cottage in the Haliburton Lakes, a condominium in Sarasota, Florida, two season tickets in the golds for Toronto Maple Leaf hockey games, and a pair of tickets for Blue Jay baseball games. He's a nut for spectator sports. He likes to fish. He likes to work. He likes to speak positively of the crown attorney's role.

Plea bargaining, for instance, that controversial tactic, the process by which crown and defence may arrive at a deal on an accused person's plea or sentence, brings out the missionary in him.

"The term itself is the worst drawback to plea bargaining," he says. "It connotes cheapness. Bad ethics. *Discussion* is a better word than *bargain*. There's discussion between the crown and the defence in somewhere from sixty to ninety per cent of all criminal cases, and about half the time the discussion leads into what I guess you'd label plea bargaining. Maybe we'll agree on the evidence — the defence will admit certain things happened without the crown's having to prove them in court the hard way — but we won't agree on the plea, whether the guy should plead guilty or innocent. Maybe we'll agree on the plea but not on the sentence. Whatever, it's just sensible to talk over things that are common ground."

Howell goes a step further. He's confident that plea bargaining, forgiving the term, results in *better* justice.

"The public has the idea we get into plea bargaining just to save time and money. Those things, really, are fringe benefits. The true advantage is that plea bargaining gives a fairer result in the end. Compare the situation with civil litigation. Civil lawyers tell me when the two sides can't agree on a settlement before they go to trial, the judge most often comes down hard on one side. That happens, and the one side probably ends up winning more than it should and the other losing more. Same thing in plea bargaining. You get both sides, crown and defence, looking at the strengths and weaknesses of their respective positions and arriving at a disposition that's fair to the accused. I'm in favour of the process. I admit it sometimes feels unbecoming, me approaching the defence to bargain, but on the whole it's better for the crown to initiate the bargaining. Otherwise, the defence might not realize that the crown is willing to settle for a lighter sentence or let the defence's client plead to a lesser charge."

Howell has one reservation in the whole delicate business of bargaining.

"It used to be, a few years ago, the crown and defence'd work out something and take it to the judge in his chambers before the case came up in court. That way, we knew what the judge thought out front. If he was against it, we'd make an adjustment. These days, the plea bargaining is revealed in open court. The result is, now and again, the judge may take a different view of the bargaining than me. He may agree with the plea I've worked out but not the sentence. So the poor guy in the middle, the accused, only gets half the deal. The wrong half. He pleads guilty to something, which is what I want, but he gets put away for a longer sentence than his lawyer told him he'd receive. When that happens I feel bad. Still, with the current system, presenting the bargain to the judge in open court, it's more acceptable to the public. They know there's no deals behind closed doors. And, after all, it's the public that I'm serving."

Ted Howell is a very correct crown.

Kathleen Wels's killer began dictating his statement to Detective-Sergeant Doug Aird late on the afternoon of Thursday, July 12, ten days after the murder.

The killer was fourteen years old.

It had been the shoe-prints around Kathleen's body that led Aird to the boy. The bicycle tracks were a clue. A bike, Aird reasoned, pointed to someone young. Maybe a kid. So did the prints from the North Star sneakers. His men fanned out through the residential areas near the scene of the killing, looking for bikes and North Star shoes, looking for kids. Not glamorous detection. More like foot-slogging.

It brought Aird to the fourteen-year-old's bedroom on Monday, July 9. He removed a pair of North Star sneakers for chemical analysis. There were blood spatters on the shoes. It was human blood, and on Thursday, Aird drove the boy to the police station.

At first the boy tried out a couple of alibis on Aird. He hadn't left his home on the evening of July 2. He'd gone no further than the tent in the backyard. And the blood on the North Stars was from rats. But the alibis were half-hearted. The boy wanted to confess, and it began to come in a rush. Aird stopped him and said he was calling in the boy's parents. The boy resisted. He wanted to speak only to the police. He couldn't face his mother and father. Aird sent for the parents, and when they arrived, the boy told his mother he hadn't meant to hurt the girl. Then he gave Aird his statement. He described the punching, the kicking, the beating with the fence-post. He said that, until the evening of July 2, until the murder, he'd never before seen the girl.

Kathleen Wels had been a stranger to her killer.

The next morning, Friday, the boy appeared before Judge Richard Donald in Durham Juvenile Court. The judge directed a probation officer named Bob Mansfield to prepare a report on the boy, then adjourned the hearing until the following Tuesday. Bob Mansfield is a former minister, a pipe-smoker in his mid-fifties, and he has a professional knack for putting people at their ease. Over the next few days he interviewed the boy's parents, his school principal, teachers, friends, and the police. He found that the boy was a passably competent pupil, that no one noticed anything special about him, that he had never been in trouble. Mansfield worked into Monday night typing his report.

The boy's parents, meanwhile, had retained an Oshawa lawyer. He was Terry Kelly, a florid-faced man with flowing silver hair, a man of two large reputations, one as a trial lawyer, the other as a sports fan. Jim Kernaghan, a writer for the *Toronto Star* sports pages, christened Kelly "Superfan", and the name stuck. Kelly once attended five soccer games in Scotland in the space of a single day. Another time, he took in four National Hockey League games in four cities in three days. His weekends are devoted to searching out sporting contests, the more remote and difficult to reach, the more satisfying. It's the "electricity" of the events that appeals to him, and he spends $15,000 a year in pursuit of his weekly charge.

His other reputation, as a lawyer, is equally grand: called to the bar in 1953 when he was a mere twenty-one, a Queen's Counsel at thirty-four. He looks at home in the courtroom and his natural gift of the gab makes him a persuasive counsel. The gift, in his case, is Irish. Both parents came to Canada from Northern Ireland, and Kelly himself travelled back to the old home for education at St. Malachy's College in Belfast. The lilt in his voice adds to his appeal as a story-teller.

"I had a client once on second-degree murder," he said one summer afternoon. "This guy, a young fella, went down from his basement apartment in Oshawa to spend Labour Day at the Canadian National Exhibition in Toronto. The fella had a dog he was very fond of, and while he was away, he left it tied up outside. He came back and the dog was gone. Hunted high and low for the mutt. Well, in the course of the search, my man had a few drinks. He went next door to call on a neighbour. This neighbour hadn't been overly keen on the dog and my man took along his gun. Silly fool, he shot the neighbour dead.

"His trial came up, and a few days before, I got my hands on the jury list, the names and addresses of all the people on the panel who might make up the twelve jurymen in my case, and I sent a friend of mine out with the list on a scouting trip around the area. He brought me back certain information, which I took with me into court. When it was time to select the jury, the crown couldn't figure out what I was doing, rejecting certain jurymen and accepting others. It was the information my friend had brought me. He found out which people on the panel owned pets and which didn't. I got eight animal lovers on the jury, and they gave me a manslaughter verdict instead of murder."

The boy in the Wels case was Kelly's third juvenile murderer. "Both the others were sent away to the Institute for the Criminally Insane in Penetang," he said. "One's out now, the other's still incarcerated in the place. I think I understand a little about these fellas."

Kelly spoke to Ted Howell. Both men wanted to move swiftly on the case. Both wanted psychiatric reports on the boy. Both wanted to avoid mistakes.

"It could have been a duplication of the Steven Truscott case," Howell said later. "That was at the back of our minds. We didn't want a situation like Truscott where years later people would be raising questions about guilt or innocence."

"It's a good thing I got into the case from the beginning," Kelly said. "It helped cool things out. It got the press quiet and the public hushed up."

On Tuesday, July 17, the boy went back to Judge Richard Donald's courtroom. Judge Donald had read Bob Mansfield's report, and he heard in court that crown and defence were of a like mind that the boy should be remanded to the Clarke Institute of Psychiatry in Toronto. He made his order, and that same day Doug Aird drove the boy from the court to the Institute.

Over the next several weeks, two things happened to the boy. He celebrated a birthday, turning fifteen on August 6, and he was subjected to a range of examinations by clinical psychologists, psychiatrists, specialists in forensic science, and social workers. The medical people reached a common diagnosis: the boy, in the words of one psychiatrist, "demonstrated a disorder in thinking and in emotions that indicates a severe pathology." They noted the boy's extreme facial mannerisms and body tics, that he became "automatic in some cases of stress" and "paced like a robot". He suffered from sexual maladjustment and he had broken down in his "coping mechanism". The psychiatrists couldn't be specific about his illness. It would take, they said, five years simply to sort out the nature of the disturbance inside him. One fact was certain. At the time of the murder of Kathleen Wels, as one psychiatrist said, the boy's "mental processes had deteriorated and he couldn't direct his mind to whether the act was right or wrong."

On the morning of Thursday, September 20, the boy appeared once again in Judge Donald's court. The judge faced a crucial decision: should he, as he was entitled to do under the provincial Juvenile Delinquents Act, hold the boy for a hearing in his own Juvenile Court or should he send him on for trial in adult court, in the Supreme Court of Ontario? Both counsel, Howell and Kelly, had already arrived at their shared view of the proper course.

"It had to be adult court," Howell said. "That's in the best interest of the boy, because if he's not guilty by reason of insanity, only the Supreme Court can sentence him to Penetang, where he'll get better treatment for his illness. It's in the best interest of the public, too, because a Juvenile Court judge can only hold a boy till he's eighteen. The public'd be revolted if the perpetrator of a crime this horrible was back on the street in three years."

"The good of the child," Judge Donald said in his courtroom, "and the interests of the community demand that the case be moved to adult court."

He remanded the boy to a hearing that afternoon in Durham County Court. Aird led the boy from the courtroom and took him to the Whitby jail, where the boy, in Aird's later words, "flipped out". He realized that he wouldn't be returned to the Clarke Institute, a place of shelter for him, and he fell into one of the robot-like states that the psychiatrists had earlier described. Aird brought the boy some lunch in a paper bag. The boy froze. He couldn't open the bag. Stress immobilized him.

A few hours later, apparently recovered, he was taken before Judge Norman Edmundson in County Court. The hearing was brief and pre-orchestrated. Howell and Kelly agreed the boy should be sent to Penetang for more tests pending a preliminary hearing on a charge of murder. The date for the preliminary, also agreed to, was Monday, November 5. Court was adjourned, and Aird drove the boy north to the Oak Ridges Mental Health Centre at Penetang.

Once again, psychiatrists peered into the boy's mind and emotions. His illness, they decided, wasn't clearcut. "Signals are present," one doctor said, "for a flowering of one or both of schizophrenia or depression." He was mentally ill, potentially dangerous, and "not safe to go out in the world". The Oak Ridges people ran a truth-serum test on the boy. It revealed a new piece of information. The boy, according to the test, had probably been searching out a girl to attack for at least a month leading up to July 2. It was on the evening when he spotted Kathleen Wels, the solitary jogger, that something went finally haywire in his mind.

Bruce Affleck made a tough act for Ted Howell to follow. He was the crown attorney in Whitby when Howell arrived as assistant crown in 1966. Affleck stayed on the job until November 1, 1977, when he resigned to go into private practice, defending criminals instead of prosecuting them, and Howell moved up to replace him in the crown attorney's office. Everything about Affleck and his history is recorded in capital letters. When he was appointed crown in 1961, aged twenty-nine, he was the youngest man to assume such a position in the country. His I.Q. is 149 and his memory is photographic. He revels in courtroom appearances, part Clarence Darrow, part stand-up comedian. He prosecuted forty-five murder charges. He survived three heart attacks before he was forty-seven. When he stepped down from the crown's job, 112 lawyers and eight judges turned out to his farewell party. They repeated what everyone had been saying for years — Supreme Court judges, opposing counsel, fellow crowns — that Bruce

Affleck may have been the premier crown attorney in all of Canada.

"Oh sure, I've had all kinds of judges tell me I'm the best man with a jury they've ever seen in a courtroom," Affleck, who doesn't mind blowing his own horn, said in his Oshawa office one autumn morning. The office reflected Affleck's ego. It was decorated with plaques of commendation from police groups, a colour photograph of Affleck gowned in court, and four framed pages from an article in *The Canadian Magazine* that described Affleck as "the winningest crown prosecutor in the country".

None of which, in Affleck's case, smacks of offensiveness. He's a likable egotist. He has an engaging style, curly hair, a stomach too heavy for a heart-attack victim, an open face, and a mouth that strews items of autobiography. About growing up in Oshawa — "a lousy place for a kid" — the son of a General Motors worker. About working his way through the University of Toronto as a night-club bouncer. "One fight, a real knockdown affair, I lost all my front teeth." About the secret of his success as a crown. "Brevity. Condensing things. If the police gave me a hundred witnesses in a case, I only called twenty-five of them. I kept things short and sweet and simple for the jury. Never used legal jargon. I didn't say *mens rea*. I said state of mind. If I used *mens rea*, the jury'd call their doctors to see if they had a dose of it."

Then the Windsor bank robbery. "One of my most outstanding cases," Affleck went on, in winging oratorical form. "The crown in Windsor was too busy and he called me to handle the prosecution. Biggest bank robbery in Canada, $1,129,000 they got. The case was ten weeks in front of a jury, and the six accused had the best counsel money could buy. I won convictions on all but one of them. Incredible trial. I had two hurdles, identification and alibi. The robbers went in wearing balaclavas, so I had no faces to deal with on identification. And, anyway, every accused came to court with alibi witnesses, people who said the robbers were somewhere else, playing poker in Toronto or something, when the hold-up was in progress. It was an enormous case for a crown. Herculean."

The Great Windsor Bank Robbery took place on December 18, 1971, at a branch of the Royal Bank. The branch happened to have on hand an abundance of cash because the nearby Windsor Raceway, suspicious that its own employees were skimming off some of the track's nightly take, had requested bank clerks to make a regular count of the money, which arrived at the bank in large bags, and compare their totals against those shown on the betting machines at the track. The robbers were professionals. They pulled off the job, in and out of the bank, in twelve minutes flat. They dressed themselves as cleaners carrying pails. Inside the pails, they hid guns and handcuffs. The caps perched on top of their heads were rolled-up bala-clavas. They entered the bank, whipped the balaclavas over their faces, handcuffed the bank employees, sabotaged the alarm system, stuck wax on the phones to cut off communications, gathered up the bags of money, and walked quickly to waiting cars. Elapsed time: twelve minutes.

The break that solved the case amounted to a piece of luck. It came when the Surveillance Squad of the Metro Toronto Police, keeping a known stick-up man under watch just on general principles, saw him hook up with another professional robber and proceed to a meeting with a third crook in a room at a suburban Holiday Inn. The police rushed the room and discovered the three heist men admiring a trunk filled with $155,000 in assorted bills. More investigation linked the money to the Windsor hold-up, and after police had rounded up the other members of the gang, the alleged robbers went on trial in Windsor County Court in the autumn of 1972.

"I was faced with a 1,000-page brief and seventy-five witnesses," Affleck explained. "That was on the Friday when I checked in at the Seaway Hotel in Windsor with the trial to start on Monday. Okay, the first problem was to identify the money the police found in the Holiday Inn as coming from the bank. I did it by the numbers the clerks wrote on certain bills. Say the bank clerks were counting two-dollar bills. They'd count them into piles of fifty and then bundle them up. But suppose they only had thirty-two two-dollar bills. When that happened, they'd mark '32' on the top bill. I called each clerk as a witness and asked him to identify this writing on any bills he marked. That tied the Holiday Inn money to the Windsor money.

"But the defence had a hand-writing expert who swore that it's much more difficult to identify a number as opposed to a letter. I didn't cross-examine the expert. Left him alone. I waited till I was addressing the jury and I said to them, 'Unless I have some illicit reason to hide something, I know my own hand-writing better than anyone, better than some expert. So if a clerk has taken the witness stand and said that's his 32, then *that's* his 32.' The jury bought my argument."

As to identification of the accused as the bank robbers, it was a matter of fitting together a jigsaw puzzle, taking pieces of testimony from many mouths and working them into a set of composites that pointed to the accused men. "Voice characteristics. Size. Body movements. Little physical quirks," Affleck continued. "I called all the people in the bank as witnesses, and among the lot of them we came close enough to satisfy the jury that we had the right guys in the prisoner's box. Besides that, we could place most of the accused in direct relationship to the money. 'Wheresoever the carcass is, there will the eagles be gathered together.' I got that out of Bartlett's *Familiar Quotations*, a biblical saying, and it's the opening line I used in my summation to the jury. They liked it."

Throwing suspicion, not to mention derision, on the robbers' alibis was an easier and flashier business for Affleck. "Take one guy. He had a woman testify he was with her on the day of the robbery in some place nowhere near Windsor. She gave her testimony very smoothly on examination-in-chief. But I trapped her on cross-examination. I produced a cheque made out to her by the guy she was alibiing for. I suggested the cheque was the first in a series of payments in return for her testimony. She had a lot of explanations for the cheque. None of them stood up. I kept hitting her with one question. 'Why? Why the cheque?' The jury couldn't understand how she could be so cool on examination-in-chief and so flustered on cross-examination. They dismissed her testimony.

"I had one other argument on the alibis that was pretty compelling. I pointed out how these guys had come forward with their alibis very late in the game. They knew about the crime. It was a famous hold-up, front pages on all the newspapers, but they kept their traps shut, these professional thieves who were known to the police, until the last minute. *Then* they produced their alibis. I told the jury they should have spoken up earlier, and the jury must have agreed because they brought in a bunch of convictions."

Five of the robbers received sentences ranging from eighteen to twenty years while the sixth, on the direction of the judge who felt the evidence against him was equivocal, walked away with an acquittal.

"There's one last mystery about the case," Affleck said. "None of the money except the $155,000 has ever turned up. Somewhere, somebody's sitting on almost a million bucks."

Even with the thrills and satisfactions of the crown's life, Affleck found himself anxious to give it up for the career of a defence counsel. "Money was one reason," he pointed out. "My last year as a crown, I made $45,000. My first year on my own, it went up to $67,000."

But there were other motives that impelled Affleck out of the crown's office, reasons that had to do with pressure and responsibility.

"Look at me," he said. "I'm just back from a two-month murder trial in London, Ontario, and it was a ball. We had eight bikers down there, eight guys from the Satan's Choice motorcycle gang who were charged with a hit on a guy from the Golden Hawk Riders. I acted for one of the Satan's Choice. Bikers are always retaining me these days because they remember how good I was at prosecuting them. I put a lot of those guys in jail. It was duck soup. I could prosecute bikers over the phone, it was so easy. If they took the stand, I'd kill them on cross-examination. If they didn't take the stand, I'd turn their silence against them. Now they ask me to defend them.

"Anyway, I was in London on this long murder case, and I realized how little pressure I had as a defence counsel in comparison to what a crown has to put up with. Jesus, it didn't even bother me that much when my guy got convicted of second-degree murder. Part of that feeling has to do with my heart attacks. I've faced death myself three times, so now it isn't such a big deal to watch a client go down as long as I've given his defence my best effort.

"But there was more to it than that, the feeling I had of being more relaxed as a defence counsel. I loved my career in the crown's office. It was second nature to me. The thing is, though, in defence you can move around more. You can expand. You're freer. You're not so much under the gun. A crown has it tough. He takes the heat."

Affleck searched for his final summation.

"As a crown," he said, "you're always on centre stage."

Nobody who deals with him in court comes away with the impression that Ted Howell, all correct behaviour and *politesse*, is a pushover.

"People always tell me how calm I am in a courtroom," he says. "I guess it's because I always try to look like I'm in control. I never shout in court. I never carry on like some hard-nosed TV prosecutor. But when I have to, I can turn on the jets."

One October afternoon he switched on his jets in Whitby's County Court, and in so doing he produced a brief episode of gripping melodrama. It was Tom McDougall who precipitated the fuss. He was a crown witness in the trial of his older brother, Andrew, on a charge of armed robbery. Eighteen months earlier, the two brothers, both stocky and glum-faced and in their early twenties, had held up the cashier at a drive-in theatre near Whitby. Tom drove the getaway car; Andrew, wearing a ski mask and carrying a sawed-off shotgun, handled the stick-up. The take was $2,600. Andrew used most of it to buy a used car and drive to Calgary. Tom hung around his home in Oshawa until the police arrested him for another crime he'd committed, a house break-in. The police had heard whispers that the McDougall brothers were behind the drive-in hold-up, and after they'd put Tom through a thorough round of questioning, he signed a statement that set out in detail the roles he and Andrew had played in the robbery. Tom went to trial, pleaded guilty to the two crimes, and was sentenced to a term in reformatory. When Andrew was finally nabbed in Calgary and brought back to Whitby for trial, brother Tom, with his signed statement to the police, was the crown's star witness.

But, once he took the stand in court, Tom balked. He wasn't going to rat on Andrew. "Yeah, I recognize it," he said to Howell when he was shown his statement, "but I don't have anything to say about it." Tom turned mute, and Howell had visions of the case, with Tom refusing to admit to the statement, evaporating before his eyes.

"Your honour," he said the the judge, a grandfatherly man named Lawson, "this witness is getting himself into a serious situation and I think perhaps he needs legal advice. May I suggest we adjourn briefly while I telephone the lawyer who acted for him on his earlier charges — that was Bill Livingstone here in town — and ask him to come down and advise this witness of his rights and obligations."

Livingstone arrived promptly, carrying an annotated copy of the Criminal Code, and spent twenty minutes conferring alone with Tom McDougall in a small room off the courtroom.

"I don't know, Ted," he said to Howell when he emerged from the conference, "the guy doesn't want to fink against his brother."

That was the moment when Howell went into his turn-on-the-jets routine.

"Bill, I want you to go back in there," he said to Livingstone, his voice tightened up, his face paling slightly. "I want you to tell Tom McDougall a story. It's about Mr. Justice Edson Haines. He had a murder trial a few years ago. Some cons from Millhaven Penitentiary were charged with killing another con. One of the witnesses was yet another inmate, but when this witness got up to testify, he suddenly couldn't remember anything. He had nothing to say. Haines charged him with contempt and told him to stand aside. The trial proceeded, and the cons were found guilty. When that was done, Haines called back the reluctant witness and gave him ten years on the contempt charge. *Ten years*. And Haines told the guy that if there'd been an acquittal in the murder case, he would've given the con a life sentence for his contempt. *Life*. You go back in there, Bill, and tell the story to our friend Tom McDougall. Tell him the story and tell him if he still doesn't feel like testifying, I'll be asking Judge Lawson for a minimum penitentiary term against him. And I think I'll get it."

Livingstone spoke once again to the younger McDougall, and later that afternoon Tom returned to the witness stand. Yeah, he said, wearing a sulky look, he remembered the statement. It was true, yeah. And, yeah, he and Andrew held up the drive-in theatre.

Judge Lawson found Andrew McDougall guilty as charged of armed robbery and sentenced him to three and a half years in the penitentiary.

At four o'clock on the morning of Monday, November 5, feeling appropriately bleary, Detective-Sergeant Doug Aird and a partner left Oshawa and drove ninety miles north to the Oak Ridges Hospital in Penetang to pick up the boy, the fifteen-year-old, awaiting his trial for murder. Five hours later, a few minutes before nine o'clock, the two policemen escorted him off the elevator on the ninth floor of Oshawa City Hall and took him to a small ante-room off Courtroom A. The corridors and the courtroom were empty. It was too early for the day's justice to begin turning over, and Aird's partner took advantage of the lull to fetch coffees for himself, Aird, and the boy. Then they waited.

Terry Kelly arrived first, dressed in a spiffy three-piece navy pinstripe suit and trailed by two students from his law firm and by his eighteen-year-old son, Tim. Kelly had put in a typical weekend. Saturday morning he drove to Oak Ridges with one of his students to talk to the boy, and that night he took in an NHL game at Maple Leaf Gardens. Next day he phoned a student at nine in the morning asking him to check a couple of points of law on insanity cases, then left for Buffalo, New York, to watch a National Football League game. He was back in Oshawa in the evening in time to catch a local junior hockey game, and before going to bed he looked over the file for the following morning's proceedings.

"The kid's never been so happy as he is up in that place," one of Kelly's students said as he waited in the courtroom. "He's been given a job as a cleaner and he really likes it. When I went up with Mr. Kelly on Saturday, it was to make sure the kid was fit to stand trial. Some of the people at Oak Ridges are awfully snapped-out, but the kid seems to understand what's going on, what the trial means and everything."

Howell arrived and spoke briefly to Kelly. The two men had been engaging in a higher form of plea bargaining over the previous few weeks, plea bargaining at its most compassionate. They had agreed to the scenario: that the boy would pursue a plea of not guilty by reason of insanity, that they would waive the preliminary hearing that morning and proceed directly to trial in the Supreme Court, that Kelly would admit all the crown's evidence about the events of the killing, that Kelly would call as his only witnesses

three psychiatrists, and that Howell would permit their
evidence to go in without serious challenge.

The courtroom was beginning to fill with people waiting
disposition of charges that ranged from impaired driving to
shop-lifting. But at 9:30 a.m. when Judge D. B. Dodds took
the bench, Howell rose quickly and asked for immediate
attention to his case. Doug Aird brought the boy from the
ante-room and stood him in front of the bench. Kelly
flanked the boy on his right side. Howell pointed out to the
judge that the boy was scheduled for a preliminary hearing
this morning on a charge of murder. The boy was waiving
the hearing. Kelly nodded to Judge Dodd. The preliminary
being waived, Howell went on, the boy was to stand trial
later in the morning at the Supreme Court of Ontario
assizes in the Whitby Courthouse. Very well, Judge Dodd
said. He remanded the case to the Supreme Court at eleven
o'clock on that same date. Aird took the boy by the arm and
steered him from the courtroom. Howell and Kelly vanished by another door. The hearing had lasted less than
three minutes, and hardly anybody in the courtroom filled
with lesser offenders was aware that a confessed killer had
been in their midst.

"This is a simple case," Howell said as he drove from
Oshawa to Whitby in his Oldsmobile station-wagon. "Simple in the sense that there's no fight. But it's complex when
you think of the old maxim, justice must not only be done
but be seen to have been done. The killing is so serious to
the community that we've got to cross the t's and dot the i's
on this one."

Gregory Evans, the Chief Justice of the trial division of
the Ontario Supreme Court, shared Howell's view, and to
avoid any risk of "another Truscott" he assigned himself to
hear the case. Evans, a medium-sized man, wears an alert
expression, but his manner in court cuts through the law's
usual formality. His mode of speech from the bench is
almost conversational, and although he sticks to the propri-
eties, his approach encourages all appearing before him—

counsel, jury, accused — to unbutton and offer the court their most open selves.

Courtroom 1 on the ground floor of the Whitby Courthouse was packed before the Chief Justice made his entrance. The boy's parents and sister were in court. Bob Mansfield, the probation officer, was there, and so was a large representation from newspapers and radio and TV stations. But most of the seats were occupied by the men and women who had been summoned for jury duty. Twelve of them would determine the future of the fifteen-year-old who was waiting in a small room off the left wall of the courtroom.

Shortly after eleven, one of the sheriff's officers who monitored the courtroom opened the door to the small room and motioned the boy to enter the court. He took a single step from the room and, seeing the crowd of press and lawyers and jury people, stunned, he stopped as abruptly as if he'd walked into an invisible wall. He turned back to his right, a move to return to the small room, then corrected himself, faced the courtroom, and paused, baffled. He looked out of place in the surroundings, a kid, vulnerable. He was wearing a dark blue suit, a white shirt, a striped tie, and a new pair of light-blue running shoes. He was tall and thin, a hint of stoop at the shoulders. His brown hair was curly and puffed, and his face was long, pale, and scared. The sheriff's officer touched the boy's arm and guided him to the prisoner's box in the centre of the courtroom.

The court clerk stood up from his desk below the Chief Justice's bench and read the charge: murder in the first degree of Kathleen Wels on July 2, 1979. How did the boy plead?

"Not guilty," Terry Kelly said, standing beside the prisoner's box.

The next piece of business was the selection of the jury. The court clerk pulled pieces of paper from a small drum and called out the names printed on them. As the jurors stepped forward, Kelly and Howell accepted or rejected them for the boy's trial. Kelly used six challenges, Howell used eight. Both rejected any young women whose names were called, any female whose looks might suggest Kathleen Wels, and, after eleven people had been chosen, Howell turned down four consecutive men in order to include as the twelfth juror a well-dressed, intelligent-looking man in his early thirties. Howell was hoping the man, whose appearance indicated he might make a responsible leader, would be chosen by the other jurors as their foreman when they retired to consider their verdict at the end of the trial.

It was shortly after noon when the twelve jurors — eight men and four women, mostly middle-aged — sat down in their box and Howell began his short opening address. He outlined the case he expected to prove and told briefly of the events on the evening of July 2. As he talked, his voice was level and concerned. There were no exclamation points at the end of his sentences. No words were underlined. His voice offered no emphasis and neither did his posture. He stood very still and confined his movements to a couple of variations in facial expression, an almost imperceptible jutting of the jaw, and an occasional tilting of his head to the right. It was as if, for the length of his address, nothing existed except the flat words. The jury hung on each one of them.

Howell called Doug Aird to the witness stand, and, displaying several photographs of Kathleen Wels taken on the night of the murder ("The photos," the Chief Justice interrupted to warn the jury, "may be a little disturbing"), Aird began to tell the jury the story of the killing. The lunch break interrupted his testimony, and the Chief Justice adjourned the case for an hour and a quarter. Howell used ten minutes of the break to eat a quick meal in the courthouse cafeteria and spent the rest of the time in his office preparing for the afternoon. When court resumed, he kept Aird on the stand for half an hour. Howell was thorough in his questioning. So was Aird in his answers, and by the end of the testimony none of the horrors of the murder had been concealed from the jury.

It was Kelly's turn. His voice was soft as he made his opening address, as if he had a lullaby in mind. He spoke of "pain" and "regret" and of the boy's "disease of the brain to the extent he could not appreciate the nature of his act". The address was short. Then he summoned, in turn, three psychiatrists to the stand, two from the Clarke Institute, one from Oak Ridges. Kelly questioned them gently — he was all too sorry to be raising such painful matters, his voice implied, but it was necessary for the good of everyone — and the psychiatrists, answering him, told of the almost unfathomable depths of the boy's illness. As each psychiatrist finished his examination-in-chief, Howell cross-examined, directing himself in particular to one issue: was it possible the boy was faking his insanity? Impossible, the psychiatrists replied.

The Chief Justice had one question for the Oak Ridges psychiatrist.

"I know how people get put in your institution," he said, "but how do they get out?"

The process is complex, the psychiatrist explained. An inmate's case is reviewed by a committee made up of one justice of the Ontario Supreme Court and two independent psychatrists who are not employed at Oak Ridges. If they find the inmate fit for release, they make a recommendation to the provincial cabinet. If it agrees, it passes on the recommendation to the Lieutenant-Governor, with whom the final decision rests.

The Chief Justice looked relieved.

When the last psychiatrist had finished his testimony, Kelly made his final submission to the jury. It lasted only five minutes. It was delivered in the same *pianissimo* manner. Kelly told the jury it could reach no other conclusion than that expressed by the psychiatrists: that the boy was not guilty by reason of his insanity at the moment of the crime. Howell's submission took ten minutes. He reviewed the evidence, reiterated the savagery of the boy's attack, but he concluded, too, with the suggestion that the jury find the boy to have been insane when he killed Kathleen Wels.

It was late in the afternoon, and the Chief Justice adjourned court until the following morning.

"My mother had an expression," Terry Kelly said in the corridor outside the courtroom, explaining his low-key approach before the jury. "She used to say, 'Don't kill dead things.' She meant, don't bother with the impossible. That's the way it is in court. It's better to admit something that's true than to fight. Admit it and get to the issues. We admit the boy killed the girl. Now the issue is his sanity. We say the lad's insane, and that's what I want the jury to understand."

At 10 a.m. the next day, Tuesday, the Chief Justice gave the jury his instructions. He told them that they must judge the facts in the case, judge them "without sympathy or prejudice". He discussed the evidence they had heard and described the murder as "vicious, brutal, and savage". He talked of the psychiatrists' testimony, and, speaking, as Howell later described it, "in lucid everyday language", he went over the technicalities of the five possible verdicts the jury might arrive at: guilty as charged of first-degree murder, not guilty as charged but guilty of second-degree murder, guilty of manslaughter, not guilty by reason of insanity, not guilty. Before eleven o'clock, the Chief Justice had finished, and the twelve members of the jury filed into a room behind the courtroom to decide on its verdict.

Everyone—lawyers, the Chief Justice, the court attendants, the police—expected the jury to arrive at a quick decision. Everyone expected a verdict of not guilty by reason of insanity. But by 12:40 there had been no word from the jury room.

"They're sceptical," Terry Kelly said. "They're weighing what the psychiatrists had to say. Juries are different these days. They've seen too much TV. They're jaded and they think these psychiatrists may be putting one over on them."

The Chief Justice, concerned, called Kelly and Howell into his chambers. He asked the two lawyers for their opinion. What did they think? Should he leave the jury to their deliberations or should he take a noon recess? Howell favoured the recess. Juries, he knew, often delayed for curious reasons, even for a meal. The Chief Justice called a recess, and the sheriff's men carried twelve cafeteria lunches into the jury room.

Howell was right. Almost immediately after the break for food, the jury announced that it had reached a verdict. The courtroom was called to order. The eight men and four women of the jury returned to their seats in the jury-box, and the foreman rose from his seat in the front row. He wasn't the foreman Howell had counted on. He was another young man. His hair was short, his face was solemn, and for a moment Howell wondered if he was a "hard-liner", a juror who took the view that the boy might be using insanity to avoid a life sentence in penitentiary. Maybe the foreman had influenced the rest of the jury to such an opinion. But, no, Howell's worry disappeared with the announcement of the jury's verdict. Not guilty by reason of insanity.

The boy's face, as he sat in the prisoner's box, gave away no sign of fear or relief or torment. It remained blank, his colour pale, his lower lip hanging slightly open. He stood up when the Chief Justice requested him to. Did he wish to say anything, the Chief Justice asked him.

"No," the boy whispered. It was the first and last time the court heard his voice.

The Chief Justice ordered the boy to be held at the discretion of the Lieutenant-Governor.

The trial had ended and the courtroom emptied quickly. The Chief Justice returned to his chambers. The boy was guided into an ante-room to speak to his parents. The jury members went in search of their coats and hats. Only Doug

Aird and his partner, waiting to drive the boy back to Oak Ridges, remained in the courtroom.

"Well, there you go," Aird said. "Two families destroyed in this case."

"I have a feeling about the boy," Terry Kelly said out in the corridor. "I think he's going to spend a very long time in Oak Ridges."

Ted Howell was back in his office, a few yards down the corridor from the courtroom. His desk was covered in phone messages, memos, files of new cases, new crimes.

"Nobody feels good about a case like that boy's," he said. "But I have other work to move on to."

Ted Howell is a perfect servant of the crown.

Fourth Adjournment

On an August Sunday afternoon, Willard Phelps steered his boat across the water with one hand and drank red wine out of a tin cup with the other. The boat was a 165-horse-power Starcraft, its name painted across the stern: *Whip-lash*. The water was Bennett Lake. Drawn on a map, its shape looks like a dolphin leaping out of the sea, head ducked down, tail flying, flippers extended. Bennett Lake is forty-five miles south of Whitehorse, close to the border where the Yukon meets British Columbia.

"All those beautiful trees up there, they were almost gone," Phelps shouted over the buzz of the Starcraft's engine. He was waving with his right hand, the one holding the red wine, at the steep, rocky hills that surrounded the lake. The hills were covered in pine and spruce, and they gave way to snowy mountains in the high distance.

"Ottawa was behind it. I came back from law school ten years ago and found that a big mining company, Bermuda Resources it was called, had the rights to cut down all the timber around Bennett and Atlin and the other lakes in this chain. The decision came from the bureaucrats in Ottawa, those buggers. Bermuda could chop down the whole lot and ship it to Japan. Well, hell, that would've destroyed the ecology around here. It'd have taken 150 years to retrieve the soil. Just a horror show. Anyway, fate intervened. Bermuda went broke in some mining venture or other and never could afford to move into Bennett. We were saved, but God only knows what Ottawa could still visit on us. That kind of thing, worrying about Ottawa, trying to preserve what we've got in the north, getting the right to run our own lives, that means my practice has to suffer. I use my legal training to help fight the battles. It takes time. It sure as hell takes time."

Phelps's roots run almost as deep in the north as history permits. His grandfather, the original Willard Phelps and also a lawyer, arrived in the Yukon from Hamilton, Ontario, in 1898, only a couple of years after George Washington Carmack and his Indians pals, Tagish Charlie and Skookum Joe, found gold at Bonanza Creek and signalled the rush on the Klondike. Willard the First set up practice in Whitehorse. He had a business on the side, running the mail from Whitehorse to Dawson, and he sat in the Territory's Legislative Assembly for twenty-two years. He was part of Yukon history. He used to tell about the early days of Whitehorse, about sitting around in the school principal's log cabin exchanging lies with the fellow who worked at the Bank of Commerce. The bank clerk's name was Robert Service.

"My dad didn't follow grandfather into law. Engineering instead," Phelps said, drinking wine in the middle of Bennett Lake, not another boat moving on the horizon. "Dad learned to hunt and fish up here with the Indians, and when I was old enough, in the 1940s and early '50s, just growing up, he passed on what he learned to me. Those years when I was young were the years that broke the Indians in the Yukon. It was never the gold rush that hurt them. Nor the Alaska Highway. It was when the world fur market went belly-up around 1950. The Indians depended on furs for their living. The market collapsed, and the federal government came along to move the Indians out of the bush and into settlements. That was for the government's convenience. Made it easier to hand out the welfare cheques. But it was devastating to the Indians' pride."

Phelps turned the boat in a wide arc to the right and headed down a bay, a part of Bennett Lake that shows up on maps as one of the dolphin's extended flippers.

"The Indian kids I grew up with, people that are in their early forties or younger now, they were the first Indians to get criminal records in the Yukon. They were the first who were taken away from the traditional ways, from the forest, and they started drinking and getting in trouble with the law. I've acted for lots of them. Legal-aid work. Pitiful. The older Indians are honest people and well-balanced people, and then you get their children, my generation, and all of them have criminal records that are horrible. What's a lawyer supposed to do?"

Phelps circled out of the bay and across the lake to the dock in Carcross where he keeps his boat. Carcross is tiny and storied. Its name is a piece of shorthand for Caribou Crossing, and its proudest landmark is a cairn that celebrates the driving of the last spike in the White Pass and Yukon Railroad on July 29, 1900. The railroad took twenty-six months to build, 110 miles of it, from Skagway, the Alaska seaport, to Whitehorse, and it provided transportation for the thousands of dreamers who flocked in to pan a fortune in the Klondike. Carcross saw plenty of traffic in its earliest days.

"Biggest disappointment in my life was when that thing stopped running," Phelps said, pointing at a huge and dilapidated stern-wheel riverboat that rested at a tilt, high and dry and forlorn, on the Carcross beach. "The *Tutshi*. It ran up and down these lakes for half a century. You had to be fifteen to work on it in the summers. All my friends had their turn. I was waiting for mine and the summer I was fifteen, 1956, they took her out of service. Broke my heart."

As Phelps spoke, a train pulled through town. The White

110

Pass and Yukon still operates, lugging tourists and small freight from Skagway to Whitehorse. The train looked cute and miniature, like something Jesse James might hold up in a Republic Pictures movie. Phelps led the way past the Caribou Hotel, built in 1911, and Watson's General Store, where they offer gold pans for sale. Beyond the post office and around the corner, he opened the door to the log cabin that has been in the family since Phelps's grandfather bought it in 1917.

"I have close ties to this land," he said, plunked in a big stuffed chair in the cabin's cluttered main room. He looked the part of a man of the north. Phelps wears a beard that's clipped like a shadow on his face. He's lean and dead-panned in the style of a hunter who'd have no trouble sneaking up on a moose, and his hands, not like any city lawyer's, are rough and scarred, the hands of someone who's baited his share of fishing lines.

He spoke a little of his history. Growing up in Whitehorse and Carcross. Leaving for the University of British Columbia where he took honours in philosophy and economics. Spending a few months working on a master's degree in philosophy at the University of Toronto. Rejecting it in favour of law at UBC. Getting called to the bar.

"I came back to Whitehorse and set up my practice," he said, sipping at the wine left over from the boat ride. "It wasn't easy to get established. I used to sit in my office on the second floor listening for footsteps on the stairs. The first four or five files I handled, I didn't get paid a nickel. It was work for the local ne'er-do-wells who dropped by my office really just for the company.

"The secret to getting started in Whitehorse is to win a few trials. That generates publicity. The thing is, Whitehorse has two daily papers, one weekly, a private radio station, and a private TV station. That's a lot for 14,000 people, and reporters'll look anywhere for a story. They love to give trials a big play. My chance came. My first criminal case. It

111

was down in Atlin and my client was charged with buggery. I drove down with the crown attorney and I only had one question for him. 'If I win this case, who's gonna drive the guy back to Whitehorse?' Well, I won, and the problem of transportation was taken care of because the guy turned out to be an escaped convict and they shipped him back east. But the trial got a lot of media coverage, people heard about me, and the business started to roll in. Corporate stuff for the companies that come up here to dig mines. Drawing contracts. Handling the disputes that the contracts sometimes produced. Court work. Enough of everything."

At the same time Phelps pitched in to community activities. He was elected to the Legislative Assembly for one term. He acted for the territorial government in negotiating Indian land claims. He helped organize the Progressive Conservative party in the Yukon ("there's a backlash up here against the Liberals because everybody associates them with the Ottawa bureaucracy that's done us in"). And he was one of three members of the Lysyk Commission. It held hearings throughout the Yukon in 1977. It visited seventeen communities and accumulated 750 pages of testimony. Its subject was natural gas, and finally, after all the visiting and the testimony, it came out in favour of constructing a pipeline to carry the gas from Prudhoe Bay in the north to the United States in the south by way of the Alaska Highway route. Phelps figures the Lysyk Commission contributed mightily to the Yukon's future.

"After I got out of law school," he said, working on the last cup of wine, "I could've stayed and practised down in Vancouver. But I looked around and realized that ninety per cent of my friends in the city were lawyers. That wasn't the way I grew up. I grew up with Indians and woodsmen and tough old ladies who made their living out of hunting and trapping. All sorts of odd ducks and real people. So I came back here. I didn't want to live an insular existence, and in the Yukon you're really no good as a lawyer unless you get out and mess around in the community with the rest of the characters. When I think about it now, I'm not sure whether I turned out to be a lawyer who hunts and fishes or a hunter and fisherman who happens to practise law."

He drained his wine cup.

"Doesn't make a hell of a lot of difference."

CHAPTER FOUR

Counsel to the Last Frontier

You can't miss the new courthouse in Yellowknife. It looks like a Brobdingnagian sardine can. It's six storeys tall, a skyscraper by Northwest Territories standards, and wrapped from street to roof in silver-colour aluminium. It glints and flashes in the sun and reflects light beams across the rest of drab downtown Yellowknife. According to one local lawyer, it was built this way, visually unmistakable, so that the Inuit and the Indians who are its most frequent customers wouldn't have any trouble locating the place.

Inside, the courthouse runs to a warmer look. The prevailing motif in décor, not surprisingly, is Eskimo Traditional. Tiles depicting Eskimo domestic scenes cover a large pillar in the centre of the building. Banners of jolly Inuit figures hang in the courtrooms. And inside a long glass display case against one wall of the lobby on the second floor, a series of small but commanding Eskimo carvings recreates significant trials from the Territories' judicial past.

One trial required three carvings of tiny, grim figures in parkas. The first shows a man with a rifle shooting another man in the back. In the second, a woman is stabbing the killer in the chest. And in the third, two children lie stricken on the ice. Beside the stark carvings, a printed card tells the story of the little figures.

Kikkik. Tried at Rankin Inlet on April 4, 1958. Half
brother of accused killed Kikkik's husband, Hallow. Kikkik then killed the half brother and then out of food
struck across the barrens in winter for help. Abandoned
two smallest children in igloo. Charged with murder and
with abandoning one child and criminal negligence in
respect to one child who died. Not guilty in each case.
Offences near Henik Lake.

"Those legal cases out there in the carvings," Jim Slaven
explained, "you might say they're what got the law started
in the north. Judge Jack Sissons heard them all. He was the
first judge up here, appointed in 1955, and he was the guy
who said we're gonna take the law to every man's door. He
meant every Eskimo's door, and he put the court on the
circuit, flying out of Yellowknife every month or so for a
few days or a couple of weeks, as long as it took to hold trials
in a bunch of communities distributed the hell and gone
across the Arctic. He started it, Sissons, and we've still got
the circuit with us to this day."

As he spoke, Jim Slaven sat chain-smoking in his office at
the rear of the second floor of the courthouse. He's a hefty
man in his early fifties, round face, short black hair brushed
back from his forehead, spectacles, and a manner that's
open and welcoming. Since 1974 he's been a Territorial
Court judge, the equivalent of a Provincial Court judge in
the rest of Canada, and he knows everything about that
unique N.W.T. institution, the circuit.

"I put in about 40,000 miles a year flying around the
Territories," Slaven said. "But it isn't the miles that wear
you down. It's the hours. The planes are so damned slow.
We fly in a Twin Otter or a DC-3, one of those old makes of
plane, and by the time the court party piles on—the judge,
court clerk, court reporter, crown counsel, and defence
counsel, plus all our robes and typewriters and food and
cases of beer—we're lucky if that plane gets up to eighty

miles an hour. We're lucky if it gets eighty feet off the ground."

The circuit splits into two basic trips. One takes the court north from Yellowknife to the Mackenzie Delta, into Inuvik and its suburbs. The other is to the east, 1,300 miles to Frobisher Bay on Baffin Island, then around the Eastern Arctic. In all, the travelling court dishes out justice to Territories citizens spread over 1.3 million square miles. Most of those miles are forest, lakes, and tundra, but one hundred or more communities are tucked into the wilderness, home to 43,000 people. About 14,000 are Inuit, another 12,000 are of Indian ancestry, the rest are white, and slightly more than 10,000 of the 43,000 live in Yellowknife, the N.W.T. capital, 600 air miles north of Edmonton, But it's the people outside the metropolis who keep the circuit in operation.

"For the way the law is administered up here," Judge Slaven said, "you have to learn how to husband your energies. It's cold in those planes, forty-five below in winter, colder inside the plane than outside. And when you get where you're going, you can't count on a hot meal, not even a cup of coffee. Sardines and crackers. Sometimes I hold court in a schoolroom in some tiny dot of a place on the map of the Arctic on nothing but some sardines and crackers all day. *Day?* In winter, there isn't any day. Just twenty-four hours of darkness."

Judge Slaven shook his head at the wonder of it all.

"When I know there's a grind ahead," he said, "I don't take a drink."

He shook his head again. "Amazing," he said.

What's amazing is that under such hectic, even primitive, conditions, the system, in one strange way or another, seems to generate justice.

"Sure it works," Slaven said, and by way of illustration he proceeded to tell the story of the sad and troubled young man of Rankin Inlet.

Like several other northern communities, Rankin Inlet is an artificial invention. It sits on the west shore of Hudson

Bay several hundred miles north of the Manitoba border, and until the early 1950s it existed only for a couple of dozen Inuit. Its isolation ended when nickel was discovered in the area, and by 1957 North Rankin Nickel Mines Limited was in business. The mine recruited Eskimos from camps and communities for hundreds of miles across the land west of Hudson Bay. They were people of different backgrounds, styles, cultures, and languages. They worked at the mine, thereby pushing the population of Rankin Inlet from almost scratch to over 1,000, until the nickel ran out in 1962. Many of the Inuit returned to their old home grounds, but a few hundred stayed on in Rankin, living off hunting, fishing, and government relief payments. The community floundered for years until Rankin was designated the regional headquarters for the N.W.T. District of Keewatin. That made it a minor centre for local government, transportation, and communications. New jobs turned up, many Inuit freed themselves from relief, and the population climbed back to almost 1,000.

Then, one shocking day in 1978, much of Rankin was burned to the ground. The damage added up to several million dollars. Arson, everybody recognized, and it didn't call for intensive police work to nail the arsonist. He was a young Inuit, mentally retarded. He was arrested, charged, and held for Judge Slaven.

The court party arrived in Rankin by plane from Yellowknife at noon on the trial date. It was an autumn day in 1978 and Judge Slaven was ready to proceed. But a group of Rankin people — Inuit — asked him to delay proceedings. They were calling a community meeting to talk about the young man and his fate.

"It was the first time such a thing had happened in Rankin," the judge said, "the first time the local people had ever sat down together. You see, coming from all various backgrounds the way they had, different strains of Eskimo, they'd never merged as a real community. There was a professor up there, fellow named Williamson from the

117

University of Saskatchewan, who'd been going to Rankin every summer for eighteen years, and he said this was the old traditional Inuit way of doing things, meeting together and looking after their own. Well, hell, under those circumstances the court was pleased to stand aside for a few hours. That might sound ridiculous to a judge in the south, but northern justice is different."

The Inuit met and the judge waited. "Had some sandwiches and cold coffee for dinner," he said. "My wife was along because it was our wedding anniversary. I told her, 'You can't say I didn't take you out for dinner on our anniversary.' "

The meeting broke up and Judge Slaven convened court. He took a guilty plea from the young man's lawyer and then listened to nine Rankin people testify, representatives chosen at the meeting. They talked of the young man's problems and his character and his family, of their wishes to care for him, to find him a job, to ease his troubles. Judge Slaven sat into the night. The witnesses' testimony was translated from Inuit into English and his comments and questions were translated from English into Inuit. The judge waited.

"Once I had to stop the trial and send for the local nurse," the judge said. "It was the boy. He was picking at scabs on his arm. They started to bleed."

The testimony ended and Judge Slaven announced his verdict. Arson calls for a jail term. No jail term, Judge Slaven told the court. Instead, probation. He put the young man in the care of the community.

"Down south," he said, "that'd raise a few eyebrows."

It was past midnight when the court party climbed on the plane to fly home to Yellowknife.

"You get better justice in the north," Judge Slaven said, lighting up another cigarette in his office at the Yellowknife Courthouse. "Look, when we go on the circuit and land at Pangnirtung or Whale Cove or Tuktoyaktuk or one of those remote spots, the defence counsel along on the trip is going to be seeing his clients for the first time. Maybe a fellow's charged with something serious—rape, or even murder—and people might think, well, hell, how's that lawyer gonna give his client a decent defence on such short notice? Easy, I say."

The judge leaned back in his chair and ticked off his reasons. "Number one, the defence counsel has more concentrated time with his client. No phones ring on the circuit. Nobody has to keep office hours. The client probably ends up with more attention from his lawyer than he'd get in Toronto. Number two, the crown attorney up here shares his whole file with the defence, which is something pretty damned unique to the north. The defence doesn't have to worry about the most remote sort of surprise. And number three, if the accused person objects, says he hasn't had enough time to consult his lawyer, I say, okay, take your time, we'll wait till tomorrow or the next day."

Judge Slaven let out a long stream of cigarette smoke. "Down south," he said, "the courts are like sausage factories, cranking out the cases. Up here, we take our time. Hell, why not? There's no place special anybody's going."

The Mackenzie Valley Pipeline Inquiry, better known as the Berger Inquiry after its commissioner, Mr. Justice Tom Berger of the British Columbia Supreme Court, began its hearings in a large public room at the Explorer Hotel in Yellowknife on March 3, 1975. Its mandate was to look into the engineering and construction of a proposed Arctic gas pipeline and to measure the impact of such a pipeline on the human, physical, and living environment of the north. The pipeline, according to plans proposed in 1975 by Canadian Arctic Gas Pipelines Limited, one of the two companies competing for the job (Foothills Pipe Lines Limited was the other), would run about 2,600 miles from Prudhoe Bay north of Alaska across the top of the Yukon and up the Mackenzie Valley to markets in the south. It would cost seven billion dollars to build, making it the largest free-enterprise development ever attempted anywhere in the world. Mr. Justice Berger spent a year and a half listening to witnesses debate the pipeline's merits. He ended up with 32,353 pages of testimony from formal hearings. He travelled into thirty-five communities in the Northwest Territories and the Yukon to hear the views of local residents, and their words added up to another 8,438 pages of testimony. When all the talk was finished, Mr. Justice Berger wrote his report to the federal government. It was dated April 15, 1977, and it recommended that, in order to protect birds, whales, and other wildlife, no pipeline should be built through the Mackenzie Delta and that the construction of any pipeline through the Mackenzie Valley should be postponed for ten years, enough time to settle the claims of native peoples to compensation for their lands and enough time to develop an orderly program for the building of the pipeline.

The years of the Berger Inquiry were years for lawyers to shine. "Other than the Indian people themselves," says Doug Sanders, a professor at the University of British Columbia law school who concerns himself with the north, "lawyers were the most visible actors in the inquiry." The motives of some of the inquiry lawyers might have been mixed. Work for native peoples, for one motive, carries with it a decided cachet. Professor Sanders thinks it has done so for a couple of decades.

"Indian work has never been disreputable," he says. "A lawyer told me in 1973 that he was doing work at cost for one of the Indian organizations because he wanted a judgeship. He thought it would look good on his record. Indian work today is probably more respectable than work for labour unions."

Then, too, many of the lawyers who appeared before Mr. Justice Berger were southerners from big firms in Toronto and Calgary. To carry the burden of its argument, Canadian Arctic Gas Pipelines turned to Pierre Genest, a prominent counsel at Cassels, Brock in Toronto and a dedicated Liberal party backroom boy. The four counsel to the commission itself came from another Toronto firm, Cameron, Brewin and Scott, where the politics, like those of Mr. Justice Berger, who was a New Democrat MP and a leader of British Columbia's NDP before his appointment to the bench in December 1971, tend to be socialist. These lawyers, outsiders to the Territories, exerted a significant influence on the inquiry—and therefore on the north— and the north reciprocated in kind.

"I spent two winters with the inquiry," says Stephen Goudge, a slim, clean-lined, intense young lawyer from the Cameron, Brewin firm, "and when I came away, I realized what a constraint the environment has on every part of your life up there, physical, mental, social, all kinds of ways. At one point, I went into Inuvik for three weeks in winter, and for three weeks there was no sun. None. It's amazing the impact that has on your psychology. I came out of there and I flew straight to Florida."

But Goudge feels the experience left him with an enormous admiration for the lawyers who practise year round in the north.

"They're dealing with problems in an area that is really the country's last frontier," he says. "There's a reordering of relationships going on between white people and native peoples up there. It's a social problem, but many of the materials they have at hand to deal with the reordering are legal tools. So lawyers are deeply involved in the crucial changes in the north, and from what I saw of them at the Berger Inquiry, they're special people."

John Bayly, for instance. He's a lawyer in Yellowknife, a crown attorney now, but during the inquiry he appeared as one of the counsel for COPE—the Committee for Original People's Entitlement—representing Inuit from several communities in the Mackenzie Valley.

"I led all the evidence for COPE at the inquiry," Bayly says, "and I handled all its cross-examination of witnesses. I knew the evidence better than anybody except Berger."

When Bayly speaks that way, as he frequently does, it's

not out of conceit but out of passion. He cares about the north and about the people who'd been living off its hard land for thousands of years before the white man began dropping in. Bayly's love of the Territories sneaks out in quiet ways. He's a phlegmatic man, dark and lightly bearded, in his mid-thirties, and he seems to enclose himself forever in pools of calm. But when he talks in his studied, level way, his concern for the north gradually becomes irresistible. He isn't one of the lawyers whom Professor Doug Sanders speaks of, the cynics who take on native clients as a career booster. Bayly cares.

"A story," he might say. "In the north, among the native people, no one knocks on doors. You walk into the house and you sit down. Nobody makes a fuss about it. Certainly not the people whose house it is. Perhaps they may not speak to you immediately or perhaps they'll pour you a cup of coffee right away or hand you a beer. It doesn't matter. All right, suppose in a community like that, where all the doors are open, a fellow walks into someone's house and nobody's at home and he sees a dollar bill or a bottle of beer and he takes it away with him. Technically that's breaking and entering, which is a serious crime with a stiff sentence. But, as a crown attorney, I instruct the police not to lay such a heavy charge. Treat it as simple theft. Call it unlawfully in a dwelling house. The point is to be aware of the difference in cultures up here. White people may not approve of friends and strangers walking uninvited into their houses, but Inuit welcome it. And we can't permit the white man's law to intrude on such a charming custom."

Bayly's background makes him an unlikely candidate for the role of passionate spokesman for ancient northern ways. He grew up in southern Ontario. His father was a deputy minister in the provincial government, and young John attended private schools—Upper Canada College and Trinity College Schools. Before his call to the bar he articled with a large downtown Toronto firm, and after his call he spent nine months as a crown attorney in Thunder Bay, Ontario.

All along, though, he carried on a romance with the far north. He worked at a federal government job in Rankin Inlet for six months in 1967. In 1972 he took a canoe trip from Great Slave Lake to the Arctic and back. "I'm an outdoors jock," he says. "I like to paddle my canoe in the summer and run behind my sled and dogs in the winter." In the winter of 1974 he decided to test his affection for the north. He joined a private practice in Yellowknife.

"I got called to the Territories bar at 8:30 on the morning of January 21," he remembers, "and by nine I was on a plane to Inuvik. It was my first circuit. It didn't pay much. The circuit never does for a defence lawyer. It's all legal-aid work. You do it because it's fun."

And there are other quaint compensations.

"I'd arrive in a community and people would be at my door. Would I draw a will? Could I take a divorce case? Fix up a partnership agreement? There's always business on the side, and I'd get paid in odd ways. A free hotel room. A pair of snowshoes. Some Eskimo carvings. I'd come home with my pockets full of trinkets. For me, that's the north."

Bayly Burrows is the north, too. It is, as the sign at the side of the road leading into the property proclaims, the Bayly homestead. It lies a few minutes north of Yellowknife near the road that turns off to Giant Mine, one of the two gold mines — Cominco at the south end of town is the other — that are among Yellowknife's major employers. The Burrows takes up a couple of acres of sloping land, enough for a summer vegetable garden, for a large pen to enclose eight sled dogs, for an area to let the three Bayly kids romp around in, and enough for the small house that snuggles up to Back Bay, a gracious body of water that eventually leads into Great Slave Lake down around the corner to the south.

"COPE consumed my life for as long as the Berger Inquiry went on," Bayly said late one summer afternoon, sitting back in a stuffed chair in the living-room of the house, sipping cups of tea, utterly at ease amid the jumble of books, toys, and Eskimo artifacts. "It was a strong little grass-roots movement, and it knew how to confront the government from past battles it had with oil companies. COPE's idea was to take the pipeline application and go into the communities and explain to the people what its coming would mean to them and to the land. These native people weren't simple. Some of them had worked on oil rigs and understood the stakes. But they were naive in the sense that they thought that if the pipeline went through, they could pull their skidoos up to its stations and fill them with gas."

COPE went into communities spread over 4,500 square miles. It assembled teams of Eskimo field workers and white consultants — biologists, sociologists, geographers, lawyers — and visited each house in each community. The visitors documented the native people's experiences and reactions. Then they returned to each house in each community a second time. No resident was left untouched by COPE's researchers. Bayly and his fellow experts prepared COPE's brief for Mr. Justice Berger and then went back a third time to the communities to search out residents who would testify before the inquiry, bringing to immediate life the information that Bayly and the others packed into the brief.

"The pipeline," Richard Nerysoo of Fort McPherson near the Mackenzie Delta told Mr. Justice Berger, "means more white people who will be followed by even more white people. White people bring their own language, their own political system, their economy, their schools, their culture. They push the Indian aside and take everything."

"Another thing I accomplished," Bayly said over his tea, "I got Berger to go with the inquiry into Inuvik for two months so he could see how hard it is to work in the cold and dark of the winter. People do silly things in those conditions, and the lawyers from the inquiry were no different. They did silly things. Bickering. Arguing. Pointless disputing. I protected myself. I took my family in for the two months."

When the Berger Inquiry ended, Bayly left COPE to return briefly to private practice and then to join the Attorney General's office as a crown prosecutor. He did not take a gung-ho spirit into his new job; in fact he carefully avoided the role of a crusader bent on ridding his bailiwick of all crime. This attitude, he thinks, found its beginnings on the day he spent in court in Tuktoyaktuk. He was working with the Berger Inquiry at the time, had a couple of free hours, and, since the court happened to be sitting in Tuk, he went by to absorb the litigious atmosphere.

"I was dismayed at how little the community was affected by the comings and goings of the court party," he explained. "It isn't a scandal in the Territories to be called to face a court. It's just something you have to go through at a certain stage of your life. It's part of the white man's way of doing things. I remember the judge made a speech to the court about the seriousness of some crime or other, about a sentence he was passing. The lawyers listened, and the police and the court officials listened, but the community people didn't think it was terribly important that some of them must go to jail or bear a criminal record. So when I came back from working with COPE, I asked myself, where's the great social significance of what I'm doing?"

One episode in the courtroom at Tuktoyaktuk left its mark on Bayly. "The main case that the community was concerned about was a bootlegging charge. This man had come into Tuk with bottles of whiskey and sold them at thirty dollars apiece. He pleaded guilty and was fined fifty dollars. The community was very upset at the lenience because they were trying to keep liquor away from the young people. They hated bootleggers but somehow the court was oblivious to the feeling in the community."

These days, as a crown attorney, Bayly comes down hard on bootleggers. "I try to send them to jail." On the other hand, he's soft on nuisance crimes, on crimes that, in his view of northern life, arise out of Inuit customs, out of, for example, their aversion to locks on the doors of their houses.

"The RCMP doesn't always understand what I mean," Bayly said, sipping at yet another cup of tea in the casual, throw-away comfort of his living-room. "You see, the policeman has changed up here. It used to be that the Mountie was the guy who went out fishing and hunting with the people. He gave the Eskimos' dogs their needles. He spoke the language. Now the RCMP doesn't even have any dogs of its own. Men aren't allowed to volunteer for service in the north. They're assigned here as part of their tour of duty, and if one of them develops an affection for the place, he's assigned somewhere else in a hurry. Can't let the police get too friendly with the natives."

Bayly shifted in his chair. "I'm in the middle between the police and the court. The way I see my job, it's to make sense of a situation before the judge gets into the picture. If there's a serious crime—murder or rape—I start the machinery turning. But for cases that I think are essentially frivolous, I'll stay proceedings or ignore the situation altogether or say to the RCMP officer who's laid the charge, look, just go back and tell the guy not to do it again. I mean, why should the court and all its apparatus charge off a thousand miles to prosecute someone for allowing dogs to run at large? All it takes is common sense to apply the criminal law to the north."

Bayly walked slowly across the living-room to the long window at the back. On one side of the room his small son lay stomach down in a playpen, stretching a shaky arm at a dangling string of coloured beads. On the other side his wife sat with her teacup under a reproduction, unframed and Scotch-taped to the wall, of an Andrew Wyeth painting, *Christina's Way*. Bayly looked straight ahead, across Back Bay. The water was flat, without a ripple, and the land beyond it was scarcely less level. Only a few scattered spruce

poked against the horizon. There were no boats in sight, no
people, no movement, no disturbance. The view stretched
to eternity.

"What's up here," Bayly said, "the land and the people and
the culture, they're all worth preserving. And preserving is
part of a lawyer's work."

Judge Slaven leaned his head and shoulders into his
courtroom, the Territorial Court on the second floor of the
Yellowknife Courthouse, from the side door, the judges'
entrance.

"Greyeyes?" he asked of any one of those scattered
through the room—court clerk, court reporter, crown
attorney, a couple of defence counsel, a half-dozen others
in the public seats. "Greyeyes shown up yet?"

The crown attorney spoke. "Nothing." He was a young
man in a tan suit and he didn't bother to stand up from his
chair. "No Greyeyes, your honour, and no word."

The judge grunted around the cigarette in his mouth and
disappeared back into his office. He looked half-dressed,
wearing his vest and dickey but no gown. Judge Slaven
doesn't run a tight ship.

"This Greyeyes," he said, settled behind his desk, "he got
banged up pretty bad in some kind of hullabaloo with one
of the guys out there in the courtroom, the accused. He's
charged with assaulting Greyeyes, but the crown's got no
case unless Greyeyes shows up to testify against him. The
really complicating factor is that Greyeyes has a civil claim
in the works for money to get himself fixed up. He looks
something fierce, I understand, but his civil claim may go
down the drain if the guy out there isn't convicted on the
criminal charge. I'm not supposed to stick my nose in all of
this, but dammit, I'm sending a search party out for Greyeyes."

In the courtroom next door, the Supreme Court, Mr.
Justice Calvin Tallis was listening to a witness, a smartly

dressed, handsome white man in his late twenties, who delivered his testimony in sentences that rose at the end to question marks.

"So Napatchie had the baby, Patrick, in her arms sitting in the passenger seat of the truck? And on the way to the airport, I was driving, and she opened the door as if she was going to jump out and harm herself and Patrick, and I had to keep one hand on the wheel and grab her back with the other? We were right at the corner where Yellowknife Motors is, going thirty miles an hour?"

It was a custody case. Robert Fitzgerald, the handsome witness, and Napatchie Sagiaktook, an Inuit woman from the Eastern Arctic, had been lovers. On March 17, 1977, a child was born, Patrick, but the couple's relationship soured. Fitzgerald worked long hours, establishing his own carpet business in Yellowknife, and Napatchie, feeling abandoned, threatened to kill herself. Fitzgerald allowed her to leave Yellowknife to return to her people in Frobisher Bay, taking Patrick with her. A few weeks went by, and Napatchie phoned Fitzgerald. She had a new boyfriend. He didn't want Patrick. She was going to give the baby to another family.

"What did you do when you got the phone call?" Fitzgerald's lawyer asked him. The lawyer's name was Susan Green, a pretty, long-haired, blonde woman wearing large tinted glasses, wide brown pants, high-heeled sandals, and a black gown. "How did you react to the call?"

"I flew to Frobisher and had supper with Napatchie's family at their house? It was crowded, thirteen people and two puppies in three bedrooms, and when I left, I brought Patrick with me?"

Napatchie Sagiaktook sat across the courtroom with her lawyer. She was a short, chunky woman. Her black hair was pulled tightly back. Her face, broad and flat, was sinking into itself in the centre. When she smiled, her mouth became a small scar.

"Once," Fitzgerald told the court, "Napatchie swallowed half a bottle of aspirin?"

In his office Judge Slaven put on his gown, and the court clerk called the Territorial Court to order.

"I've got partly to the bottom of this," the judge said, speaking directly to the crown attorney. "A woman who used to be one of our court reporters, native woman, seems to have told Greyeyes that it wasn't necessary for him to appear today. Don't know where she got the notion, but Greyeyes has gone into the bush."

He shifted his attention to a man sitting in the public benches. "George," the judge said. The man stood up, a black man as tall as a basketball centre, erect and dapper and poker-faced. "George, you're acting for Greyeyes on the civil end. See if you can track him down, and in the meantime I'm adjourning for another half-hour."

Robert Fitzgerald's wife testified in Mr. Justice Tallis's courtroom. She was a schoolteacher, a composed and proper woman. She'd married Fitzgerald a few months earlier. She put Patrick in a day-care centre each school day, she said, answering Susan Green's questions, and she and Robert spent the evenings and weekends playing with the boy.

"Patrick especially likes outdoor games," she said.

Napatchie nodded slowly in a motion that seemed as ancient as the north.

Judge Slaven was on the phone. "Well, George, if he can't come out of the bush, that's the end of it. The accused's from outside, as you know, Edmonton or some place, and I can't drag him back up here again for the trial, all that expense." He paused to listen. "I worry about Greyeyes, too, George." He hung up and let out a soft moan.

Mr. Justice Tallis adjourned the custody case to Frobisher Bay at a date five weeks later. Napatchie, her lawyer told the court, was also recently married. Her husband, a Hudson's Bay store manager at Wakeham Bay in

Northern Quebec, couldn't afford to fly all the miles and hours to Yellowknife. Frobisher, a ninety-minute flight from Wakeham Bay, was more convenient. The husband wanted to testify that he and Napatchie could make a good home for Patrick if they were awarded custody of the boy.

"That's the court's policy," Susan Green told the Fitzgeralds after Mr. Justice Tallis had left the courtroom. "The court travels to the witnesses instead of making them come to it."

Judge Slaven's court was again called to order.

"Greyeyes," the judge said, "has got a job in the bush. George Carter spoke to his employers and they'll fly him out if that's what he wants, but there's no telling whether he'll still have the job when he goes back. So he'd better stay put."

The judge looked at the crown attorney. "What does the crown have to say?"

"The crown is offering no evidence in this matter, your honour."

"Very well. The crown offering no evidence, the charge is dismissed."

Judge Slaven banged his gavel and whisked out of his chair in one swift, practised motion.

"You can't help it up here," he said, back in his office. "There's bound to be some collision between the whites' and the native peoples' cultures. The industrial system coming into the north and all the rest of it, the liquor, and now the Montreal drug dealers are doing their business over in Frobisher. How're Indians and Eskimos supposed to cope with that? How's an ordinary fella like Greyeyes supposed to figure out what the courts are trying to do for him? Bound to be collisions."

Mr. Justice Tallis's court flew to Frobisher Bay and sprang a surprise. The judge was impressed with Napatchie Sagiaktook's husband and his testimony. He thought that Napatchie and her husband were fit parents for her young son, that they should have a chance to raise him. Custody of the boy, Patrick, Mr. Justice Tallis announced, was awarded to his mother.

As for Greyeyes, he vanished into the bush.

Judge Jack Sissons' work and reputation are in the process of being shredded. It was Sissons, appointed the first judge in the Territories on July 1, 1955, who handed down the original body of judicial decisions that attempted to adapt the white man's laws to keep alive the customs and culture of the northern people. Sissons, a stubborn, independent Scots-Canadian, was moved by an immediate affection he found in himself for the Inuit. "Eskimos," he wrote in his memoirs, "have as much promise for Canada as Scots have had for the rest of the world." And during his eleven years on the Territories bench he was partly successful in his campaign to preserve the Inuit way of life. But in recent years other lawyers and judges and civil servants have begun to rethink his decisions, and Judge Sissons, now dead, is a man whose proudest monuments are being torn down.

"What's happening with Sissons' laws," John Bayly says, "reflects the changes in attitudes to the people up here. Sissons was famous because he bent the rules to fit the northern situation. Now we're trying to pretend that the north is no different from the rest of Canada."

Sissons was a lawyer and judge from the Peace River country of Alberta. He was a Presbyterian and a Liberal. He walked with a limp from a childhood attack of polio, and he rejoiced in his mother's family relationship — cousins — with David Livingstone, the African explorer. When the federal government asked him to take over the Territorial Court he was sixty-three years old. He said he welcomed the adventure.

From the beginning, Sissons announced that his would be a travelling court, taking justice to the people, and from the beginning, too, he showed his compassion for the Inuit he encountered on the circuits. Kikkik, the woman whose ordeal is charted in the small carvings on display at the Yellowknife Courthouse, felt Sissons' compassion. At an isolated winter camp near Henik Lake in the Eastern Arctic, Kikkik's half-brother shot her husband dead. Terrified, Kikkik stabbed the half-brother and set off with her five children for a Hudson's Bay Company post twenty miles across the tundra. Partway on the journey, out of food and moving too slowly, she left the two smallest children under caribou skins and an improvised shelter of blocks of ice. She reached the post, but five days later when she returned to the makeshift igloo, the youngest child was dead. Kikkik was charged with murder, criminal negligence, and abandoning a child.

"Justice," Judge Sissons said in his address to the jury at Kikkik's trial, "demands that we revert in our thinking to an earlier age and try to understand Kikkik and her life and her land and her society."

He suggested to the jury it might find that Kikkik had acted in self-defence and in defence of her children.

The jury's verdict: not guilty on all charges.

So it went with Judge Sissons. In the case of Noah, he held that marriage by Eskimo custom, without ceremony or legal sanction, was still valid in Canadian law. In the case of Kolitalik, he found that three men, Amah and Avinga and Nangmalik, had, as charged, assisted the old and sick chief of a camp of fine Inuit hunters on Igloolik, an island off the northeast coast of Melville Island, to commit suicide, but he suspended sentence against the three because, he told the court, he had no wish to break up such a splendid community. And in the cases of Jimmy Kogogolak and Michael Sikyea and Matthew Koonungnak and Francis Kallooar, he held that the Inuit and the Indians are not subject to the hunting ordinances which restrict white men and that their ancient rights to hunt and fish for food remain unbounded.

The judgments in the hunting cases began the reaction against Sissons. "Crackpot law," David Searle says of the judgments. Searle is entitled to his opinion, since he had a close-up view of Sissons in action. He served as the Territories' crown attorney for five years, 1962 through 1966, when the judge was blazing his trail of controversial decisions.

"Sissons was a hard guy to be in daily contact with out on the circuit," Searle remembers. "He was forever taking reporters along — Farley Mowat, people from *Life*, a reporter from the *Globe and Mail*. He'd play to the media, and he'd trample all over established law to make himself the protector of the Eskimos."

These days, Searle is the senior partner in the biggest law firm in the Territories. It's called Searle, Richard and Kingsmill, and it practises out of smart offices in the Gallery Building on Franklin Avenue, Yellowknife's main drag. Searle handles a big load of corporate and commercial work on behalf of the mining and development companies that are moving into the north. He appeared for the Northwest Territories Chamber of Commerce at the Berger Inquiry, and he's a director of Pacific Western Airlines. Searle is as visible and as influential as a lawyer can get in the Territories.

"Oh, but I still take a couple of capital cases every year," he says. "The life on the circuit gets into your blood no matter what nonsense you have to put up with."

He laughs. He's a hearty laugher. He's a large, convivial man in his mid-forties. He's restless. He prowls the room when he talks, and when he reaches the punch lines of his stories, he hovers over his listener waiting for the reaction. Then he laughs.

"Sissons used to load the dice against the crown," Searle says. "He'd look through the reports from justices of the peace around the Territories for convictions of Eskimos on charges of hunting out of season. Then he'd instruct an appeal to be brought before him, and he'd promptly acquit. It was a no-win situation for the crown."

That wasn't Searle's only complaint.

"We wanted to take Sissons' decisions to the court of

appeal, but he'd fox us. He'd hold in those hunting cases that we hadn't proved any facts. You can only appeal on matters of law, not on the facts. So he'd rule we hadn't proved the identity of the accused. He'd rule we hadn't proved that the accused shot the musk-ox. He'd rule we hadn't proved that the musk-ox *was* a bloody musk-ox. We had no case at all when Sissons had finished with us, nothing to apply any law to and no law to appeal on."

The frustration ended one day in July 1964 when an Eskimo named Sigeareak from Whale Cove on Hudson Bay shot some caribou, cut out their tongues, sliced off a few other pieces of meat, and left the rest of the caracasses to rot.

"A blatant case," Searle says, happy at the memory. "A blatant, lovely case. Just took the tongues. A great delicacy. Tasted them myself. Absolutely delicious."

Sigeareak was charged with "killing and abandoning game fit for human consumption contrary to section 15(1)(a) of the game ordinance". But before his trial, Searle called on the magistrate who was to hear the case, an experienced northern hand named Peter Parker, and suggested a piece of strategy designed to outfox Sissons.

"I wanted an acquittal the first time round. That's odd for a crown counsel, eh? But it was part of the plan. I wanted Peter Parker to find that all the facts had been proven, that is was Sigeareak who'd shot the caribou and abandoned them. Then he had to find that on the basis of Sissons' decision in *Regina* v. *Francis Kallooar*, one of those damned pieces of law that said Eskimos aren't bound by the game ordinance, he had to acquit Sigeareak."

Which is precisely what Magistrate Parker ruled.

"Then the crown, which was me, appealed by way of stated case. That's where you appeal against any proceeding in a magistrate's court on the ground that what he held was erroneous in law."

The appeal from Magistrate Parker's decision went before Sissons in a stated case that asked the question: "Was the magistrate right in holding that the game ordinance and particularly section 15(1)(a) thereof does not apply to Eskimos?"

"Ah, it was diabolical," Searle says. "I knew we had Sissons. He had to affirm Parker's decision, which he did, and then at last we had some law to take to the court of appeal."

On the appeal, William Morrow acted for Sigeareak, thus in effect arguing Judge Sissons' view of the law. Morrow was a distinguished counsel from Edmonton who was later to follow Sissons on the bench in the Territories and even later to be appointed to the Alberta Supreme Court. But in the Sigeareak matter he was unsuccessful in protecting Sissons' string of decisions in the hunting cases. The court of appeal upset Sigeareak's acquittal, and so, on further appeal, did the Supreme Court of Canada.

"I think it is desirable to say specifically," Mr. Justice Hall wrote in the highest court's judgment, "that insofar as *Regina* v. *Kallooar* and *Regina* v. *Kogogolak* hold that the game ordinance does not apply to Indians and Eskimos in the Northwest Territories, they are not good law and must be taken as having been overruled."

Judge Sissons was heart-broken.

"With the words of Mr. Justice Hall," he wrote in his memoirs, "it seemed...that my campaign had failed and the seven years' war had gone to the bureaucrats."

"Oh yeah, he was furious," David Searle says today. "In one fell swoop we reversed all his earlier decisions. And he never knew who the Machiavelli was behind the whole plan. I never told him it was me and he went to his grave not knowing. But, lord, I'd had my gut full of all those years of taking his crackpot law."

Searle's delight in his ultimate triumph over Sissons doesn't spring from revenge realized or any other malicious motive. Uh-uh, he says. The point, according to Searle, is that Judge Sissons, good-hearted man that he may have been, wasn't reading the drift of the northern times correctly.

"All right," Searle says, "maybe twenty years ago people in Baker Lake and all those other places were living in ice houses. But that was ending in Sissons' day, and now everybody has a home made out of wood and bricks. The young people speak English. They don't know the Eskimo tongue. And hunting and fishing, my lord, it's only the very old people who live off the land in this day and age. The era of bringing up defences for Eskimos that Sissons raised is long gone."

Even the notion of the circuit, as established by Judge Sissons, is falling at least partly into disrepute. John Bayly thinks so.

"Sissons was right to have the court go into the communities," he says. "But it's got out of hand. Now we fly in for trivial matters when we shouldn't. It'd be better for the people if they called on the travelling court much less and if the local justices of the peace handled everything except fraud and rape and murder."

Alas, there are problems. The JPs, to cite one difficulty, are reluctant to judge their neighbours, especially at the fees they're paid. How come, the JPs argue, they get five dollars per case while the judge from Yellowknife gets $35,000 a year in salary, and gets to fly in a big plane and to wear a beautiful gown?

"So," Bayly says, "the justices of the peace are refusing to sit whenever anybody enters a not-guilty plea, and our court is kept on the road. It gets silly. Once, two little boys in a community in the Eastern Arctic got into some mischief, set fire to a tree, and fed the dogs some fish that had glass in it. Instead of scolding the boys, the community called in the court. It cost $5,000 just to put the plane in the air. That's what Sissons started for us."

But at least some of Sissons' work remains intact and on display. Mike Sikyea's duck, for example. Mike Sikyea is an Indian from Yellowknife who shot a duck six miles north of the city one day in the summer of 1962. Unfortunately for Mike a Mountie happened on the scene and charged him

136

with hunting a duck out of season contrary to the Migratory Birds Convention Act. The charge came before Judge Sissons, who ruled that the Act didn't apply to Indians engaged in their age-old right to hunt for food in all seasons on unoccupied crown lands. The crown attorney appealed, and over the next few years the case wound its way up to the Supreme Court of Canada, where Sikyea was ruled guilty of the offence. The case, appeals and all, cost the crown $250,000 to pursue.

The duck that gave rise to the charge, the duck that prompted Jack Sissons' decision and the crown's appeal, has been stuffed and placed in the glass case on the second floor of the new Yellowknife Courthouse. And these days, whenever Mike Sikyea pours himself a few drinks, he leads his friends on a brief conducted tour of the courthouse.

"That duck up there," he'll say, stopping in front of the display case, "that's my quarter-of-a-million-dollar duck."

"Absurdity," John Bayly says, "pervades a lot of what the law and lawyers do up here in the Territories."

Fifth Adjournment

Wellington's Court Restaurant in downtown Toronto is a place of maroons and browns and muffled atmosphere. It's favoured by corporate lawyers who like quiet and discretion with their lunch. Let the high-profile corporate guys eat at Winston's where the proprietor, John Arena, guarantees a flurry of attention for anyone with a Name. John Turner of McMillan, Binch has a favourite Winston's table. Jim Arnett of Stikeman, Elliott, Robarts and Bowman prefers Wellington's Court and generally begins lunch with a soda-water.

"I got into corporate law because I had a romantic notion of it," he said one noon hour, waiting for his soda-water. "You're involved in power. You're involved in the corporate planning process right alongside the senior management of multinational companies. You really see what's happening in the business community. You have the perspective that maybe, say, a deputy minister in Ottawa has. It's heady stuff. It's like I thought at the beginning. Romantic."

Jim Arnett is a slim man in his late thirties with a quality of purity about him, something hard and clean and exact in his personality. He studied law at the University of Manitoba ("worst law school in the Commonwealth"), took classes at Harvard, including some Henry Kissinger seminars, and then went searching for a career. He spent a year at the Department of Justice in Ottawa, entered private practice in Winnipeg, and defected briefly to the advertising game with the Vickers and Benson agency in Toronto ("I decided advertising was frivolous") before he arrived at the Stikeman firm and romance in 1974.

"Of course, there's no way to get around working long hours in this end of the law," he went on. "You're not cutting the mustard unless you show up at the office on weekends. It's the unspoken pressure that makes you put in the time. You have to keep track of the hours you spend on all your files. That's for the purposes of billing the clients. You bill by the hour. All the statistics, that's the hours and billings and so forth, are fed into a computer. Which means that everybody else in the office can check at a glance on how much you're working. There's the unspoken pressure."

He took a swallow of his soda-water. "In any corporate firm a junior lawyer, the person just getting off the mark, is expected, or *required*, to show 1,600 billing hours a year. You don't chalk up big figures like that by working day to day. It stands to reason there's a disproportionate number of workaholics among corporate lawyers."

Arnett ordered a julienne salad and talked of his firm's history. It began in Montreal in the 1940s with Heward Stikeman, the first lawyer in Canada to make a reputation as a tax expert. He built a formidable Montreal firm, then looked to expansion. First, an office in London, England ("A gold mine of business for us with the multinationals," Arnett says. "Fifty per cent of my time is on London work"). Next, Toronto. In the 1960s Stikeman opened a Bay Street firm, now up to two dozen lawyers, in partnership with John Robarts, who brought with him the contacts of ten years as premier of Ontario.

"The big corporations we have as clients rate lawyers on the basis of how fast they can move paper around," Arnett said, forking his salad. "Multinational executives think in terms of logistics. It's all very well to have a document properly drawn, but if it isn't in the right place at the right time, then it's no good. What it means is that we only spend half our time on substantive stuff and the other half on things like how to get a paper signed in Vancouver and on somebody's desk in Ottawa a day later. It gets complicated when your client has a head office in London, a branch in Tampa, Florida, a tax accountant in New York City, and turns out his products on the west coast. But that's corporate law."

Arnett asked for another soda-water. "In multinationals it's hard to find who's running things. The executives do a lot of ass-covering. They're always drawing memos to set down their position on any given situation just in case there's a bomb that might go off and blow them out of the water. They look for lawyers to buttress them. One executive'll phone a lawyer in our firm and report back to his company that the lawyer said to go ahead and follow XY course of action. Another executive'll phone another lawyer in the firm and report back that he said to take YZ action, something very different. What's happened is that the first executive has talked to somebody in the corporate end of things over here and the second executive has talked to somebody on the tax side. There may be two quite different reasons, corporate and tax, for taking two different courses of action. There's a lot of politics at work in the situation, what with the two executives jockeying for their positions, and it's part of the law firm's job to make sure that things don't fall between the cracks. We have to provide the overview so that the tax and the corporate reasons for taking different steps get reconciled in the best interests of the client. The client, you know, isn't really a monolith. It's individuals."

Arnett had vanilla ice cream for dessert. No coffee, thanks. "Hardware's important. Crucial, in fact. Telex, computers, word-processing machines. Some days my secretary spends three or four hours at the telex. That's how you get things done. Using the hardware. It's the major revolution that's come along in corporate law in these last few years, but to me it's second best. Marshall McLuhan, you know, says you don't need to talk personally to anybody these days because the phone and telex and the rest are contemporary man's substitute. But nothing's as good as a face-to-face meeting, not even a bunch of people on a conference call. It's not the same dynamics. Some element escapes you."

Arnett polished off the ice cream. "Corporate lawyers are different from other lawyers. We aren't concerned with justice. We're solicitors. That's the starting point, and then it's almost as if we're becoming part of the international business bureaucracy. Not quite, but we're getting there."

Arnett walked out of the dim of Wellington's Court into the shiny glass and silver metal of the skyscraper above the restaurant, the Commerce Court West. He rode an elevator to the forty-ninth floor, back to Stikeman, Elliott and the romance of moving paper.

CHAPTER FIVE

Tory, Tory

The New York businessman was in a hurry. He wanted to wind up the deal, the acquisition of a Canadian company, in time to avoid an American tax deadline that was not much more than a week away. He arrived in Toronto and rushed to his Canadian lawyer, Jim Tory, at Tory, Tory, Des-Lauriers and Binnington. It was a small gathering in the Tory offices — the American businessman, Jim Tory, a couple of lawyers from his firm, and the president of the Canadian company which was to be the subject of the swift acquisition. The Canadian president had been summoned to the meeting on such short notice that he hadn't brought along his own lawyer. That worried him.

"I don't know," he said. "It looks like a good deal, but the speed of it all kind of gives me concern. I don't have anybody here advising me."

He looked at the deed of sale on the table in front of him, freshly drawn and lacking only his signature.

"I'll tell you what," he said. "I respect Jim, and if Jim says I should sign the deal, I'll sign."

Tory shifted in his seat.

"Well, I've got to point out there are certain negatives in the sale from your side," he said to the Canadian president, and over the following few minutes he proceeded to outline the "negatives".

"Yeaa-ahh," the president said, stretching the word into a couple of syllables. "I didn't recognize any of those things myself, not till you put your finger on them."

He nudged the deed of sale across the table.

"In light of all this," he said, "I don't think I'm going to sign the deal."

He left the meeting.

"Wait a minute," the New York businessman said to Tory, "whose lawyer *are* you anyway?"

And he went home to New York without his Canadian acquisition.

Tory, Tory, DesLauriers and Binnington is a remarkable institution for two reasons. To begin with, it is a "hot" firm, Canada's consummate corporate-commercial law firm of the 1970s and early '80s. Its lawyers, over fifty of them in mid-1980 with the body count threatening to rise, act for, among other distinguished clients, Wood Gundy (stocks and bonds), the International Thomson Organization (newspapers, oil, and sundries), Reichhold (chemicals), Rogers Cable Telecommunications (radio and television), and Simpsons-Sears (merchandising). It provided the legal brains behind the key corporate takeovers of recent years: the Bronfman family's conquest of Brascan, the Thomson purchase of the Hudson's Bay Company and the FP newspaper chain. It dispatched senior partners on assignment, both temporary and permanent, to run some of the country's most powerful corporations and public bodies, Jim Tory's twin brother John to the Thomson organization, Trevor Eyton to Brascan, Jim Baillie to the Ontario Securities Commission. Tory, Tory, DesLauriers and Binnington is, in short, omnipresent in the Canadian corporate world. That constitutes its first point of distinction. Its second, perhaps surprisingly, is that it is a firm of lawyers who are honest and responsible and decent. Tory, Tory is, also in short, a place of nice guys.

"Jim and John Tory," Trevor Eyton says, "don't have a

mean bone in their bodies, and they're the people who established the standards the firm goes by."

Dick Gathercole agrees. He teaches at the University of Toronto Law School after a career in practice that included a half-dozen years at the Tory firm, and although his personal politics (middle left) make him a natural debating opponent for Eyton (far right), he too recognizes "the personal integrity of the Tory brothers. The spirit and excellence of the firm come from them, and so do the things that make it such a *good* place to work."

It's Jim Tory who is chiefly responsible for setting the moral tone, at least since John departed in 1973 to serve as senior financial advisor and all-round *éminence grise* to Kenneth Thomson, the second Lord Thomson, in the management and expansion of the empire he inherited from his father, Roy, the first Lord Thomson. John's name remains in the firm title and he stays in regular communication with Jim on matters legal, business, and social. But it's Jim who heads the firm, and for a standard-bearer and shining example to his peers and juniors he is a curiously anonymous man. He is fifty, has blond hair, a roundish face, a shy smile, and an unfailing talent for hiding his light under a bushel. (John is darker, slimmer, and almost equally self-effacing.) Jim's suits, no matter how freshly pressed in the morning, look slightly rumpled by noon hour. His notion of the ideal Saturday is to put on his thick old white wool sweater-coat and take his wife Marilyn shopping at the St. Lawrence Farmers' Market, then settle in at a modest restaurant called the Old Fish Market for a lunch of beer and scallops. His private life — "private" in the sense that Margaret Trudeau would never grasp — is all of a piece. When he and John turned fifty in March 1980, friends organized a party of celebration at an inn in a development ninety miles north of Toronto for family skiers called Cranberry Village. The party invitation, written by one of the friends, read "Dress: T-shirts. No gifts." The wording seemed appropriate on every count.

144

What Jim Tory, with his probity and, to be sure, his brains (he was the silver medallist in the year of his call to the bar), has most significantly managed to shape at Tory, Tory is a true community of corporate lawyers. The firm displays among its members a series of interconnections and mutual passions and a commonality of interests that are almost uncanny and that beyond question contribute to the firm's *esprit* and success. Bill DesLauriers and Art Binnington grew up three houses apart on Hillhurst Boulevard in an unpretentious North Toronto neighbourhood. The two Torys, DesLauriers, and Binnington were University of Toronto fraternity brothers at Psi Upsilon, not a frat of the first, snobbish rank but one that mixed jock activities, gregarious weekends, and ties that bind. The list of items-in-common, large and small, among Tory, Tory partners runs on from past to present: Paul Moore is the Akela, scouting language for adult leader, of his son's Wolf Cub pack in Mississauga, and Brian Shields used to hold the same title and responsibility, dressing up one night a week in the costume decreed decades ago by Lord Baden-Powell, for *his* son's pack at Lawrence Park Community Church.

Ah, Lawrence Park. It's another piece of togetherness that several members make their homes in Lawrence Park, a subdued, leafy residential district on the outer fringes of Toronto's north end that in recent years has unobtrusively slipped past Forest Hill and Rosedale as the city's most desirable address. Shields lives in Lawrence Park. So do Bill DesLauriers and John Tory. Jim bought his Lawrence Park home in 1959, a comfortable-old-shoe of a house, substantial and three-storey, that's handy to a park, the subway, and the Rosedale Golf Club. Tory uses all three. It's gratifying, too, but hardly essential, that Ross Le Mesurier, corporate finance chief at Wood Gundy, lives next door to Jim, and that Dick Thomson, chairman and chief executive officer of the Toronto-Dominion Bank, has a house around the corner.

But the factor that binds Tory, Tory's senior partners

145

most intrinsically is their common beginnings at the University of Toronto Law School during the years — the 1950s and early '60s — when it was tiny and renowned for its legal scholarship. Of the firm's eight pace-setting members from the period around 1960 — the Tory brothers, DesLauriers, Binnington, Eyton, Shields, Jim Baillie, and Gordon Coleman — all but one, Shields, who studied at Osgoode Hall, proceeded downtown from the U. of T. Law School. It was no coincidence. The Tory firm had a self-appointed talent scout at the school — Bora Laskin. In the years long before his ascendancy to the Supreme Court of Canada, Laskin lectured in labour law, property law, and constitutional law at the university law school, and his concern for the bright students who passed under him was genuine and abiding. The Tory boys ranked among his favourites, and in the years when they were building the firm, Laskin operated as a faithful recruiter.

Trevor Eyton was one of the recruits. Eyton is a husky man — he puts on a Santa Claus suit for the annual Tory Christmas parties — with unblinking eyes that could look holes through a corporate adversary, and he remembers that Laskin was single-minded when it came to Tory, Tory.

"It was a custom in third year at the law school," he says, "that all the students would go to Bora and he'd give each one a list of three or four law firms that he thought would be appropriate places for them to article. He'd say, check out these three or four and make a choice among them. Bora was very well-connected downtown. He knew every firm and he knew his students. He had a sense which students and which firms would mix.

"In my third year, I waited until three-quarters of the class had been to Bora before I went to see him. I sat down in his office. He had this enormous room, but the desk was positioned right up at the door, which was always open, so he could see the students passing by and call them in for a chat. I sat down and he leaned over and patted me on the knee and said, 'You go to Tory's.'

146

" 'But what about a few other firms?' I said. 'What about Blake, Cassels or McCarthy and McCarthy?'

" 'Never mind the others,' he said, and he patted me on the knee again.

" 'Tory's,' he said.

"Of course he was right. Bora Laskin is one of my heroes."

At the other end of the pipeline, down at Tory's, it was John Tory who took charge of the hiring for several essential years. "If you look down the list of the first twenty-five names on the firm letterhead today," he says, "you'll see my handiwork." He used two criteria in selecting students and young lawyers. Marks came first. "That may be élitist," he says. "But by taking the students with the best marks, I knew I was starting with people who'd already proved they knew how to work. I used to phone up the secretary of the law school—she was a wonderful woman and very good to me —and I'd tell her to send me down the top twenty-five people from third year. I guess I had kind of an inside track there, an advantage over the other firms."

The second criterion was more amorphous. It had to do with nerve and personality. "Corporate lawyers have a closer relationship with their clients than other sorts of lawyers," Tory says. "A person charged with a criminal offence doesn't have to *like* his lawyer. He just wants somebody who's going to do something to get him off. But in corporate law there's so much give and take, back and forth, exchange of ideas, intimacy, and so on, that lawyers and clients have to get along. That's what I looked for in students and juniors, all-round types who showed the potential to hit it off with company presidents and corporate executives." Those people, after all, don't like to suffer fools gladly.

What has emerged from the various links, from the coming together of lawyers who have shared over the years an educational institution, a neighbourhood, good deeds, and one another's respect, is a law firm that boasts more rah-rah than most college football teams. The spirit pervades the office—partners gather each Friday afternoon in a small conference room off the main boardroom for drinks and conviviality—and it extends outside the firm to the clients that Tory, Tory elects to take on.

"You might as well work for people you have respect and affection for," Eyton says. "If I don't like a client, I'll send him to someone else in the firm—or more likely out of the firm. The point is, you're going to be working hard, you're going to be working through the night on many, many occasions, but you never think about the effort when you're tied into clients who are appreciative and supportive. When the client sees you pressing yourself to the limit, he'll remember it and like it. And he'll have a short memory when things don't end up right. That's the way it goes at the firm. Jim Tory, the man at the top of the list, the senior guy, he feels the pressure of doing the job. He *feels* it. The clients recognize that, and in return the corporate world is full of people who'll do anything for Jim."

The man at the top, Jim Tory, typically waves aside anything that hints at personal glory and prefers to speak in praise of the "team concept" in the practice of corporate law. He elaborates:

"Suppose we're into an important transaction at the firm, a takeover or something. Well, you start off with the lawyer who's the over-all director of the deal. He's the generalist. As a lawyer, I'm a generalist. I don't think I'm an expert in anything, but I know a little bit about a lot of branches of commercial law.

"So, on the deal, the generalist seconds to himself a tax man and a securities man, people in the firm who are specialists in those areas. Some lawyers do nothing but securities work. They know all about the stock exchange, about what the Ontario Securities Commission will permit, about how many days you have to accomplish certain aims. They're experts. Maybe the generalist'll also need a person from the real-estate department in the firm to handle a land aspect of the deal. If some sort of opposition is expected in the course of the operation, he'll get a litigation man to stand by. He'll pull in two or three young fellows, junior lawyers, who can draft all the paperwork that's inevitably involved. Pretty soon we'll have maybe eight to ten lawyers gathered together, and they'll be devoting seventy per cent of their working time to the one transaction.

"That's what the team concept amounts to. I don't know how it feels at other firms, but to collaborate with good people from our office, go along with them on a deal that's important to a client, the whole thing amounts to, ah, a very satisfying experience."

"*Satisfying* to work with people at Tory's?" Trevor Eyton says. "I'll put it this way — of the eight or nine or ten people in the world I most respect and love, the high percentage are at that law firm."

Paul Moore may be the quintessential Tory, Tory partner. He has been a member of the firm since his call to the bar in 1967. He ranks as one of the senior Tory men on one prime account, Wood Gundy. And he's a lawyer who registers as positively evangelical when talk turns to the grandeurs of corporate practice.

"I want to be a productive member of society," he explains. "When I was in law school, I was torn between criminal litigation and commercial law. I had a conversation with a crown attorney and he told me ninety-five per cent, maybe more, of the people who come up in criminal court are flat guilty. How could I be a productive member of society defending guys who're already guilty of something? I joined Tory's and burned the midnight oil learning about corporate securities work. That was a very right decision on my part. It's the business aspect of Canadian life that produces the country's wealth. I mean everybody from the Avon lady to the guy who runs a Becker's store to the Bronfman family. I work for those people. I'm loyal to business. That means I'm socially useful. And it doesn't hurt to get paid well for it either."

Moore's personal pride in the Tory firm is immense and specific. "I can name on the fingers of both hands the number of law firms in Canada who do the sort of work we do," he says, "and I can name on the fingers of one hand the number of lawyers who are really good at it. Most of the latter are in this firm."

His pride begins when he surveys the elegant Tory offices. They're on the thirty-fourth and thirty-fifth floors of the Royal Bank Building, which is plainly the jewel among Toronto's downtown towers. On the outside it has a shimmery copper gleam, and, rather than being of a conventional boxy shape, it boasts exterior walls that take off in cunning zigzags. Inside, the entrance lobbies are all mirrors and potted plants and splashes of colour from the tapestries by Jack Bush and Jack Shadbolt. The effect is one of calm and order, a peace altogether alien to the commerce that is the building's reason for existence.

Upstairs, the Tory floors maintain the building's mood. The atmosphere is muted. The hallways are not in the usual bowling-alley style but repeat the zigzag patterns of the outer walls. The colours of the carpets and the interior surfaces run to beiges and pale browns. A pair of contrasting landscapes, a traditional A. J. Casson oil and a large, ethereal work by Takao Tanabe, face each other over the knubby blue chairs and couches in the clients' reception area. Paintings catch the eye everywhere; Tory, Tory owns enough Canadian art, tastefully chosen, to make a serious collector wince in envy. The individual offices, also slightly eccentric in shape, come in three sizes: large for a few senior men, medium for the middle-level partners, smaller by a degree for juniors and students. Most of the senior and middle-level offices face south over a splendid view of Toronto's harbour and islands. Paul Moore's office, medium-sized and next door to Trevor Eyton's (now rarely occupied while he presides over Brascan Limited), looks slightly east.

"There's a reason why I chose this location," he said in the office one bright November afternoon. Moore, chunkily built, likable, and a natural enthusiast, is in his early forties and could pass for ten years younger. His face has clung to boyishness. A lick of reddish-brown hair falls over his forehead. He likes to chew gum. "The reason is, the sun shines in from the south, and that does two things, drives up the temperature in the offices and blinds you to the view. I wasn't keen on either prospect."

Moore pays attention to such matters of detail in his life. "In the mornings, I pace myself through the *Globe and Mail*," he said. "Front page and comics at home. On the bus ride from the house to the commuter train I chat with my neighbours. The quiet half-hour on the train, which I treasure, I use for a quick look at the sports and for studying the *Globe*'s "Report on Business" section. That's essential. I'm behind if I don't read the ROB. It tells me what the Ontario Securities Commission did the day before, what other corporate lawyers are up to, what new ideas may be floating around the business community. I get off at Union Station and I'm ready for the day until I catch the 6:23 train back home at night."

Moore was an outstanding student at the University of Toronto Law School. He stood number one in first year and again in second year. In third year, he scored five A's and two B's on the final exams. So did Dick Gathercole. But Gathercole's marks were marginally higher and he finished first in the class, Moore second. Moore went downtown to article with a well-regarded commercial firm, Campbell, Godfrey and Lewtas, while Gathercole, along with another top graduate from the U. of T. Law School, Gar Pink, proceeded for his articles to the Tory firm.

Gathercole, a man whose social views put him much in contrast with Paul Moore, pops up in illuminating ways in Moore's early legal career. When Moore took his call to the bar and was casting around for precisely the right firm to practise with, he spent an hour chatting in John Tory's office. He took immediately to Tory's solid ways. Tory found Moore long on intelligence and efficiency and short on stuffiness, surely a man for Tory, Tory. But was there room to take on a new junior when the firm had already elected to hire Gar Pink and another articling student, Bob Torrens? Ah, but Dick Gathercole, a third candidate for the firm, was leaving for a year's study at the London School of Economics. Room was made, and Moore joined Tory's. Twelve months later, so did Gathercole. He wasn't enthusiastic about corporate work and concentrated on the firm's new litigation department. He resigned in 1971 to work for a free legal-aid clinic, then for the Ontario Attorney General's office, then for his old law school. Unlike Paul Moore, Gathercole, a big, soft-spoken man, given to sweaters and corduroy pants, bright, an idealist, was not at heart a Tory, Tory lawyer.

"Those offices in the Royal Bank are like a sealed spaceship," he says. "That's how they strike me when I visit my friends at the firm. At least when I look out my window at school I see other people. They look out and see other buildings full of other lawyers. The office is cut off from the real world, and it explains why the lawyers in it don't understand that certain problems exist — for example, that in Ontario most ordinary citizens have no real access to the legal profession."

Gathercole makes clear his respect and affection for the Tory partners as lawyers and as people. But corporate law, put simply, isn't his bag. "It's typical of Jim Tory," he says, "that he let me do work on firm time for Digger House, a place for kids with drug problems, and Theatre Passe Muraille, a sort of adventurous theatre company. In fact, he encouraged me. But I've never been enamoured of multinational corporations. I couldn't see the significance in two huge companies fighting it out. I didn't really care who won. To work at the Tory firm successfully, you have to believe in the capitalist system."

Paul Moore, a capitalist without apology, takes satisfaction in his dealings with big corporations and the men who run them. "I was at a meeting over in the Wood Gundy boardroom not long ago," he said. "Some senior Wood Gundy people were there and a few executives from a corporation that we were working out a deal with. We had complicated matters to go over and the hours crept along until it was getting to six o'clock and nothing was close to being wound up.

" 'Listen,' I said finally, 'it's six, this is Tuesday, and I have to leave the meeting.'

"Why? Naturally they wanted to know why.

" 'Because Tuesday is my Cubs night. I'm the Akela of the pack and I have to be there.'

"Well, we're in this magnificent boardroom, we're talking a $5 million deal or something with very important businessmen, and the next thing that happens is Ross Le Mesurier, one of the head people at Wood Gundy, is down on his haunches, the way kids do at Cubs, with his fingertips spread out touching the carpet and he's giving the Cub yell: 'Dib, dib, dib, Akeee-la!' Right in the boardroom. He remembered his Cub days. Some of the others did too. I left the meeting and everybody understood."

Moore chewed on his gum. "The businessmen I deal with aren't the fat cats you might imagine if you went by the wheeler-dealer standards of a TV show like *Dallas*. They're friendly and decent and have all their brains in place. No profanity. No drunkenness. They're the people who make the products and furnish the jobs in this country. They run the companies, and corporate lawyers are the guys who provide the grease that keeps the companies carrying on business. Corporate-commercial law is all about getting things done."

Which, according to Moore, isn't as routine as it sounds.

He has put in his share of consecutive round-the-clock sessions to wrap up a transaction for a client. He sets aside one hour at home each evening to retreat to his den, a room that *does* look directly over Lake Ontario, to check office files. He reads in his field constantly — the *Economist* ("for its politics, not its economics"), the *Financial Post* and the *Financial Times* ("to find out what my partners are doing"), the *Canada Business Law Report*, the *Canadian Tax Journal*, the bulletin from the Ontario Securities Commission ("because the law changes so rapidly in my field"). And he keeps up with the barrage of new and revised federal and provincial statutes, the Securities Act, the Business Corporations Act, the Income Tax Act, the Bank Act, the Foreign Investment Review Act.

"Where the pleasure comes in my practice is in being innovative," he said, slumping into a comfortable posture in his chair. "You never do the same deal twice. You always think of new ways of accomplishing the client's objective. If you repeat yourself, then your practice is getting old hat. There's bound to be some fresh twist."

He offered an example.

"In the last couple of years, traditional corporate financing has dried up. So if one corporation wants to acquire another, that route is closed off. But what's replaced it is the takeover business, and there are all sorts of variations on it. One way is for the buying company to offer to purchase all the shares in the target company and be successful in getting 90 per cent of them. Then, by statute, the offerer can go to court and get an order directing the other shareholders, the people holding the 10 per cent that didn't accept the original offer, to sell to the offerer.

"Okay, we had a deal where our client wanted to make a takeover by this method, but we knew that a large block of stock in the target company, 25 per cent of it, was in the hands of one shareholder. That could have been bad news. Suppose we started buying stock around the majority shareholder but didn't get him. We'd be in a bidding war. So what we did first was approach the majority stockholder and take an option on his shares. It was subject to certain conditions and time limits and so on, but we had him tied up. Then we went after the other shares. We got 93 per cent of them, including the one guy's 25 per cent. Then we squeezed out the remaining 7 per cent. Our client started with nothing and ended with 100 per cent of the target company."

Moore shifted position in his chair, swivelling to look out his window, the panorama of the city to the east free of glare. "If the squeeze-out method isn't available, there's the amalgamation tactic. What happens there is that the client company sets up a subsidiary company and it enters into an agreement to amalgamate with the target company. You only need to get two-thirds of the target company's shareholders to approve the amalgamation for it to be binding on the minority one-third. That makes it relatively simple, but there are plenty of variations you might have to work on the transaction. Maybe you'll offer the holders of shares in the target company redeemable preferred shares which are redeemed in cash. That makes it inviting for them. Offering cash in some circumstances is innovative. The cash has interesting capital-gains implications. Everything depends on the mix, whether you offer money or shares. You work out the tax consequences and make it appealing to the shareholders in the target company. That's what lawyers are for.

"In one case," Moore went on, his boyish smile turning on at the memory, "we did a deal where we used takeover *and* amalgamation. These were two separate transactions but we packaged them. We sent to each shareholder in the target company a cash offer conditional on the amalgamation's being approved. It was an innovative idea. It worked. Our client got control of the company he needed to round out his business picture."

Moore was still smiling. "The way I feel after a deal of that kind is the way I always expected to feel in law. Like a productive member of society."

Robert and Anorah Tory worked a farm at Guysborough, Nova Scotia, in the mid-nineteenth century. Along with their crops they raised three sons whose lives read like chapters from Horatio Alger. James Cranwich Tory became Lieutenant-Governor of Nova Scotia. Henry Marshall Tory founded the University of Alberta, took office as its first president, and was later head of the National Research Council in Ottawa. John Alexander Tory, born in Guysborough in 1869, went into insurance with Sun Life of Canada. "Life insurance," he once said, "is something that enables one generation to hold out a helping hand to the next, and so assist the carrying out of the Divine purpose of humanity's progress toward the ideal." That lofty philosophy peddled a record number of policies for John A. He moved to Toronto in 1908 and built his Sun Life division, the Western Ontario Branch, into the most remunerative life-insurance agency in the British Empire. When he stepped up to a Sun Life directorship in 1938, his branch was too lively for one successor to manage. Western Ontario had to be split into six branches.

John A.'s son inherited his father's energy and his uncle Henry's scholarship, and threw in his own dash of flamboyance. John Stewart Donald Tory, born in 1904, graduated at the stop of his class at Osgoode Hall Law School, 1927's gold medallist, and the following year took a doctorate in law and business administration at Harvard. He went into practice with the venerable and respected Toronto firm headed by W. N. Tilley, a legend at the Toronto bar. By 1941 Tory had acquired the expertise and confidence to strike out on his own. He formed a new firm with his name at the front end. Its specialty was corporate law and it thrived.

It was J. S. D. Tory who tended to Massey-Harris's corporate work in that company's great years. Tory shared the load of legal advice to the E. P. Taylor interests with another firm, Fraser, Beatty, and when Taylor formed the Argus Corporation in 1945 he placed Tory on the board. Tory looked after Abitibi, the colossus in pulp and paper, and in 1952 he shepherded Simpsons through its merger with Sears, Roebuck and Company of Chicago. He was at his zenith in the early 1950s, a member of the boards of over thirty companies in fields as diverse as aviation and publishing, oil and life insurance (Sun Life naturally), and he reigned as indisputably the most sought-after lawyer-director in the country.

J. S. D. lived well. He bought five hundred acres of land in King, an area of rolling hills and gentleman farms northwest of Toronto. He stocked his spread with Aberdeen Angus and Guernsey cattle and with Yorkshire hogs. He kept horses, too, and each morning J. S. D. would rise with the sun, take a long canter, then settle in for a session of general reading—books, magazines, some legal documents—until it was time for his car and driver to transport him to the firm's offices on King Street in downtown Toronto where he'd go about the business of spreading his influence.

"J. S. D. Tory was a rare man, like one of those old-time tycoons you saw in the movies," one of his former law associates says. "He liked his drink and liked his pleasures, but most of all, I think he enjoyed the exercise of power."

Trevor Eyton remembers a small but all-so-typical sample of J. S. D.'s flourish when it came to wielding power.

"Mr. Tory and some other leading Toronto businessmen, very big names, wanted to put together a charity to help a university in the Caribbean," Eyton says. "The problem was that to get a deduction for the charity with the beneficiary outside of Canada, they had to get status as a charity inside Canada. A slightly tricky business, establishing exemption from the usual charitable status. Mr. Tory called me into his office—this was around 1960 when I was still a student—

and turned the job over to my humble talents. I embarked on a program of correspondence with civil servants in Ottawa and I got exactly nowhere. I was crushed; here I was failing all these important Toronto businessmen, and after four months, I went back to Mr. Tory and confessed my failure.

"He sat me down in his office and had his secretary put him through to the Deputy Minister of Revenue in Ottawa. The Deputy Minister came directly on the line. That was the first thing I noticed. The second thing I noticed was that Mr. Tory called the Deputy Minister by his first name and the Deputy Minister referred to Mr. Tory throughout as 'Mr. Tory'.

" 'Are you against communism?'

"Those were the first words Mr. Tory spoke to the Deputy Minister, and naturally the answer was, 'Yes.'

" 'The only way we're going to keep communism out of the Caribbean,' Mr. Tory said, 'is by giving those people down there some university education.' And he went on to explain about the charity he and his friends wanted to establish and he asked the Deputy Minister what he intended to do about it.

"There wasn't any hesitation from the other end. 'I'll put your charity on the exempt status, Mr. Tory,' the Deputy Minister said, and I walked out of Mr. Tory's office with a better understanding of what power was all about."

J. S. D. and his first wife had twin sons, John Arnold Tory and James Marshall Tory, born March 7, 1930. The boys' mother, Jean Arnold Tory, is in her different way as remarkable as their father. A woman of pride and industry, she has given much of her life to community work: "not just sitting on boards," one of her friends says, "not showcase performances, but going out and slugging for her causes." To this day, in her seventies, Mrs. Tory keeps active—she plays golf several times a week at the Rosedale club, pulling her own cart around eighteen holes—and conducts herself with immaculate style. "A lot of the sons' definitive genes come from her," the friend says, "the ones that have to do with decorum and grace and that side of life."

Jim and John went to the University of Toronto Schools, a fiercely competitive high school for brainy kids. At UTS, the yearbook for the Tory boys' graduating class quoted John as planning a career in medicine. A son of J. S. D. Tory evading the law? Hardly. Indeed, the haste with which the boys were pointed into law school bordered on the unseemly. They took only two years in arts at the University of Toronto, then switched to the university's law school, taking advantage of a regulation that permitted enrolment in law without an undergraduate degree.

"I'd never do it again, miss out on a complete background in the arts," Jim says. "But it was, well, *suggested* to us that it'd be a good idea at the time."

The brothers got their call to the bar in 1954 and entered the firm founded by their father. It was a period of flux. Jim and John were absorbing the intricacies of corporate-commercial law through the late 1950s, while in the same years J. S. D.'s health and his enthusiasm for practice were on the wane. A couple of important clients — A. V. Roe Ltd. was one — took their business elsewhere. The firm endured upheavals. In 1957, a group of lawyers left the Torys to form a new firm, Miller, Thomson, Hicks. In 1961 — the firm was then titled Tory, Arnold, Wardlaw and Whittaker — Wardlaw and Whittaker departed. They tried to persuade a pair of the Tory firm's young whizzes, Trevor Eyton and Jim Baillie, to join them. The pair declined. Perhaps they saw the glory years ahead under Jim and John.

Failing health and all, the senior Tory never lost his panache. In 1965, facing death, he scheduled four short board meetings for one day, gatherings of directors of companies he had served and guided for years. At the conclusion of each meeting, he walked around the table and shook hands with his fellow directors.

"Thank you," he said to every man. He was driven home,

and not long after, he died. Responsibility for the firm passed finally and officially to J. S. D.'s sons, thirty-five years old at the time, an outrageously tender age by the ancient standards of Bay Street.

"On the day Mr. Tory died," Eyton remembers, "four or five of the leading businessmen in the country phoned John and Jim and said they'd leave their accounts with the firm. That's a measure of the respect they'd had for the old man. But there was an unspoken rider on the commitment — the firm had to do the job of keeping the clients happy."

"Hectic" is how John Tory remembers the years immediately after his father's death. "With everybody leaving the firm or dying," he says, "there weren't many of us left, about eight or so lawyers. The firm was small and very young. The work got absolutely hectic but it was exhilarating. Enough hours in the day were the problem. I used to come home at night and sit in a chair in the den and read over letters of opinion that junior lawyers had drafted for clients. I'd suggest changes, write in new proposals, kind of redraft the letters, and next day I'd tell the juniors to get the letters retyped and be sure to send them out under *their* signatures. It wasn't that I didn't have pride of authorship in what I'd written. It was just that when the client called back I wanted him to phone the lawyer who'd signed the letter. I didn't want him to phone me. There weren't enough hours in the day."

Despite the burden of youth, the Torys and their partners delivered the corporate goods. Through the late 1960s they gave their clients intelligent advice, long hours, a deep helping of integrity, and, it seems clear, some additional measure of service, something with a touch of mystique. The extra ingredient, in John Tory's view, is nothing less than "creativity".

"People don't realize what's involved in the process of corporate law," he says. "Other lawyers, the ones in criminal law or civil litigation, deal with problems. There's nothing creative about that because what they're in fact dealing with is something that's already happened. In corporate-commercial law, on the contrary, you tangle with events that haven't yet occurred. *That's* creative. You've got a corporate reorganization or a corporate acquisition coming up, and you have to project yourself into the future and visualize all the possibilities, good and bad, that might happen and then figure out the ways to avoid the bad and capture the good."

Tory took his lessons in corporate finesse from an old master, Roy Thomson. It was Thomson who came out of Northern Ontario in the 1940s to put together an empire based initially on a chain of Canadian newspapers but later including everything from insurance companies to *The Times* of London, from travel agencies, truck lines, and Scottish television to North Sea oil. Roy Thomson and J. S. D. Tory enjoyed a close business and social relationship, and by the mid-1960s Thomson, by then Lord Thomson of Fleet, had begun to hand on direction of his empire to the two men's sons, Ken Thomson and John Tory.

"Talk about creative, that was Roy Thomson," Tory says, "and he forced me to be the same way. I was a young lawyer and he'd come to me and say he wanted to accomplish a certain end in a business deal, an acquisition maybe. I'd look into it and tell him it couldn't be done the way he wanted to do it. 'Find another way,' he'd say. And I'd have to. Roy never accepted that something couldn't be done. He was like most corporate clients—he knew where he wanted to end up. He knew where he wanted to go at the end of the road. It was my job, the lawyer's job, to find the road-blocks along the way and pick a route through them. I think that's not a bad metaphor for creativity."

One problem, according to Tory, is that there's just a single way to acquire a corporate lawyer's thinking processes. "Not from law school. The only training you can count on is the kind that comes from working with corporate lawyers and clients who already know the ropes. Under those circumstances, corporate-commercial practice gives the most scope of any kind of law for people to demonstrate creativity, even people who aren't at all naturally creative. That's strange but true. Law school, though, fills in none of the background for that. You get called to the bar and you start from scratch."

J. S. D. Tory, for his part, liked to compare law school to a boxer's training-camp, a place to get in shape and develop an edge. It wasn't, however, the real arena. It wasn't the marketplace where the corporate lawyer has to confront and sell. Corporate law, J. S. D. said, was selling. He had another theory: he kept in his law office a complete set of *Fortune* magazines, and he used to insist that any man could make himself into a sound corporate lawyer if he did nothing except read every issue of *Fortune* from cover to cover. That done, J. S. D. contended, a man would develop an understanding of how commerce works, how management functions, how presidents think, and how corporate lawyers sell themselves.

Trevor Eyton tends to agree with J. S. D.'s approach to corporate law. "Actually I'm appalled at how little we lawyers really know," he says, "and how well rewarded we are for the small areas of work we cover. But commercial lawyers, if I was summing us up, have to be persuasive. We have to be people who can look other people in the eye."

Looking people in the eye, Tory, Tory grew. Some favoured keeping the firm small and specialized, an impossible aim. Too many factors compelled it to expand almost in spite of itself. The ambitions of such Tory clients as the Thomson organization demanded that the firm hire new lawyers to handle the fresh volume of business. The increasing complexity of government regulations affecting large corporations called for more manpower at the firm. And the swelling reputation of Tory, Tory inevitably attracted new clients. New clients meant more lawyers.

"The firm had to expand in ways nobody might anticipate," Jim Tory says. "For example, our litigation department. For a long time, whenever one of our clients got into something that called for litigation advice, we'd send them over to another firm, Kimber, Dubin, where they specialized in that sort of law. But after a while we felt that wasn't good enough. We had to be in a position to give our clients the whole range of service under one roof."

Thus, in the late 1960s the Torys reached for another old classmate from the University of Toronto Law School. He was Frank Callaghan, who had been for years a counsel in the office of the Ontario Attorney General. Almost immediately the provincial government retained Callaghan and his new associates at Tory, Tory to handle a complex pollution lawsuit against the Dow Chemical Company. The litigation department needed more bodies. When Callaghan left in the early 1970s to become deputy attorney general, the Tory firm absorbed Kimber, Dubin with its five litigation specialists. When Charles Dubin left to take a seat on the Ontario Supreme Court, the firm hired Lorne Morphy, a counsel with a strong reputation based on years of outstanding court work at a variety of major Toronto firms. Today Morphy heads a litigation department that numbers a full dozen lawyers.

"At first we were just used to having litigation people around," Jim Tory says. "Now we've got a department that's about as good as anybody's."

For all its diversity of services, it is of course Tory, Tory's skill in corporate-commercial law that distinguishes it. Corporate takeovers, corporate acquisitions, corporate restructuring—the firm blankets the field. Peter Bronfman, for one, knew who to turn to when he and his brother Edward, nephews of the late and mighty Sam who launched the Bronfman dynasty, developed a yen in 1979 to take over Brascan Limited. He turned to Trevor Eyton.

The Bronfman vehicle for the Brascan adventure was Edper Equities Limited. It is two-thirds owned by the Bronfman brothers and one-third by Patino N. V. of the Netherlands. Eyton, who dished up legal guidance to the Bronfmans almost from the beginning of his Tory career, had introduced the Bronfmans and the Patinos, just another piece of astute lawyerly service, and the two families hit it off. Edper's assets included Place Ville Marie in Montreal, assorted shopping plazas across Canada, and some choice Calgary real estate, but the Bronfman-Patino-Eyton forces figured Brascan was ripe for plucking. It possessed, as one attractive feature, a hefty bank account. Brascan, a Canadian company that dated back to 1899, had originally built itself on investment in the power utility of Brazil and later expanded to take in a variety of holdings in Brazilian and Canadian companies (John Labatt, Consumers Glass, London Life). In late 1978 it sold off its ownership in Light-Servicos Electricidada S. A. of Brazil for $447 million. That put cash in its bank account. That made it appealing to Edper.

On April 5, 1979, Eyton met with Brascan's chairman of the board, Jake Moore, and his legal advisor, a senior man from Blake, Cassels and Graydon (over one hundred lawyers, offices in the Commerce Court West), in a suite at the Royal York Hotel. Eyton looked Moore in the eye and told him Edper intended to pursue a controlling interest in Brascan. Moore, none too happy and prepared to resist, contented himself with a noncommittal expression. End of meeting and commencement of what was later variously described as "the largest and most controversial deal in recent Canadian business history" (*Maclean's* magazine) and a "ruthless takeover" (*Toronto Star*).

The struggle, "testy" at times in Eyton's word, lasted for almost three months, but it was essentially a no-contest affair. Edper had on its side too much nerve, moxie, and money. On April 30, Edper purchased 2.4 million Brascan shares on the American Stock Exchange in New York, the largest single transaction ever in AmEx history. Edper kept buying—3.3 million shares from various sources on May 1 —until it had spent $340 million, cash on the barrelhead, for 13 million Brascan shares. Other large shareholders in Brascan, correctly reading the drift, cast their lot with the

Edper team, and by June 14 Edper had passed the 50-per-
cent mark in its holdings of Brascan stock. Takeover, in
effect, completed.

Jake Moore stepped aside as Brascan's chairman of the
board on June 29, taking with him payment of a year's
salary ($250,000) and a juicy lifetime pension ($100,000 per
annum), and later in the summer Eyton moved his talents
from the thirty-fourth floor of the Royal Bank to the forty-
eighth floor of Commerce Court West as Brascan's new
president. He trimmed the company's staff by 50 per cent,
streamlined the enterprise, and completed the conversion
of Brascan from an operating company to a holding company. Eyton knew where he was going. He's always known
where he's been headed.

"When I was in high school, Jarvis Collegiate in Toronto,"
he said one winter morning after he'd occupied his Brascan
chair for six months, "the guidance counsellor asked me
about my plans. This was all part of the routine in discussing your ambitions and future occupation and so on. I
looked at the guidance person and said, 'I'm going to be a
corporate lawyer for the CPR.' I don't know about the CPR
part, but I got the rest of it right. At the time, I was thirteen."

In the same years as the Edper action, in 1979-80, the
Thomson organization was spending some of its money in
the interests of corporate reorganization. It bought 75 per
cent of the Hudson's Bay Company for $641 million in
April 1979 and it purchased FP Publications Limited for
$165 million in January 1980. Both transactions involved
struggles, with Galen Weston (of the Weston conglomerate
that includes Loblaw's, National Tea, Weston Bakeries, and
another half-hundred subsidiaries) over the Bay, and with
Howard Webster (a Montreal financier who once owned
the *Globe and Mail*) over FP. Both were engineered by John,
with the support of Ken Thomson and the constant legal
ministrations of Tory, Tory ("On the Bay deal," John says,
"my brother and Gar Pink and a couple of other fellows did

practically nothing else for a whole six weeks"). And both were part of a larger scheme to bring a chunk of the Thomson money and authority from the United Kingdom back to Canada.

"The corporate restructuring of the Thomson organization has taken me two years," John Tory explained one Sunday afternoon in March of 1980, sitting with a drink by a grate fire in the den of his Lawrence Park home. "I had to consider corporate implications and tax problems. I had to look at everything from the U.K. standpoint and the Canadian standpoint. And I had to use lawyers from both countries to work through the maze. I'm a lawyer, but in this case, over the two years, I was looking at the job as a client. What I was doing — this made me feel pretty good — was asking lawyers to be what clients used to ask of me. To be creative."

The Tory, Tory success story shows no indications of running short on future chapters. "The young guys," John Tory says, "the young lawyers they send up to me from the firm to help on different deals, are smarter than they used to be in my days at the firm. They haven't got the experience or the flexibility, but they've got the brains. They amaze me."

One of the young guys happens to be John's son, John Jr., who entered practice with the family firm on March 3, 1980. Jim has a son at law school. He also has a daughter who is a chartered accountant and another daughter who spent much of 1979-80 in a community outside Peking pursuing her research in Asian studies. But for now it's John Jr. who's the prime candidate to carry on the Tory legal tradition. He has already recorded an intimidating share of accomplishments, a range that includes seven years as an on-air announcer at Toronto radio station CHFI and management of two federal election campaigns, one win, one loss, for Ron Atkey, Joe Clark's immigration minister. At his high school, UTS — where else would a Tory prep himself? — the school's director of Student Counselling Ser-

166

vices, Clare Pace, once asked John Jr. the same question Trevor Eyton's guidance counsellor had directed at him. Where was he headed? What was his ambition?

"I'm going to be prime minister of Canada," the boy answered without a modest moment of hesitation.

Clare Pace thinks John Jr. might make it.

Sixth Adjournment

It was the morning Jack Johnson's picture turned up on the front page of the Calgary *Albertan* that signalled the end of his career with Chambers, Might, Saucier. This was in 1969, and Johnson, then in his mid-thirties, had been a member of Chambers, Might, the richest and most influential corporate law firm in Calgary, for ten years, a partner for almost two. But Johnson led a double life. By night and on weekends he dabbled in mildly leftist politics. He handled work for the Company of Young Canadians. He urged social changes to help the poor. He heckled Pierre Trudeau's government. And one Saturday evening when Trudeau dropped in to Calgary for a fifty-dollar-a-plate dinner, Johnson and some like-minded friends organized a "Beggars' Banquet" on a downtown Calgary corner, urging Trudeau to detach himself from the fat cats long enough for an exchange of views with the ordinary folks out on the street. While the people at the Beggars' Banquet waited for Trudeau to show up—he later made a brief appearance— Johnson and other organizers of the banquet took turns haranguing their supporters. A photographer from the *Albertan* happened to catch Johnson in action, hollering through a bullhorn from the back of a flatbed truck. The picture made the front page on Monday morning.

"Do you realize you're threatening my living?" one of the

senior partners told Johnson that afternoon. "I've worked in this firm for years. I've made an important position for myself in the community. Now you're trying to tear it all down."

"They kind of over-reacted at the firm," Johnson says, looking back. "It was as if they'd suddenly discovered Karl Marx in their midst. The other partners turned cool to me overnight, and it was obvious that I had to shut up about my views or leave the firm."

Johnson left, and in the years since his departure he has accumulated an intriguing bundle of experience in Canadian law. For two years he stayed on in Calgary, practising criminal and family law, "poverty law", as he calls it. He taught at Queen's University Law School in Kingston, Ontario, for a few years, instituting a course titled simply "The Legal Profession" which took a sociological look at lawyers and their work. He spent four years with the Canadian Radio and Television Commission in Ottawa and another eighteen months as co-director of Parkdale Community Legal Services in Toronto, the pioneering free-law clinic for the poor in Canada. And in January 1980 he returned to government work, the director of legal services for the Ontario Ministry of Energy.

"Maybe if I'd stayed with Chambers, Might I'd have developed tunnel vision the way so many lawyers do," Johnson said, sitting in the living-room of his handsome old brick house in mid-town Toronto one morning close to Christmas. "Lawyers reach a point where they can't conceive of anything outside their specialty. They become part of the system. They're *used* to the system, no matter how much that system may be fucking up. They're beyond any critique of it. But for me, moving around the way I have, I can bring a degree of perspective to the profession."

Johnson is slim and grey and, at least in manner, the antithesis of the flaming radical who threatened the partners at Chambers, Might. He speaks in a low monotone that wouldn't reach past the front row of any political gathering not equipped with a microphone. He's imperturbable and calm at the centre. He's also stubborn and possesses no shortage of nerve. That's made clear in his description of work at the Ministry of Energy.

"I like to have input in policy," he said. "You're not supposed to get that at the ministry, not as director of legal services. But by nature people like to pass the buck. If you don't mind the buck, you can move into the policy area. I don't mind the buck."

Johnson is not an alarmist, too cool for that, but the deliberate hodgepodge of the last dozen years of his career as lawyer-teacher-bureaucrat have left him uneasy about a drift he thinks he's spotted in the profession.

"I can see a split developing in the way law is practised in Canada, almost as if there are two different kinds of law," he said. "The separation is by intelligence. The best and the brightest graduates from the law schools are going to the big firms, and the rest set up business in an office on the second floor of a shopping plaza or something like that. The big firms don't care to know anything about a student except what his marks were. If he's in his class's top twenty, then the firm takes him, and the student, he wants into the big firm. He wants the action and the income."

In some ways, Johnson figures, the separation by intelligence determines the quality of service that clients can expect from their lawyers. "In the big firms the lawyers have an incentive to do a bang-up job because they know their clientele is going to be around with more work tomorrow and next month and a year later. They maintain a continuing relationship with their clients. But the guy in the shopping plaza handles one-shot stuff — a house purchase, a divorce, a motor-vehicle accident — for a client who comes into his life for a couple of weeks and then vanishes. The lawyer in the big firm goes past the point of just servicing his client. He'll read a new piece of legislation from the federal government, write a memo about it, and send it to the client, telling him how to conduct his business

170

in light of the legislative changes. That's sharp law. That's preventive law. The guy in the shopping plaza has no time for that. He moves business in and out with a speed that's almost mindless. It's the only way for him to make a buck."

Johnson found the same division—bright students versus the rest—at Parkdale Community Legal Services. The Parkdale clinic, founded in 1971, was the joint brainchild of the Osgoode Hall Law School and Parkdale, a neighbourhood in an old section of west Toronto identified by boarding-houses and immigrants, high density and low income. The clinic is mainly funded by the Ontario government—$405,000 in 1979—and it operates out of storefront quarters that have about them a whiff of mould, sweat, and bad nerves. Five full-time lawyers run the place, and they're backed by third-year Osgoode students, twenty-one at a time, who have selected as one optional course a four-month semester of working six and seven days a week at the clinic guiding people who've run into grief with their landlord or their spouse, the finance company, the Workmen's Compensation Board, or the police.

"I never looked at the marks of the kids who chose the clinic," Johnson said. "But I had the feeling they weren't the top students in academic terms. The A students would stay at Osgoode and take another optional course, probably a seminar in Advanced Business. I don't mean that the kids we got at the clinic were lemons. I felt encouraged about them and about what they learned from their experience with us. I've seen a lot of young lawyers arguing cases before judges in Provincial Court, lawyers five or six years older than our kids, and these people's credibility as counsel was the shits. That's because they've never had any feedback on how they're performing. They blow the case for their client by lousy cross-examining or by not knowing how to read a judge. At least the kids from the clinic go into the legal world with solid critical faculties when it comes to the whole judicial process. They'd take a landlord-and-tenant case into court and the judge might behave like an animal to

171

them. A stupid judge. So many of them are. And the kids might think, wow, I can't argue any law in front of this guy. But by the time they were finished at the clinic, they'd learned when it was wise to go along with the judge, trim their sails, and sit down and when it was important to say 'fuck it' and plunge on. That's a good lesson. That's bringing value into the practice of law."

Johnson looked for a conclusion.

"I'm not a pessimist," he said. "I just want to see things run right in the profession."

CHAPTER SIX

The Doctors' Man

There's a theme that runs through Jack Major's stories.

"What's remarkable," he said one gleaming January after-noon in his office on the thirty-second floor of the Shell Centre in Calgary, "is that the law works so well."

Then he told the story about the circumcision that went wrong.

"I had an Edmonton doctor for a client who messed up his very first operation. Unfortunately it was a circumcision. The patient was a truck driver in his twenties, and when my doctor was finished with him, he wasn't especially fit for sexual intercourse. His penis gave him a lot of pain when it was erect and it tended to dart to the left. My doctor had used something in the operation he called 'Bell's Tech-nique'. I consulted another doctor as an expert witness and he said, 'I never heard of Bell's Technique but remind me not to use it.'

"So it was clear my doctor was negligent and the only real issue was the amount of damages the truck driver should collect. The judge hearing the case in the Alberta Supreme Court was a fellow named Riley. Dead now. He had a drinking problem, but he was a pretty good judge. Used to need a couple of Scotches to steady his hand when he wanted to sign an order. Anyway, we weren't more than an hour in court on this case when Riley called me and the

173

truck driver's lawyer into his chambers and said let's settle the damages.

"Riley asked me how much? I said $3,500. I knew that was a low figure. He asked the other lawyer the same question. He hemmed and hawed a little. He said the truck driver was a simple guy and sexual intercourse was his only hobby and he ought to be compensated in the neighbourhood of $12,000. Riley said that was too high.

"Riley pulled a coin out of his pocket, a quarter, and he said he was gonna flip. If the truck driver's lawyer won the toss, the damages would be $6,500, and if I won, they'd be $4,500. Riley flipped the coin and the other lawyer called heads.

"Heads it was. The truck driver collected $6,500, and that was what I'd call a perfectly fair settlement. Justice prevailed. The law worked. But when you think about it, it was all so damned ludicrous."

Jack Major practises with Jones, Black and Company. The firm, now the largest in the west, has a history that reaches deep into Calgary's past and is enlivened by one memorable feud. Senator Sir James Lougheed, grandfather of the man who became Alberta's premier in 1971, began the firm's story almost a century before Peter Lougheed was elected. He set up practice in the old west and benefited from the good fortune of acquiring the Canadian Pacific Railroad as a client. Lougheed gathered distinctions along with clients. He was the last man named by Sir John A. Macdonald to the Senate and the first Albertan named by England a Knight Commander of the Most Distinguished Order of St. Michael and St. George. He built himself a twenty-six-room sandstone mansion in 1891 and shone as the leading light in Calgary's legal community.

In the winter of 1897 the senator brought an impecunious but promising young law graduate from the Maritimes into the firm. The young man was Richard Bedford Bennett, and in the twenty years that followed his arrival in Calgary, the firm prospered. Bennett, as he rose to become

174

a senior partner, prospered more than most, partly because he cozied up to the widow of E. P. Eddy and eventually inherited money from the Eddy Match fortune. No one questioned Bennett's legal abilities, but he was not an entirely popular boss around Lougheed and Bennett. His puritanical ways rubbed raw. Bennett used to insist that the annual bonuses be handed out to the firm's lawyers and employees in the office first thing on New Year's Day morning. It was his method of ensuring that the partners didn't carouse too late or too disgracefully the evening before, although one nervy junior, Harry Nolan, made it his custom to show up for the bonus ceremonies still decked out in his white tie and tails.

By the early 1920s some of Lougheed and Bennett's lawyers saw their chance to rid themselves of Bennett's burdensome presence. He had often been absent from Calgary in the preceding years. Politics took him to Ottawa, where he served as Minister of Justice in Sir Robert Borden's Cabinet, and an acute case of Anglomania took him on frequent and lengthy visits to England. The dissident lawyers approached Lougheed to move against Bennett, dissolve the partnership if necessary, and regroup without Bennett's inclusion. The senator agreed, and the plan to shake Bennett seemed to be in place. But the plotters had reckoned without their most junior colleague, a young opportunist named Orrin Might, who telegraphed word to Bennett in England alerting him to events back home.

Bennett returned and joined battle. The senator brought a simple action in the Supreme Court of Alberta for dissolution of the firm. His Statement of Claim in the case was a mere three pages long. Bennett, outraged and resolved to crush his adversaries, filed a Statement of Defence and Counterclaim that ran to forty-five pages. He summoned the firm's clients and directed them to choose between himself and Lougheed. He was relentless and a trifle malicious. The senator, in his seventies and frail, had no zest for the struggle. Bennett triumphed. The Lougheed faction, defeated, willingly split away, and Bennett kept as clients the CPR and most of the banks. The faithful Orrin Might continued by his side.

Bennett remained long enough in Calgary to ensure that the firm was headed in a direction congenial to his bank account and then returned to politics. He was elected prime minister of Canada in 1930, and the firm fell into the hands of three men. Might, whose legal acumen never matched his eye for the main chance, was one. Jack Saucier, a talented litigation specialist until an attack of ulcers persuaded him to switch to corporate work, was another. And Everett Chambers was the third. It was Chambers who steered the firm into its salad days after the Second World War.

Even Jack Johnson admired Chambers. Johnson's abrupt leave-taking of Chambers, Might, Saucier in 1969 didn't blind him to Chambers' lessons. "He was an influence of competence and real honesty," Johnson says. "He was very conservative — all of them were — but he got across the message to me and everyone who came in professional contact with him that there was only one kind of work worth doing in the practice of law. First-class work."

The secret to Chambers' dedication was ulcers. Like Saucier, he was their victim, but his struck at an early age, the mid-twenties. With strong drink, exotic food, and high living denied to him, he turned to work. "He was fanatically devoted to his practice," Jack Major says. "If he had nothing else to do, he'd sit at his desk in the evenings and memorize all the boring clauses in a mortgage deed. There wasn't anything he didn't know about corporate and commercial law." Chambers set the pace and the firm grew in ability and clients.

When he was sixty-five, Chambers booked himself into the Mayo Clinic in Rochester, Minnesota, and returned home with his ulcers cured. He tasted cocktails for the first time in forty years and found the experience so delightful that he made them an increasingly regular item on his daily schedule. By then, however, the firm he'd built was sturdy.

176

Chambers died, Might died, and Saucier retired. Junior partners assumed leadership, new names appeared in the firm's title, and today Jones, Black and Company has over fifty lawyers and includes among its clients the Bank of Commerce, Imperial Oil, Dome Petroleum, and Shell Oil. It's a power in the west.

Jack Major is the star of the firm's twelve-man litigation department and one of the west's most respected counsel, and he is also the resident realist at Jones, Black. He grew up in the Northern Ontario town of Espanola, the son of a railroad man, and he hustled to finance his way through Loyola University in Montreal and the University of Toronto Law School. He headed west in the summer of 1957, intending to spend a couple of years, but never got around to turning back east. Along the way, he developed antennae for the absurd in his profession. The law is to be respected, he says, but there's no reason not to laugh at its nonsensical ways. Major, a lean, dark, angular man who wears an expression of perpetual amusement, likes to laugh.

"I was representing a lawyer who sued a newspaper for defamation," he said on the January afternoon in his office. "This was when I'd just got started in court work, and I was totally ignorant about the tactics you use in selecting a jury. The case had a jury with six people on it, and essentially what I did was accept the first six who were called. Another lawyer, an experienced counsel who was in court that day, not on my case, looked at the jury and said to me out in the corridor, 'That stinks. How'd you let it happen?'

" 'What's so wrong?' I asked him.

" 'Look at them,' he said. 'You got three women on your jury wearing dresses from Kresge's. Ladies like that, Kresge's dresses, cheap, they never award anybody a dollar.'

"I felt mad at myself for getting into such a rotten position with the jury and I went in expecting the worst. We were ready to settle for an apology from the newspaper anyway.

177

We really didn't figure on much in the way of money. So I was kind of surprised — this is putting it mildly — when the jury gave us $25,000 damages.

"Well, a couple of years later I ran into the guy who was foreman on that jury. We started talking about the case, no reason not to, and he told me when the jury went out to consider its verdict he was personally in favour of giving my client no more than $5,000. That was tops. He said he got out-talked and out-voted in the jury room. Who by? The ladies naturally. It was the Kresge's dresses who held out for the $25,000. Isn't that just goddamned ludicrous?"

Major closed the venetian blinds on his office window, shutting away the view of the Rocky Mountains to the west, and rode the elevator to the Shell Centre's basement garage. His car is a Fleetwood Cadillac, dark brown, and he drove it out Elbow Drive, past the Calgary Golf and Country Club, to Bel Aire, a neighbourhood of post-1960 houses, generous-sized and good-looking. Major's is painted white and shows all the signs of conscientious maintenance.

Inside, the house radiates a sense of harmony, a trick that Major's wife, Helen, a warm and attractive woman, pulls off without any visible fuss. Their four kids — a daughter and three sons, early twenties to pre-teen — are talkative, polite, and rarely get out the front door until their clothes (tidy) and hair (medium short) have passed Helen's scrutiny. Everybody goes to mass on Sunday, and Major plays golf with his two teen-aged boys at the Calgary Club. He reads the *National Review* and *U.S. News and World Report* and keeps plenty of liquor around the house for guests. He doesn't drink. He runs a few miles most days of the week, and he completed two marathons in his mid-forties. Life around the Major home is controlled, conventional, and happy.

Major settled down in the den, a room of books and golf trophies, and talked about doctors. "It's kind of enlightening to defend them in court. They get more upset than almost any other clients. It's because they're a bit spoiled.

Nurses are respectful to them at the hospital. Everybody defers to them, nobody questions what they do. All of a sudden a former patient sues them. They're served with papers that say they've been negligent. They're terrified they're going to lose their right to practise after all those years of school. Right before your eyes, suave medical men turn to jelly."

Major knows doctors up close. About fifty per cent of his practice is given over to defending them. He is the Alberta counsel for the Canadian Medical Protective Association, a venerable and hard-nosed organization run by doctors from national offices in Ottawa and dedicated to guiding its members through lawsuits. The CMPA is not an insurer. It's a mutual-defence outfit, and in return for annual fees of about $300 per doctor the association extends assistance to its troubled members, mostly by retaining counsel like Major.

"What I like about the CMPA is that they give me a blank cheque to go all out and defend the doctors," Major said in his den. "As long as the association is satisfied the doctor hasn't been grossly negligent, they'll fight. That's a different system from the set-up in the United States. Down there it's insurance companies that cover the doctors and they'll always pay something to the plaintiffs. A guy sues an American doctor for $10,000 and his insurance company gives the guy $500 just to go away. That encourages people to issue claims, and the result is there are far more malpractice lawsuits in the States and the awards are astronomical. The premiums their doctors have to pay are rising out of sight. Insurance companies nick neurosurgeons in California for $30,000 a year."

As a client, the CMPA is a tradition around Major's firm. Harry Nolan, the counsel whose nerve used to challenge R. B. Bennett on New Year's Day, acted for the association. So, in later years, did Jim Milvain, then Herb Laycraft. Nolan eventually worked his way to a judgeship on the Supreme Court of Canada. Milvain became the chief justice of the trial division of the Alberta Supreme Court in the 1970s, and Laycraft sat under him as a puisne judge on the same court. Now the old client has become Major's preserve.

"It's common-sense work," Major said. "Get the doctor to explain in detail what went on and use a book called *Schmidt's Attorney's Dictionary of Medicine* to figure out what he's talking about. I develop a pretty solid knowledge of each particular medical situation that stays with me for a week, long enough to finish the trial. Then I forget it. It's the way I wrote exams at law school. I used to put off studying until the last possible moment. I'd piss around till eleven o'clock the night before the exam. Then I'd spend all night learning the subject, brush my teeth, write the exam, and forget it. Pretty much the same principle in a lawsuit."

That analysis brought Major to a summary of his attitude — singularly independent and irreverent, as it happens — towards the men who practise his own profession.

"Nobody's yet shown me a reason for lawyers to take themselves seriously. A guy who performs brain surgery, maybe I'd take him seriously, or the guy who works out the theory of relativity. But not the lawyer who argues a case in court. You're not going to sway anyone with your eloquence. Handling a case is nothing except common sense. Keep your perspective, show a little common sense, and don't get pompous about it. Oh, hell, lawyers are all right. It's the rare exception where you find one without a sense of loyalty to his client. Lawyers may be incompetent but they're trustworthy. And most of them have complete confidence in their own judgment. For myself, I believe I come to the right decision a hundred per cent of the time. If a judge disagrees with me, he's wrong."

Major was interrupted to tend to some peripheral matters. He kissed his youngest son good night, stroked the family kitten, and took a long-distance call from a client in Toronto. It was Barney Danson, the former Cabinet minister in the Trudeau government. Danson was making a pitch to launch a new airline in Ontario and had retained Major to represent him at the hearings before various government agencies. Airline law is another Major specialty. He satisfied Danson's immediate problems on the phone and returned to a discussion of malpractice suits.

"They bring out the weird side in everybody — doctors, patients, the judges even. You can never predict who's going to sue or why. Some guy may be horribly smashed in a car accident and the doctor performs miracles of surgery on him and the guy comes out in one piece except he's got a slightly bent arm. He's lucky to be walking around, but he still sues over the bent arm. Other people take much worse abuse from a doctor and never say a word. It has something to do with the doctor's bedside manner. If he's good with his patients in a psychological way, makes them feel content even while he's messing them up physically, he won't get sued. Patients know him, probably he's the family physician, and they wouldn't dream of taking him to court. Specialists get sued the most. They work the hardest and perform the most complicated surgery, but the patients don't know them, not like their regular doctors. So they gun in on the poor beleaguered specialists and let the family doctors off the hook."

Major laughed. "Doctors think it's the end of the world when a case against them gets reported in the newspapers. But people don't pay attention to that stuff. Nobody cares. In one way, maybe it'd be better if doctors' lawsuits got wider coverage, better for prospective patients, I mean. When a doctor's sued, the best time to visit him is in the next few months because that's when he's being extra-careful.

"You have to keep your sense of humour about the medical world. There was an eighty-year-old guy over here in the Foothills Hospital for a cataract operation. Something went wrong with the flow of oxygen from the wall tank. The auxiliary tank turned out to be empty, and while they were scrambling around for a replacement, the old guy suffered brain damage, went into a coma, and died. His family put a death notice in the paper that ended, 'In lieu of flowers, please send a donation to Foothills Hospital in the hope of promoting better medical care.' Foothills didn't care for that. No sense of humour."

Major fetched himself a glass, some ice cubes, and a bottle of Sprite.

"*Lepp* v. *Hopp*," he said. "It's a case that shows you how judges get tangled up in malpractice suits. I act for Phillip Hopp, the doctor, and right now the case is on the list for hearing by the Supreme Court of Canada. I don't know what they're gonna make of it, not after the horsing around at the appeal-court level."

Hopp set up his shingle as an orthopedic surgeon in Lethbridge, Alberta, in the early winter of 1974. He was busy developing his specialty when Ernie Lepp presented himself at the local hospital on February 25 of that year. Lepp complained of crippling pain in his lower back. He was a semi-retired farmer, sixty-six years old, and he said the agony had come on him suddenly the day before, hitting him in the left upper thigh, hip, and groin. The pain immobilized him. Hopp ran a myelogram and diagnosed the problem as "a disc prolapse or protrusion in the area of the fourth lumbar vertebra causing a portion of the disc to protrude into the spinal canal and to exert pressure on the spinal cord carried in the spinal canal." In layman's terms, Lepp suffered from a severe "slipped disc". Hopp operated on March 20 and removed parts of the protruding disc.

In the days that followed, Ernie Lepp said the pain hadn't entirely vanished. It hurt too much to take the physiotherapy that Hopp prescribed. Hopp shipped him to a Calgary hospital where a more sophisticated examination revealed that there was a larger protrusion, more bone than perhaps Hopp had been able to see on his equipment, still pressing on Lepp's spinal cord. The Calgary doctors removed it. Lepp came out of the second operation free of most of his pain, but he continued to list several complaints. He felt numb in the buttocks, penis, and testicles. He needed a cane to get around. And, most galling of all, he was impotent.

"Two or three times a week," he said, speaking of his life before February 24, "I had wonderful sexual relations."

Lepp decided to sue Dr. Hopp for negligence and assault.

"There's one hell of a crucial point in the case as far as all doctors are concerned," Major said, drinking his Sprite. "It was Hopp's first operation as an orthopedic surgeon. He'd done fifty or sixty of these slipped-disc jobs while he was training in Edmonton, but this was the first on his own. The plaintiff's lawyer, guy from Lethbridge named MacLean, made a big deal out of that. He argued it was Hopp's duty to inform Lepp he was going in for number one. He said if Lepp had known it was Hopp's first operation — Hopp didn't see any reason to mention it — he wouldn't have given his consent to the surgery. That's how the assault suit came into it. Where the person being operated on has consented under something like incomplete information or false pretences, then the doctor has in effect committed an assault when he touches the guy with his surgical instruments. The consent is cancelled out. So Lepp was asking for damages on two levels, negligence and assault, and the argument about the first operation tied into both of them. Does a doctor have a duty to tell a patient he's making his debut on the patient, so to speak?"

The trial took place in Lethbridge over four days at the end of April 1977 before Mr. Justice William Brennan of the Alberta Supreme Court. "My argument was pretty straightforward," Major said. "Hopp had spent four years getting himself qualified as an orthopedic surgeon, and since he was certified as competent in his specialty, he didn't have to tell Lepp whether it was his first or his four-hundredth slipped-disc operation. And I said he'd carried out the surgery properly at the time. No negligence." Mac-Lean, the plaintiff's lawyer, hammered at the first-operation issue in his examination-in-chief of Lepp at the trial and his cross-examination of Hopp. But the judge wasn't buying MacLean's argument.

Mr. Justice Brennan's judgment came down on Major's side at every point. He held that the extra protrusion in Lepp's spine, the one that the Calgary doctors ultimately removed, might not have been present at the time of Hopp's operation. It might have been a subsequent development. But even if it was present from the start, Hopp had made the only reasonable diagnosis of Lepp's condition and had carried out proper surgery. What's more, Lepp had suffered no damage from any of Hopp's actions since Lepp was already in physical trouble on the day he presented himself at the Lethbridge Hospital before Hopp had laid eyes, let alone scalpel, on him. Hopp, in Brennan's judgment, came up roses.

On the crucial question of disclosing the fact of the first operation, Brennan offered one word:

"Ridiculous."

Hopp was under no obligation to go into detail about the number of previous slipped-disc operations he'd carried out.

"Were I to hold otherwise," Brennan wrote in his judgment, "it could lead to a requirement that every doctor would be required to keep track of each and every operation of each and every type that he ever performed, so that he would then be in a position to fulfil the obligation upon him of informing the patient prior to performing a proposed operation of the number of such operations he had done in the past. To my mind, this would be nothing short of a ridiculous situation."

But MacLean appealed on behalf of Lepp, and two years later, in March 1979, after Major and MacLean had reargued the case before three members of the Alberta Court of Appeal, Hopp — and, by extension, the rest of Canada's surgeons — was back behind the eight ball.

"It was kind of a silly situation," Major said, still working on the Sprite. "The judges who heard our argument were Morrow, Prouse, and Haddad. Morrow's the famous judge. He used to act as counsel on the important Eskimo cases up in the Arctic, and before he got the job on the Alberta Appeal Court he was the judge in the Northwest Territories, Jack Sissons' successor. Morrow's wife once said about him, 'It's tough to be married to a man who's a legend in his own time.'

"What happened was that Prouse handed down a fast and short decision backing up everything that Brennan held at the trial. Morrow went off on a completely different tangent. He wrote a long twenty-one-page judgment that reviewed everybody's testimony. Well, he didn't say in so many words that Hopp had an obligation to tell Lepp it was his first operation, but he got on to the 'seriousness' of the surgery. He said Hopp failed to let Lepp know how *serious* the operation could be, and that was reason enough for Morrow to overrule Brennan. He found negligence and assault against Hopp and awarded Lepp $15,000 in damages."

Major straightened up in his chair, Sprite glass clutched in one outstretched hand.

"At that point," he said, generating suspense as he talked, "we're tied. One judge for Lepp, one for Hopp. But how about the third guy, Haddad? No word from him. Three, four, five days went by. He hadn't made up his mind. Who knew what was going on behind the scenes? Finally we got Haddad's decision. It was two words. 'I concur.'"

Major paused to rekindle the suspense.

"Who *with*?"

Major leaned back.

"With Morrow."

Lepp was now the winner. But later in 1979, Major went to the Supreme Court of Canada and won leave to appeal the judgment of the Alberta Appeal Court. He returned to

Calgary to sit out the long wait until the Supreme Court's docket allowed room for argument on *Lepp* v. *Hopp*.

"In the meantime," Major said, "the issue about first operations is still up in the air. Morrow didn't really decide whether a doctor has to advise his patient on that. Nobody knows the answer."

Major shook his head.

"Hopp, after the trial when he thought he was ahead, Hopp said to me, 'I'm going out tonight and get drunk.' He'd been under a lot of pressure and he was kind of a loner.

" 'All right,' I said, 'you ought to go with your friends, people from the hospital maybe.'

" 'I haven't got any friends,' he said."

Major polished off his Sprite.

"You never think of doctors as people with problems."

Next morning, another frigid and shiny Calgary day, Major opened a thick file of legal documents and spread them across his desk at Jones, Black.

"*Ares* v. *Venner*," he said, sweeping his hand over the documents. "Landmark decision in the Canadian law of evidence. It started out as simple malpractice, and when the Supreme Court of Canada got through with it, they'd overruled a decision in the House of Lords, the highest court in the common-law world."

Major sketched in the bare-bones facts of the case. Ares was a college kid, George Armand Ares, and one Sunday afternoon in February 1965 he went skiing on the hills near Jasper in the Rockies. He fell during a run at the end of the day and fractured his right leg a few inches below the knee. A ski patrol trekked him to the local hospital, Seton Hospital, run by the Sisters of Charity of St. Paul, where a doctor, one Albert Venner, a Jasper general practitioner with a specialty in internal medicine, put Ares's leg in a cast from toes to upper thigh. So far, so good.

In a couple of days, however, Ares's toes turned blue and

swollen. On Wednesday night Venner split the entire cast, didn't like what he saw, and dispatched Ares to a hospital in Edmonton. An orthopedic surgeon ran an arteriogram that revealed a block in circulation at the fracture site. Gangrene had set in. The leg deteriorated, the muscles wasting away from lack of blood, and on April 5 the Edmonton doctors amputated the leg at a point midway between the knee and the ankle. Ares sued Venner for negligence.

"When we got to court," Major went on, "it was before an Alberta Supreme Court judge named Michael O'Byrne, and my argument for Venner was that the lack of circulation in Ares's leg, the thing that led to all the trouble, was caused internally by something that broke in there in the impact of the skiing accident, something nobody could see. The cast, I said, the way Venner put it on, had nothing to do with the blockage or the circulation problem. We had an expert witness, a specialist who looked over the charts and the X-rays, and he testified that the lack of circulation had internal origins. No negligence on Venner's part. He followed proper procedure. That was my case."

Major sat very still in his chair as he talked. He's a steady man in more ways than one, a person of "equilibrium", in a favourite phrase of the west.

"The nurses' notes were the problem. These were the nurses at Seton Hospital in Jasper, and strictly as part of the routine, they made notes about the look of Ares's leg outside the cast. Turning blue, swelling, no feeling in the toes. Naturally I didn't want O'Byrne to hear that. The notes'd make Venner look bad. So I wasn't going to call the nurses as witnesses. Now, Ares's lawyer, Harold Veale from Edmonton, he didn't want to call the nurses either, because in malpractice cases nurses are always friendly to the doctor. But Veale was lusting to get those notes in evidence. How was he gonna do it without the nurses? Big question.

"Well, when we'd had discovery of Venner before the trial, Veale examining Venner under oath about different matters preparatory to the trial, the notes were tendered as part of the discovery. At the trial, Veale told O'Byrne he wanted to read Venner's discovery into the trial record. That was okay. But he wanted to read the *nurses' notes* as part of the discovery.

"I was on my feet in a flash.

"'Stop right there,' I said, self-righteous as hell because I knew the case law supported me. A long line of cases back to damn near the beginning of the common law held that notes like those were hearsay. That means they were second-hand evidence and only admissible as evidence at a trial if they're put in through the testimony of the people who made them, namely the nurses in this instance. I cited all the authorities to O'Byrne and sat down.

"Son of a bitch if he didn't rule against me. He let the notes be read from Venner's discovery and that was the turning-point for the case. O'Byrne looked at the stuff in the notes and said all the classic signs of circulatory impairment were right there for Venner to see back at Seton Hospital — the blue, the swelling, the numbness in the toes. He held that Venner had been negligent and gave Ares $29,000 for his amputated leg.

"I went straight to the Alberta Court of Appeal, and they said, hell, O'Byrne was crazy letting in the notes. All the case law was against O'Byrne, they said, and they ordered us to go back and start all over again at a new trial. Veale wasn't going to sit still for that, and he appealed the Court of Appeal's decision to the Supreme Court of Canada. We trucked down to Ottawa in the middle of February 1970. Jesus, it was cold. Anyway, this turned out to be the time when the Supreme Court decided to take poor old Venner and make his little case into a landmark judgment in the law of evidence."

Major pulled a thin bundle of papers, stapled together, out of the file of documents on his desk. He leafed quickly through the bundle and folded back a sheet at a paragraph marked in dark blue Pentel.

"Hospital notes," the marked section read, "including nurses' notes, made contemporaneously by someone having a personal knowledge of the matters then being recorded and under a duty to make the entry or record should be received in evidence as *prima facie* proof of the facts stated therein."

"Those are the words of Mr. Justice Hall," Major said. "He wrote the Supreme Court's judgment, and what the judges said they were doing in this decision was a little judicial trail-blazing. They looked at a 1965 judgment in the House of Lords that went the other way on hearsay evidence, the traditional way, and they said in so many words, the hell with it. Hall wrote that the courts had to keep up with the modern world. Maybe Parliament and the ten provincial legislatures could pass laws changing the rules of evidence as they relate to certain kinds of hearsay, but the Supreme Court wasn't going to wait for the legislatures to act. That's what Hall wrote. They were going to lay down some judge-made law. Too bad for Venner. The nurses' notes were now a fresh exception to the hearsay rule. They didn't have to be put in evidence through testimony from the witness stand. O'Byrne's judgment in the trial court was restored, and Ares collected $29,000."

Major stood up and adjusted the venetian blinds to let the view of the Rockies into his office.

"Well, okay, but the sad part of it to me is that something got lost in the shuffle of all the judicial juggling. It was Venner's reputation that got pushed aside. Temporarily, anyway. The Supreme Court was so busy settling the great evidence question that they made Venner out to be a worse doctor than he really is. He suffered because the judges were so preoccupied with the evidence question."

Major began to tidy up the stack of documents.

"Just to rub it in, the Supreme Court took a couple of months to arrive at their decision, not till late April, and somehow the judgment got into the newspapers before my

189

copy arrived in the mail from Ottawa. Venner didn't hear
about it in advance from my office. He read it on the front
pages. He was mad as shit at me. Can't blame him. He said
his kids were taunted at school that their father was a lousy
doctor. He moved his practice from Jasper to Edmonton.
Poor bastard. He's a perfectly competent doctor."

Major laughed. "Ares, the plaintiff, Jesus, I don't know
what he had in mind for his future before he lost half his
leg, but where he ended up was in law. He's practising today
with the Durocher firm up in Edmonton."

Major laughed again at something he'd almost forgotten.
"Ares's father got some yards out of the case. He's a chiropractor, and what with all the carping that chiropractors take
from doctors, he took the opportunity to get some of his
own back about the negligence of certain doctors."

Major folded shut the file cover on *Ares* v. *Venner*.

"Some of these cases," he said, "they're so damned
ludicrous."

Seventh Adjournment

Mal Kronby, short, dark, and looking like a better-groomed Al Pacino, strolled in straight from court, still wearing his gown, and sat down for lunch.

"Family law is the human comedy," he said, all very naturally, "and the case I got on today is something from the Marx Brothers."

This was in the lawyers' dining-room on the second floor of Osgoode Hall. It's a room that makes the law inescapable. The walls are lined with shelves of case reports. The vaulted ceiling suggests a Dickensian courtroom, and the stern portraits of nineteenth-century judges that ring the room might be characters from *Bleak House*. All of them, that is, except the dashing fellow in the painting at the north end of the chamber, William Osgoode himself, a mere thirty-seven years old when he was named first Chief Justice of Upper Canada in 1792.

"Kraft and Kraft," Kronby went on. "Nobody's over five feet and everybody delivers lines out of *A Day at the Races*. The issue is actually very simple. Mrs. Kraft obtained an interim judgment in 1973 for alimony from my client, Mr. Kraft, $100 a week. He didn't pay a penny. He went to Honduras and got mixed up in the fruit-juice business. Six years later the wife brought another action, this present one, to collect everything Kraft owed her and more.

Kraft's answer is he has no money. He lives on a pension from his son. Simple issue — what can Kraft pay today? But Mrs. Kraft's lawyer insists on parading through witnesses — I see Chico, Harpo, Groucho, even Margaret Dumont — and they all talk about big money deals that may or may not have taken place in Honduras in 1975."

Kronby raised his hand to signal for a menu, and the waitress placed it in front of him before he'd bothered to finish the gesture.

"By my count, we already have two witnesses who are skating at the edges of perjury, one who's making the noises of a double agent, and Mrs. Kraft's lawyer has taken the distinctly unusual step of impeaching a prime witness for his own client. This fellow — he's the suspected double agent — just will not give the answers from the stand that the lawyer has been led to expect, something about the witness standing guard in a Honduras hotel room over a pair of Mr. Kraft's pants from which he was temporarily absent and which were alleged to contain $20,000 cash. Is *that* the Marx Brothers or isn't it?"

Kronby unreeled a few more episodes. "Mrs. Kraft demands a Yiddish interpreter when she testifies, but she's answering in English before the interpreter starts translating. And her witnesses, the businessmen from Honduras, these are men with single-track minds. I can only get one answer out of them on cross-examination.

" 'What time of day is it?' I could ask.

" 'Kraft is the most evil bastard in the whole entire world,' they'd answer.

"It could only happen in a matrimonial case. The human comedy."

Kronby consulted the menu. It conspicuously omitted any mention of beer, wine, or spirits. Once, briefly, in the 1960s, the Osgoode dining-room offered alcoholic beverages at noon, but sales stuck at a figure far below the profit level. A few lawyers braved one dry sherry per meal, but the great majority were reluctant to be observed imbibing at midday by their peers or, more risky, by the judges who traditionally took lunch at a select table near the back entrance. The exception was an Irish professor from Osgoode Law School, a dazzling raconteur named Desmond Morton. He regularly washed down his lunch with three or four ales. Morton was the secret envy of the lawyers' dining-room.

"Cheese omelette and coffee, regular," Kronby ordered.

Mal Kronby grew up lower-middle-class, the only Jewish kid in the Beaches section of east-end Toronto. The rest of his life has been spent putting distance between himself and the old neighbourhood. He's managed it effortlessly. Class clings to the man. He's articulate, a lawyer who speaks in paragraphs. He dresses in combinations of tweed jackets, Cacharel shirts, and figured ties, a look of sophisticated *sportif* that would make Fred Astaire sigh in appreciation. He's a nice player of racquet games and cooks a fine Chinese meal in a wok. Consider his wife, Mimi, vivacious and bright, she puts in a full and admirable day as a social worker. Their two teen-aged sons go to schools for smart kids. Kronby is a flutist and every second Sunday afternoon sits in on a two-hour jazz workshop. Once, in some spare time, he took a solo flight in a single-engine plane.

"It was a hell of a rush, very exciting," he says. "But after that moment of glory I didn't see much point in continuing the exercise."

Kronby was called to the Ontario bar in 1959, and not much later, when he was working in a small general firm in downtown Toronto, an annulment case walked through the door that changed forever the direction of his practice.

"To call it an annulment case is to call Château Lafitte Rothschild a wine," he said. "Husband and wife were married in Canada. Husband at the time was ostensibly divorced, wife was indisputably widowed. Eventually they separated, and husband sued, alleging adultery on the wife's part. Wife — my client — denied the adultery. More to the point, she said, was that husband had a prior subsisting marriage from 1941 in Lithuania, that wife number one was still alive, and that husband and wife number one had never been divorced under Lithuanian law.

"We therefore counter-claimed for annulment on the grounds there had been no valid marriage in Canada, asked damages because the husband's allegations of adultery had tainted my client's reputation in the small Toronto Lithuanian community, and claimed more damages for assault on the basis that my client only consented to have sexual relations with him in the belief, which we could now show to be erroneous, that she was legally married to him.

"I looked at the facts and said to myself, 'This isn't a real case, this is a question from the Family Law exam at school.' And there was *more*. The husband admitted his 1941 Lithuanian marriage, but he raised a marvellous defence. He said the marriage wasn't valid because wife number one, at the time he married her, was still bound by a marriage she'd entered into in *Siberia*. Therefore he was free to marry wife number two in Canada. It was a gorgeous crossword puzzle.

"I had to make myself into an expert on marriage and divorce in Lithuania, *circa* 1941, and in the end I satisfied the court that the husband's Lithuanian marriage was still valid. The husband couldn't prove the Siberian marriage. We won.

"Years later, by a coincidence I relished, another case involving a marriage in Lithuania came into my office.

" 'Ah yes,' I said to the client as I reached very suavely for these old documents on my shelf, 'the Lithuanian situation. Very unique.'

"He was impressed."

Not long after the case had taken hold of Kronby's imagination, he and another lawyer opened their own firm with an eye to building a family-law practice. "Matrimonial law is like crabgrass," Kronby says. "Once it flourishes, it pushes everything else out." By the late 1960s Kronby's reputation as one of the three or four most accomplished lawyers in the Toronto divorce business was secure.

"The majority of lawyers avoid matrimonial law," he said, testing the texture of his cheese omelette. "Compared to it, commercial litigation is a picnic. Maybe a matrimonial case isn't always as complex in law, but that doesn't make it easy to deal with. It's the blood and hormones of the practice that most lawyers can't stand."

Kronby amplified.

"I handled a separation agreement for a woman. Reasonably routine. I sent her a modest account. She returned a cheque for half the amount along with a letter that said she was happy with the result and the service and the fee. She had nothing to complain about except that I wasn't—her words—*supportive enough*. Where did I fail her? I couldn't imagine. All I'm certain of is that more than in any other kind of law, clients look to you to be accessible. Pats on the back. Sometimes they call you at home for a pat on the back at three o'clock in the morning, which, all things considered, is a fairly likely hour for matrimonial emotions to run rampant."

Worst grief of all for a lawyer, Kronby went on, are divorce actions where custody of the children emerges as a raging issue.

"Higher authority," Kronby said, happy enough with the omelette. "That's who to turn to. In a custody action, naturally you have to protect your client's interest. Why else has he retained you? But you try to steer the client in a direction that will most help the kids, and that's the point at which you look to higher authority."

Such as?

"Here's a typical scenario. Husband and wife split. Wife wants to take the kids. Husband is ninety-nine per cent agreed. But husband's mother is screaming in his ear, 'What, Eddie? You're crazy! Leaving the children with that bitch? You're a better parent. Eddie, get the kids. For your

195

mama, Eddie.' All right, the lawyer on the other side and I convince our clients to let a psychiatrist assess everyone, and he comes down with a definitive analysis, the wife should have the children. Eddie heaves a sigh of relief. He's off the hook. He goes to his mother and says, 'It's for the best, ma. Higher authority.' "

As Kronby talked, another gowned lawyer passing by on the way to pay his lunch bill patted him on the shoulder, and smiled.

"Jim MacDonald of MacDonald and Ferrier," Kronby said when the man was out of hearing range. "He's one of the reasons why matrimonial practice is respectable and respected these days."

True enough, divorce lawyers of a couple of decades back carried an image of sleaze. Rigged adultery. Shady ladies. Private detectives breaking into hotel rooms with flash bulbs blinking at the evidence in the bed. The Archbishop of Canterbury, of all people, helped ease divorce out of the shadows with his 1966 pronouncement that irretrievable marriage breakdown was "an appropriate ground of divorce". The Divorce Act, largely the work of Senator Arthur Roebuck, followed in Canada a couple of years later, making it no longer necessary to base divorce on one party's fault. Grounds other than adultery—indeed, "irretrievable marriage breakdown"—put the private eyes and shady ladies out of business. And for Kronby and other Ontario matrimonial lawyers, the province's Family Law Reform Act, a 1978 statute, brought another measure of civility to their practice. Designed to avoid endless litigation, the Act declared that, at the break-up of a marriage, family assets must be equally divided and non-family assets might be divided at the court's discretion in shares between the former spouses.

"Then there was Jim MacDonald," Kronby said. "He made matrimonial law a specialty. It was principally through his pioneering that now we've got an excellent matrimonial bar in this city. It works to the advantage of both sides in a divorce action to hire lawyers who know the territory. Good matrimonial lawyers, specialists, identify the issues and move toward a settlement in a hurry. Get some general practitioner on a case, in over his head, and there's trouble."

Kronby loaded his coffee with cream and sugar. "A guy phoned me the other day, lawyer I know. He's acting for a husband and he says he doesn't think the wife's lawyer has read the Family Law Reform Act. 'The wife is settling for half the family assets,' he says, 'but she helped the husband set up his business, kept the books for a few years, and she's probably entitled to a share of the non-family assets. What do I do?' I told him he was under a duty to his client. If the case gets to court, the judge'll spot the discrepancy. It isn't the responsibility of the guy who phoned me to make the wife's case. Too bad she retained the wrong lawyer."

Kronby made the point that matrimonial lawyers routinely settle cases involving a couple of hundred thousand dollars. "It's easy to accumulate that much in family assets. But suppose that sum, $200,000, was the subject of dispute in a commercial case. The lawyers'd be overwhelmed by such a staggering amount and they'd fiddle for years over motions and pleadings and delays. In a matrimonial case, $200,000 is everyday money."

Seven hundred and seventy-four thousand dollars, on the other hand, is a figure that raises even Mal Kronby's cool a degree or two. It was the package amount, $774,000, he won for Mildred Bregman in a 1978 action against Sidney Bregman. "A very interesting little case," Kronby says, using his understated smile.

Sidney Bregman is a partner in Bregman and Hamann, a Toronto architectural and engineering firm that, among other lucrative jobs, served as project consultants on the Toronto-Dominion Centre and First Canadian Place and handled the engineering work for the Eaton Centre. By the time of the divorce action, Mr. Bregman had accumulated net assets of $2.8 million and enjoyed a gross annual income of $500,000. Mrs. Bregman, as the marriage disintegrated, wanted her share of the loot. Just before the contest went to trial, Kronby offered to settle at $900,000, a figure that included a division of the family assets, maintenance payments for the wife, support for the one child still at home, and a share of the business assets. Sidney Bregman's lawyer wouldn't move above $650,000. The parties went to court for five days in June 1978, and in the end Mr. Justice David Henry struck the bargain at $774,000.

"Maybe what the case is most illustrative of is the discretionary component the judge has under the Family Law Reform Act," Kronby said over his coffee. "This was a situation where the wife had worked while the husband finished his last couple of years at university, then stayed at home and looked after the kids while the husband went out and became a rich and famous architect. Beyond half the family assets, what's the wife's compensation?"

In Mr. Justice Henry's discretion, it was $300,000. "In my opinion," he was at pains to write in his careful forty-four-page judgment, "it would be inequitable in this case to limit Mrs. Bregman's share of the total assets to her share of the family assets. Taking Mr. Bregman's worth at $2.8 millions, I consider it fair to say that Mrs. Bregman's contribution to his ability to achieve it [and] her assumption of responsibilities [leaving] him free physically, intellectually and mentally to work at his profession and to manage his personal investments which are considerable entitles her to a share of the non-family assets accumulated by him to the extent of $300,000."

"As well," Kronby said, "we engaged in those intriguing wrangles over assets that might or might not have been considered part of the family property and therefore equally divisible between the two parties." The Oriental rugs, for example, and the Picasso and the forty-two-foot racing boat. Once again, after all of counsel's arguments were tallied up, it remained to Mr. Justice Henry's discretion to divvy the spoils.

Bregman got the boat. Value: $160,000. "I find," the judge wrote, "that this boat has been used almost exclusively by Mr. Bregman for sailing and entertaining. He is a serious sailor who participates in racing during the season from May 1 to mid-October. He uses it also as a means for entertaining business clients." But Kronby's arguments on behalf of Mrs. Bregman prevailed when it came to the Picasso, a $24,000 gouache. It had hung in Bregman's office for two years after its purchase in 1970, then in the study at the family home in the plush Forest Hill section of Toronto for three years, until, with the marriage disintegrating, Bregman spirited it back to his office. "I infer on all the evidence," Mr. Justice Henry held, "that Mr. Bregman, for whatever reason, decided in 1972 to make the Picasso part of the furnishings of his home, that when he removed it in 1975, that was an attempt, too late in the day, to alter its status again."

On the Oriental rugs, Kronby broke even. Bregman developed a passion for Oriental rugs as his career entered its harvest period. He hunted them down, studied them, coveted them, bought them. He had sixty of the rugs by the time the marriage ended, worth either $160,000, if Bregman's courtroom testimony were accepted, or $200,000, if the testimony of a rug expert called by Kronby were believed. Mr. Justice Henry went for the $200,000. But, his lordship pointed out, there were two categories of Oriental rugs in the collection. Some were on the walls and floors of the family home; others were kept in boxes by Bregman for "occasional inspection and display to guests and collectors". He held that the former were properly family assets and the latter belonged exclusively to Bregman. A saw-off.

"Needless to say," Kronby said, finishing off his coffee, "I found the case a challenge and a delight."

He paid for lunch and made his way to a courtroom on the fourth floor of the building across the street from Osgoode Hall. Kraft and Kraft, the version of matrimonial law's human comedy according to the Marx Brothers, was resuming after the noon recess. One of Mrs. Kraft's witnesses, another of the bitter business rivals of Mr. Kraft, was on the stand, a crumpled man with the face of a failed vaudeville performer. Kronby cross-examined him.

Kronby: "You started an action against the Home Juice Company, the Honduras company with which Mr. Kraft was associated, in January 1979. Is that correct?"

Witness: "I did. Yeah."

Kronby: "An affidavit of merits was filed on behalf of the defendant in April 1979, right?"

Witness: "Yeah."

Kronby: "Since then, nothing has proceeded. What has happened to your case in the last six months?"

Witness: "It slept."

Kronby turned slowly and looked at the man in the witness stand.

"It slept," Kronby repeated. "Ah, *le mot juste*."

He wore a look of deep appreciation.

CHAPTER SEVEN

The Children's Crusader

It was on the day of the old man's heart attack that life seemed to turn finally hopeless for "Jim Oliver" (not the boy's real name). He was twelve years old when the old man had the attack, on a snowy day in December 1977, and he'd already seen a share of trouble. Earlier in the year the police caught him with a trail bike that had been stolen from another boy. A Family Court judge heard the police's evidence and decided Jim was guilty of possession of stolen property. The judge declared Jim a juvenile delinquent. His mother and father found him sniffing glue. His father strapped him. At school Jim was placed in a class for slow learners. He couldn't read, not even street signs. Other kids called him a dummy. Life was sour. And then the old man had the attack.

It happened after school. Jim was in a gang of boys who were packing snowballs and hurling them at any handy target, themselves, street lights, houses. They threw at one house and the old man who owned it came out of his door and chased the boys down the street. "Get away, you little buggers," he yelled. The boys ran out of his range and the old man turned back home. He climbed the stairs to his front door, grabbed his chest, and fell down. He was dead.

Someone told the police that Jim was in the gang, and a constable from the Youth Bureau was in the Oliver house by dinner-time. "Why do you pick on Jim?" Mrs. Oliver said to the constable. "He's told me what happened. There were other boys in on it. Why are you here? At this house? Why *Jim?*" The constable took Jim to the police station and asked him questions. He didn't lay a charge, but the police kept an eye on Jim in the following months, and on February 9, 1978, he was back in the same Family Court, accused of stealing a package of Export A cigarettes from an A & P store.

It was Judge Warren Durham's Family Court in Brampton, Ontario. Brampton is the judicial centre for the Regional Municipality of Peel in southern Ontario. Much of Peel is made up of Mississauga, a sprawling, densely populated community next door to Toronto on the west. Many of its residents commute from Mississauga to jobs in Toronto. Jim Oliver's father is one of them. He works as a mechanic. He and Jim's mother moved up from Nova Scotia in 1964 with their children, all ten of them. Two of the older kids had run into grief with the law. Michael, in his twenties now and settled down to a job in a warehouse, spent two months in training-school for stealing a car when he was younger. Paul, three years older than Jim, was put on probation for stealing a motorcycle. Jim was the youngest and the most troubled.

Judge Warren Durham thought so. He's a soft-spoken, gentle man in his early fifties. He wears a neatly trimmed beard that gives him a dashing look, and in the summertime he likes to push off in his sailboat, the *Jennie*, and cruise down Lake Ontario. He practised law in the town of Oakville, just west of Mississauga, specializing in family litigation, and he was appointed to the Family Court in Brampton in the spring of 1974. His manner is leisurely, as if nothing—no senior judge, no overloaded court docket, no anxious lawyer, no disturbed kid—could push him to an unconsidered decision.

In Jim Oliver, he recognized, he says, "a boy who was suffering, the kind of thing I'm too familiar with in this job." Jim appeared in his court four times from winter to early summer of 1978 as Judge Durham searched to find help for him. Jim was locked into the system. Once a boy has been declared a juvenile delinquent under the provincial Juvenile Delinquents Act, a step that a Family Court judge may take when he's convinced the child has committed a criminal offence, then the judge can shuffle him into all sorts of slots. He can place the kid in a foster home, commit him to an industrial school, leave the child at home on condition that he report to a probation officer, or improvise some other solution.

"The potential power I have over a kid is enormous," Judge Durham says. "I can keep jerking him back into my court till he's eighteen years old."

When the judge first saw Jim on the charge of the stolen trail bike and declared him a juvenile delinquent, he merely adjourned the case *sine die*, to a future indefinite date that might never arrive. He was giving Jim another chance. Jim couldn't handle it, and when he came back to court, pleading guilty to stealing the Export As, Judge Durham ransacked his options for another answer.

Nothing worked.

A new school didn't work. For the last few months of the school year, April to June 1978, Jim was switched to a school that ran a special class for kids with learning disabilities. He was baffled. He reacted against the class. He'd chew gum and blow bubbles. He'd pretend to faint and crash from his seat to the floor. The other kids laughed, and the teacher of the special class threw up his hands.

The Clarke Institute of Psychiatry in Toronto didn't work. A psychiatrist talked to Jim and the rest of the Olivers and wasn't optimistic. "The relationship between the Oliver children," the psychiatrist wrote in his report, "tended to be superficial. Each seemed to go his own way. Weak members are not carried and in the case of Jim are allowed to go it alone." But, the psychiatrist wrote, "the snowball incident had a profound effect on them all, particularly Mrs. Oliver.

They suddenly became very aware of Jim's problems and very guilty because of their earlier lack of concern. They are dealing with this guilt now by becoming very protective of him and projecting their anger at outside agencies, particularly at school. At present, they feel hopeless."

Judge Durham adjourned Jim's case from February 9 to April 6 to June 16 to July 27, each time hearing reports on Jim's stumbling life, each time postponing his final decision, each time looking for help in finding a solution.

"All right," he said in court on July 27, "if ever a child needs a child's advocate, someone who acts for him in court and for no other individual or agency or bureaucracy, then that child is Jim."

He adjourned the case once again until Jim had a lawyer of his own. The lawyer turned out to be Jeffery Wilson, and it was Jeffery Wilson more than anyone else who directed the rescuing of Jim Oliver.

Wilson looks like a kid himself. He's in his late twenties, and he has a slight build, a heart-shaped face, and a big puff of dark hair. His words rush when he talks, and what comes out is a jumble of eagerness and expertise. He's smart and he's competitive. Another lawyer, a slightly older man who, years ago, was Wilson's counsellor at summer camp, remembers this of him as a camper: "Jeffery went all out in everything, every sport, every activity, but you couldn't call him an over-achiever because he achieved anything he set out to do."

Wilson practises alone in a bright, airy set of offices in the ancient and refurbished Gooderham Building in downtown Toronto, built in 1892 and nicknamed the Flatiron Building for its curious wedge shape. The décor in Wilson's own office reflects his passion. On the walls there are framed black-and-white photographs of kids playing games, kids hugging adults, kids laughing so loud you can almost hear their voices in the room. A copy of Lewis Carroll's *The Annotated Alice* lies on a shelf behind Wilson's chair, and Mordecai Richler's *Jacob Two-Two Meets The*

Hooded Fang cozies up to it. Wilson earns his money by handling divorce actions and drawing separation agreements, but he puts his emotions — along with his brains — on the line when he acts for kids like Jim Oliver.

"People come in here with a big alimony case," he says, "and I tell them, 'The fee you pay me will help some kid.' I lose money on the children and pay the freight with the adults."

Wilson is a founding member of Justice For Children, an outfit that, in the Ralph Nader style, takes on causes and cases on behalf of kids. He wrote a textbook for lawyers, *Children and The Law*, nine chapters, 367 pages, eighteen pages of indexes and eighteen of cited cases, all the law there is that touches on children and on, as Wilson writes in the book's preface, their "powerless and repressed status". That's Wilson. With no prompting he'll make statements like this, the words tumbling over one another: "Everybody has his agent in society. The worker has his union, the manager has his corporation. But who's the child's agent? He's got none. At the very least, when he comes before a court, *any* court, Family Court, the Supreme Court, when his parents are arguing over his custody, he should have representation. If he isn't part of the decision-making process, then whatever decision is arrived at isn't going to work."

All of which leaves a question. Why? Why does Wilson say such sensible and unexpected things? Why Justice For Children? Why *Alice* and *Jacob Two-Two*? Why? Wilson's a bachelor. Why the kids?

Maybe part of the answer surfaces from his past. When Jeffery Wilson was a boy, not yet a teenager, one of his parents died. Some months later, the surviving parent died. At the second funeral, as the service was about to begin, young Jeffery ran down the aisle.

"You promised me," he cried. "You promised me it'd never happen again."

"That cry," someone who was at the funeral remembers, a

friend of Jeffery's older brother, Steve, "that cry was the most heart-rending sound I've every heard."

An uncle looked after Steve and Jeffery. He was a social worker and the director of a summer camp, and the two brothers turned out just fine.

Wilson got his call to the Ontario bar in March 1978, and from the start he geared himself to represent kids in court. He acted for thirty of them during his first year of practice. Most arrived in his office through referrals from other lawyers. A few came because they'd seen him on television championing Justice For Children. In Wilson they recognized someone dramatically different from their notion of a lawyer.

"The use of the child's advocate is still very limited," Judge Durham says. "In my court there are exactly twelve lawyers, busy practitioners, who'll give their time to act for kids. That's because it takes a special breed of cat to do the job. Family Court isn't a place for the adversary system. You don't want to waste a lot of ammunition trying to prove the kid isn't technically guilty. Ninety-five per cent of them plead guilty anyway. The reason the child's advocate is in court is to come up with ideas that'll help the kid after he leaves here."

When Judge Durham asked in court for a lawyer to represent Jim Oliver, his words were more a suggestion than an order, since he had no power to compel a child to be represented. But a student from Osgoode Hall Law School was in court that day. Judge Durham encourages law students to hang around his Family Court on the premise that maybe they can help a kid who needs a steer in the right legal direction. The student at Jim's hearing left the courtroom and phoned Jeffery Wilson, whose reputation he knew. A meeting was set up with the Oliver family, and, since they couldn't afford to pay a lawyer's fee, the Ontario Legal Aid was rung in. By September 13 Wilson had a certificate from Legal Aid to take on the case.

He interviewed the Olivers in their home. He spent time

with Jim. And he came away convinced of a couple of things.

"Jim's problem has everything to do with learning," he said. "I saw that right away. He's one of those sad kids who can't make connections in his head. He can be taught to do it by people who really give a damn about teaching him. But he isn't getting it right now. That's his trouble. All the other stuff, stealing the cigarettes and fooling around with the trail bike, they're just a reflection of his frustration with an educational system that can't even teach him to read."

Maybe, Wilson figured, the Toronto Learning Centre had an answer to Jim's problem. The Centre makes a specialty of reclaiming kids, usually kids with learning disabilities, whom public schools have failed to reach. "Most of our youngsters," said Ray Carlaw, TLC principal at the time Wilson approached it on behalf of Jim, "come to us in a rather demoralized state. They're the losers of the world. They've been dumped off in basements or they've been given the back room of some place because, you know, we really don't want to expose learning-disabled youngsters to the normal kids in the world." The TLC isn't a back room. It operates out of tidy and tranquil quarters in an office building in North Toronto. It gets results through patient, upbeat, and concentrated teaching methods. It has a staff of forty for 154 students. It exudes optimism. It is very expensive — $6,800 per student per year.

Wilson inspected the Centre and persuaded it to inspect Jim. Inspecting Jim wasn't easy. "When you talk to him," Carlaw said, "you must refocus him in to you constantly in order to get him to look at you and talk to you, snap him back into what you're doing because he tends to wander." Still, Carlaw was confident that, sure, the Centre had a program that would equip Jim to deal with words and numbers and street signs. One problem, though, Carlaw told Wilson. He'd better move fast or two things might happen — there wouldn't be room for Jim at the Centre and, besides, it could be too late for Jim.

And the money? The Centre's $6,800 tuition fee? Who was to come up with the cash for Jim?

"That's where things may hit the fan," Wilson said. He had a brainstorm. It was to ask Judge Durham for an order making the Region of Peel responsible for paying Jim's way at the TLC. He'd rely on Section 20(2) of the Juvenile Delinquents Act, which says that "In every case it is within the power of the Court to make an Order upon the parent or parents, or *upon the municipality to which the child belongs* [italics mine], to contribute to the child's support such sum as the Court may determine...." The potential flaw in Wilson's scheme lay in the word "support". Did the definition of "support" include education? Wilson thought the answer ought to be in the affirmative. But would Judge Durham agree with him? Wilson set to work preparing his argument. There were, alas, no cases that defined "support", and no other lawyers, it seemed, had tried to use Section 20(2) of the Juvenile Delinquents Act to manoeuvre a municipality into paying for a child's education. Wilson was starting from scratch. He needed Scotch tape and paper-clips to hold his argument together. There was only one element that was certain — the Regional Municipality of Peel would oppose the role of paymaster that Wilson was about to assign it. When it got notice of the Jim Oliver case, things would heat up.

The Brampton Courthouse, where the case was heard on November 7, 1978, is a smart new two-storey brick building that sits in strange isolation in fields far south of Brampton's business and residential areas. Inside, Judge Durham's Family Court is small and functional and hints at friendliness. The docket showed eleven cases for the seventh, a busy day, but the judge was prepared to give all the time and attention that was necessary to get through the Oliver case. It began at ten o'clock and continued past the lunch break until 2:20 before Jeffery Wilson had finished calling his witnesses and presenting his arguments.

As Wilson performed, Jim Oliver sat beside him at the

counsel table. Jim worked on his nails, not randomly and nervously but with a surgeon's dedication. He'd study one nail for two or three minutes, then bite it sharply with his front teeth. More study, more trimming, then a close inspection to ensure that all nails were retreating toward the quick at the same rate. His face, hunched over the nails, gave away no expression. It kept to a protective blankness. It was a wary teenager's face. It had a light touch of acne. His body showed the same signs of adolescence, of new muscles growing. He was slim, about five feet five, and wore his dark hair in a neat and conservative cut. He was neatly and conservatively dressed, too. A patterned shirt, jeans, white socks, and soft Hush Puppies. He worked on his nails.

Wilson called six witnesses: the principal of the Peel school that Jim attended during the last three months of the previous spring; Ray Carlaw from the Toronto Learning Centre; the executive director of a counselling agency for teenagers in Peel; a social worker from the Peel Board of Education; Jim's mother; and, very briefly, Jim himself. A simple pattern emerged from Wilson's questioning. Peel's public schools, the witnesses told the court, couldn't teach Jim. Jim would benefit from the Toronto Learning Centre's methods. And when he began to learn to do things he'd never managed before, to read, then his hassles with the police would fade away.

"I think Jim's behavioural problem is a manifestation of incorrect educational programming," Ray Carlaw told the court in his testimony, echoing Wilson's own earlier analysis. "I don't believe he really is a behavioural problem. I think he's acting out of frustration, and I think if I was as learning-disabled as he is, I would act out as well."

Carlaw made a strong witness, confident and skilled, occasionally angry, sometimes dramatic. Wilson asked him to outline to the court a program for Jim at the Centre. Carlaw's answer was long and thorough, but at one point it boiled down the Centre's approach to a few powerful words.

"I would set Jim up in a program where first of all we will have optimum success," Carlaw said, his voice rising, the volume stepped up. "Optimum success. We will not allow failure. Failure will *not* occur."

Wilson smiled at the words. Judge Durham quickened his note-taking. Jim's attention switched off his nails and focused on Carlaw. The other witnesses, sitting on the public benches, shifted and stirred. something unmistakable filled the courtroom. It was nothing less than a sense of hope. This kid, this Jim whose life had been so irredeemably lousy, so drenched in defeat, was going to be rescued. Carlaw's words represented a turning-point in the hearing. From the moment he spoke them, the odds began to run in Jim Oliver's favour, and everybody in the courtroom recognized the rising sense of hope.

Policewoman Grant recognized it. She spoke for the crown at the hearing, a correct, no-nonsense woman in her forties who worked for the Peel Youth Bureau. She sat at the crown's table, serving as the Family Court equivalent of the prosecutor, but she called no witnesses, cross-examined Wilson's witnesses perfunctorily, and when it came time to present the crown's argument, told Judge Durham that "I can only say from what I have heard this morning that I really cannot disagree with Mr. Wilson in terms of what is in Jim's best interests." Policewoman Grant wasn't going to quell the sense of hope.

Wilson's argument lasted almost thirty minutes. His job was to provide Judge Durham with precedents in earlier and accepted law that he could rely on to make an order directing Peel to pay for Jim's tuition at the Learning Centre. Wilson talked first of a "necessary". The word came from an 1891 English decision by the Court of Queen's Bench. It held that, for an infant, education was like food and clothing, a "necessary". Aha, Wilson was saying to Judge Durham, you *see*. The Ontario Juvenile Delinquents Act says you can order a municipality to pay for a delinquent kid's "support". And how is "support" to be con-

210

strued? Very broadly, broadly enough to include education, as broadly as the way in which the old Court of Queen's Bench construed "necessary".

Wilson, standing at the counsel table, making sudden hand gestures at the stack of papers in front of him, bending over quickly to check a reference in a case-book, his body in constant, tense movement, cited more old decisions. And more. Sometimes he'd disappear into a thicket of case law, out of the sight and comprehension of everyone in the courtroom except Judge Durham. Then he'd reappear with a few sentences that would unmistakably link Jim Oliver's immediate situation to the musty concepts left over from century-old English judgments.

"In Jim's circumstances," he said, still hammering at the union of "necessary" and "support", "he will not be able to learn a trade without the special education he needs. I asked the question specifically of Mr. Carlaw, who gave me a very blunt response that if Jim does not get the education he needs, then his chances of succeeding in society — and I'm just recollecting this — it was something like nil."

"Support", Wilson was saying in short, equals "necessary", and both embrace education.

Judge Durham nodded.

Wilson took on Section 20 of the Juvenile Delinquents Act, the section under which the judge would make his order. He had more cases. He had Ontario Supreme Court decisions to show that when a Family Court judge makes a support order against a municipality, thereby compelling the municipality to spend taxpayers' money, he should balance "the child's own good and the best interests of the community".

"Well, I argue most respectfully," Wilson said to the judge, "that this is a case where these two things — child's own good and best interests of the community — absolutely coincide. This community will suffer if the interests of this child are not satisfied with a proper education."

Wilson sat down.

"This is indeed a sad court," Judge Durham said. "It's a place where the community regularly brings their frustrations."

The two sentences began his judgment. He could have adjourned the hearing for a couple of weeks and mulled over the judgment in his chambers. Instead, he chose to wing it, to dictate his decision off the top of his head for all in the courtroom to hear and for the court reporter to record. It took more than half an hour. Judge Durham liked to ramble and to touch all bases. He reviewed each witness's testimony in detail. He unloaded a blast at the Peel Board of Education. "I don't know that Jim has failed school," he said. "I think the school system has failed Jim." He offered his own definition of education and praised the Toronto Learning Centre. He began to wind towards the nitty-gritty of his decision. Wilson moved restlessly in his chair. Judge Durham said he liked the 1891 case from the Court of Queen's Bench that Wilson had brought him. "I notice one of the judges was talking about the circumstances of being 'in this working-class England where it's so necessary to learn a trade', and I was impressed in thinking how strongly those words carry on almost ninety years later."

Yes, Judge Durham went on, education is a "necessary" for Jim. Yes, he needs this support. I will order it, and, yes, Peel must pay. He moved swiftly to the end of his judgment. He was using Section 20 of the Juvenile Delinquents Act to direct Jim to attend the Toronto Learning Centre for the balance of the school year beginning the very next day. He ordered the Regional Municipality of Peel to send a cheque to the Centre for $5,780 covering tuition for the balance of the year. And he adjourned the case until June 28, 1979, when all parties would once again appear before him for another assessment of Jim's situation.

Judge Durham smiled at Jim and banged his gavel.

"His judgments," Wilson said in the corridor outside the

courtroom, "they're like the *Whole Earth Catalogue*. You read through a lot of philosophy and sociology before you finally get to the law. But, hell, he's on the same wavelength as me. Thank God."

Jim stood in the corridor with his mother. He was wearing his blank expression. Ray Carlaw walked up to him. He shook Jim's hand and said he looked forward to seeing him in school the next day. Jim smiled. His face revealed something no one in the courtroom had seen. Two deep dimples.

Back in his office, Wilson waited for trouble. "Quite frankly," he wrote later in the week to one of Jim's teachers at the TLC, "when I cynically consider the worthwhile and beneficial implications of this decision for the purpose of ensuring all children an education, I would not be surprised if this bureaucracy, as with others, strains the success of the decision by various appeals to higher court."

Within a few days, Wilson's mail turned up a letter from Osler, Hoskin and Harcourt. It ranks among the two or three most high-powered law firms in Toronto. It boasts seventy-three lawyers and two floors of slick offices in First Canadian Place on King Street. One of its clients is the Regional Municipality of Peel. The letter let Wilson know that Peel had instructed Osler, Hoskin to launch an appeal of Judge Durham's decision. But, the letter went on, the appeal would be delayed because the member of the firm's litigation department who tended to Peel's business, J. Edgar Sexton by name, was tied up for several weeks running a complicated prosecution on behalf of the federal government under the Combines Investigation Act.

"Those guys, they're wheeling out the heavy artillery," Wilson said, and he set to work moving paper in and out of his office. Letters, legal memos, notes for his argument on the appeal. He exchanged several letters with Osler, Hoskin to arrange for Peel to pay Jim's tuition at the TLC even while the appeal was in the works. He drew his bill for fees and disbursements in Jim's case and mailed it to the Ontario

Legal Aid, $1,031.56—or about thirty-five cents an hour for all of Wilson's time. He wrote letters recruiting witnesses to appear at Jim's June hearing before Judge Durham. He received a note from a woman named Rosemary Underwood of the Ontario Association for Children with Learning Disabilities saying she'd heard about the Oliver case and offering her expertise. Wilson sent back a letter welcoming her aboard. And he enclosed a cheque for fifty dollars, a donation to Mrs. Underwood's association.

Early in March, Osler, Hoskin served Wilson with its Record in *Peel* v. *Oliver*. The firm's first step in the appeal procedure was to bring a motion before a judge of the Ontario Supreme Court requesting leave to appeal. If the judge decided there was merit in Osler, Hoskin's argument, then he'd send on the case for a full-scale appeal hearing before another Supreme Court justice. The Record set out the argument that Osler, Hoskin would present on the first motion. It came bound in bright blue covers, forty-three pages of submissions and cited cases and quoted law.

Wilson was impressed. "Some of it makes me edgy," he said. "I mean it's strong, especially the stuff about necessaries."

He was referring to paragraphs 39 and 40 of the Record, the crunch in Osler, Hoskin's argument.

39. It is submitted that insofar as schooling of the Respondent Oliver may be considered a necessary of life, this schooling is provided by the public education system at no cost. The public education system in the Province of Ontario provides both regular programs and special education programs for children with learning disabilities such as that experienced by the Respondent. It is submitted that education as a necessary of life for the Respondent should be interpreted as restricted to these programs provided in the public education system. Anything more is not educational as a necessary of life, but remedial treatment.

40. It is submitted that the parents of the Respondent should pay for any special private schooling of the Respondent over and above that provided by the public education system.

"Maybe they're right," Wilson said. "Right in law, I mean."

He stayed in his office late into the night for most of a week preparing his reply to Osler, Hoskin's arguments, his Respondent's Statement. It ran to thirty-eight pages, enclosed in a tan folder, and it repeated in different phrasing all of the points he'd made to Judge Durham. He read it over several times, made changes, inserted new case citations, had his secretary retype it, and then, struggling against his reluctance to let the Statement out of his hands, released it to be served on Osler, Hoskin.

"Fat's in the fire now," he said, shrugging.

In the meantime, through the winter and spring, Wilson checked in regularly with the Oliver family. The reports on Jim's progress were positive. He'd missed only two days of school at the Learning Centre and he was beginning to find a handle on books and the printed word.

"He likes school, he smiles a lot," Wilson said. "But he thinks the cops are out to get him because he's doing such neat stuff at the Centre."

The cops got him. On April 21, a month after Jim's fourteenth birthday, he walked out of a Canadian Tire store with a tail-light and a generator for a bicycle. He hadn't paid—$5.18—and a security guard spotted him. The police laid another delinquency charge against Jim. Wilson arranged to have it dealt with during the June appearance before Judge Durham.

And there was another problem. Ritalin. It's a drug that acts as a calming agent on children who might otherwise be restless or hyperactive. The TLC used Ritalin on Jim, 120 milligrams a day in pills that he took at nine in the morning, noon, and three in the afternoon.

"At the Centre," Wilson said, "they prescribe Ritalin like

jelly beans. I worry. I'll fight like hell to keep him in the place, but I'll fight like hell to get him off Ritalin. I hate drugs."

Osler, Hoskin's motion for leave to appeal reached court on May 29. It was to be heard at Osgoode Hall in Weekly Court, a forum where lawyers appear before a Supreme Court judge, without clients or witnesses present, to argue issues that have to do more with procedure than with substance. Wilson arrived at Osgoode at 9:15 that morning carrying a fat briefcase and accompanied by a bearded law student who was along to help with the manual labour, running for books and chasing down last-minute references. The two men collected armloads of case-books from the Osgoode library and carried them into the courtroom where Mr. Justice Richard Holland was presiding over Weekly Court. The room was small and elaborately decorated in gilt and in regal colours. The judge, a man with a plummy accent and the face of a basset hound, sat high on his bench at one end of the room, and below him the well of the courtroom was crowded with lawyers in long black gowns, vests, tabs, and winged collars. The Queen's Counsel occupied the front of the court, beyond a low barrier, and the rest of the counsel distributed themselves on benches that sloped upwards toward the back of the courtroom.

J. Edgar Sexton wasn't among the lawyers on either side of the barrier.

"Steve Smart," a brisk young man whispered, sliding onto a bench beside Wilson and holding out his hand. "Osler, Hoskin. Sexton's out of town. Matter of some importance. We're asking to have the motion adjourned."

Wilson looked unperturbed. "Sure," he said. "Okay."

Smart waited his turn on the list of matters scheduled for hearing that day.

"M'lord," he finally began, pausing while an elderly and vague court clerk handed up to the judge the thick stack of documents in *Peel* v. *Oliver*. "M'lord, we are respectfully requesting an adjournment."

Smart's voice took on an even, measured quality, a drone, and the lines came out of his mouth at a practised clip as if he'd mastered them long ago.

"Case of real importance," he told the judge. "Constitutional questions ultimately involved...motion will need several hours to argue...our Mr. Sexton to take the appellant's brief...held up out of town under circumstances of some urgency...."

Mr. Justice Holland seemed relieved. The list of cases was already long enough, and he'd grant the adjournment. Wilson got to his feet and requested protection for Jim during the adjournment. He got what he wanted.

"I'm endorsing the papers," the judge said as he wrote on a document in front of him, "with an order that the Family Court judge's program in respect to the Respondent is to go ahead until this court, the Supreme Court, orders him to stop."

Wilson and Smart bowed in the direction of Mr. Justice Holland's bench and headed quickly out of Osgoode Hall, gowns flying, to the building across the street. They were going to ask the Registrar of the Supreme Court to assign them a special Weekly Court date when the motion could be heard.

"No way I'm gonna do that," the Registrar told them in his office. He had a W. C. Fields air. He'd seen it all and wasn't impressed. "You say it'll take half a day to argue? That means *all* day. I don't believe anything lawyers tell me. I'll put you on the list waiting for cancellations — *Peel* v. *Oliver* is it? — but you're way down the line."

There was a sense of anticlimax to the morning — all that preparation, all that machinery cranked up, for a motion that wasn't heard and now might be heard only in the unpredictable future — but Wilson gave off no sense of exasperation.

217

"Part of the law business," he said. "You wind yourself up and then nothing happens. Osler was entitled to an adjournment. It was only the first time up for the motion. I expected anything to go on. Or nothing."

Wilson walked back to his office.

On June 27, the day before Jim's case was to return to Judge Durham's court, the Supreme Court of Canada got into the act. That was the date it handed down its oral decision in the case of *Viking Homes* v. *Peel*. It was another case that originated with Judge Durham. In January 1975 and again in April 1976 he had acted under that handy section of the Juvenile Delinquents Act, Section 20, to commit two delinquent kids to the care of a group home for troubled adolescents run by a private company called Viking Homes. He'd also ordered Peel Region to pay $43 per day for each kid's upkeep. Peel, represented by J. Edgar Sexton, appealed the decision. Mr. Justice John Holland — no relation to Mr. Justice Richard Holland — held that Judge Durham had exceeded his authority. Under Section 20, Mr. Justice Holland ruled, Judge Durham could commit a delinquent child to an industrial school or a foster home or a children's aid society, or to a parent or a probation officer, or to any "other suitable person". But he couldn't commit the child to a group home like Viking because it didn't qualify as "other suitable person". Viking took the case to the Ontario Court of Appeal. The Appeal Court agreed with Mr. Justice Holland. So, as of June 27, did the Supreme Court of Canada.

Judge Durham had been slapped down by the highest court in the land, but he'd long since made a new legal play under Section 20. Shortly after Mr. Justice Holland's decision in the Viking case in the spring of 1977, Judge Durham ordered a young girl who appeared before him, a suicidal teenager, to be delivered into the care of a former policeman named Tom MacKenzie. By no coincidence, Tom MacKenzie happened to be a supervisor at Viking Homes. More ways than one to skin a cat, Judge Durham said, as he

218

directed MacKenzie, who qualified, in the judge's view, as an "other suitable person" under Section 20, to take the suicidal teenager to live at Viking Homes under his supervision. And who was to pay her expenses, $43 a day? Why, the Region of Peel.

Peel once again appealed Judge Durham's decision, and while the appeal was winding through the judicial system, the judge received an unexpected visitor. Madame Justice Mabel Van Camp of the Supreme Court of Ontario came calling on him in his chambers at the Brampton Courthouse. It was a winter day close to Christmas 1977, and Madame Justice Van Camp had no appointment and had sent no advance notice. Supreme Court justices, according to fixed custom, don't just drop in on lesser members of the bench, announced or unannounced.

"I couldn't figure it out," Judge Durham said afterwards. "She chatted for twenty minutes. She said Supreme Court people didn't get out of their courts enough and see the world. She was interested in the dynamics of my court, how I function, that kind of thing. Strange visit but, you know, *nice*."

During the chat, Judge Durham didn't mention the Viking case. He had no reason to. Madame Justice Van Camp didn't mention it either. She had a reason for her silence. Not long after her visit, a decision came down from the Supreme Court on Peel's appeal of Judge Durham's order placing the young girl in Tom MacKenzie's custody. The decision turned down the appeal, holding that this time Judge Durham had acted within his powers under the Juvenile Delinquents Act. Tom MacKenzie qualified as an "other suitable person" in Section 20's terms and Peel must pay for the girl's upkeep in the Viking home. The decision was written by Madame Justice Van Camp.

"Now that," Judge Durham said, "*that* caught me by surprise."

"What a humane thing to do!" Jeffery Wilson said when he heard the news of Madame Justice Van Camp's visit to

219

Judge Durham. "But, you know, it was a real break that the appeal went to Van Camp. Just mention kids in her court and her eyes water up."

Peel took the Van Camp decision to the Ontario Court of Appeal. But the appeal hadn't yet come on for argument by June of 1979, and, going into Judge Durham's court, Wilson was left to contend with the Supreme Court of Canada's ruling in the first Viking case.

"Sure, it says a Family Court judge can't commit a kid to a group home," he said. "But the Toronto Learning Centre isn't a group home. My situation is different from the Viking case. If it comes up in front of Durham, I can distinguish it. No problem."

He paused.

"I don't *think* there's a problem."

Wilson wasn't bothered either by Jim's fresh trouble with the Peel police, the $5.18 theft from the Canadian Tire store. "It's one of those situations," he explained, "where I say, 'Oh, you naughty boy,' but inside I'm glad because this new charge'll help me argue that Jim ought to be kept at the Centre till his head is really straight."

The hearing on June 29, a serene summer day, got under way in Judge Durham's courtroom at two o'clock in the afternoon. Jim Oliver sat beside Wilson at the counsel's table. He'd grown since the previous November. So had his fingernails. He looked huskier, a little taller, and he'd abandoned the surgeon's approach to his nails. His face, though, still gave away no emotion. His mask was in place, and if he'd grown to trust the people in the courtroom he wasn't letting them know.

Two men took their places at the crown's table. One, bulky, wearing a snappy sports coat and a genial expression, addressed the court only once during the afternoon. "I'm just here about the money," he told Judge Durham, smiling. He was a lawyer from the Peel offices and his job was to report back to his bosses on the sum Judge Durham might order the municipality to pay for Jim's schooling.

The other crown representative was from the Peel Youth Bureau, Sergeant Tom Crossin, a heavy man in his early fifties, deadpan expression, greying hair cut short, the look of an intimidator. But, like Policewoman Grant at the November hearing, Sergeant Crossin took a distant second place to Jeffery Wilson in the proceedings. At one point Sergeant Crossin suggested to Judge Durham that Jim might be better off in a training-school learning a trade, and he raised an objection to the cost of the Learning Centre, now up to $7,400 a year. Judge Durham brushed him off. Gently.

"Crossin's a nice guy as these people go," Wilson said during a short recess in the hearing. "I've seen cops in that job who'd say, 'Okay, Jim, you got off this time, but wait'll you turn sixteen. We'll be watching for you.'"

Wilson called seven witnesses to the stand.

"Jim was a problem when he came to the Centre," Jim's teacher, a dark, handsome woman in her early thirties, testified. "He was learning at a mid-grade-one level. Now he's at the grade-three level with potential for grade five, and he's one of the most conscientious workers I've come across."

The second witness heaped more praise on Jim. She was the head of the Centre's junior school, a bright-faced, confident woman. "When Jim came, he was a hunched-over, defeated-looking young man," she said. "Later I saw a big smile on his face, and I came to know him as an outspoken, polite, and charming gentleman."

A psychologist from the Family Court Clinic at the Clarke Institute testified about the effects of Ritalin. "It's positive for Jim," he said. "It gets at an organic problem. Jim's mind, you see, jumps around. That's reflected in his physical jitteriness. Without the Ritalin he's mentally all over the place. But as a permanent solution, well, research is just starting on whether the need for Ritalin is everlasting."

What about the stealing, Wilson asked, the theft from the Canadian Tire store?

221

"It's remarkable he hasn't done more than just take a bicycle generator," the psychologist answered. "The thing is, he knows there's a chance he may not go back to the Toronto Learning Centre, and that's upsetting him. The stealing was a way of asking for help."

Rosemary Underwood stepped to the witness stand, an assured woman wearing a frilly dress with a flowered pattern. She told the court she was executive director of the Ontario Association for Children with Learning Disabilities. "A learning disability," she said, "has to do with the neurological or nervous system. With Jim it affects his ability to listen. It's as if there's a part in him missing, and he has trouble just paying attention."

Is there an answer, Wilson asked, a solution for Jim?

"For children with learning disabilities," Mrs. Underwood answered, "you can't just get at the social and emotional factors. You have to get at education, and group homes and training-schools are no good for that. They just lead to frustration and failure. This $7,400 at the Toronto Learning Centre isn't out of line for helping Jim. If he was taken out of the Centre at this stage, society would end up paying a lot more in welfare and crime and unemployment insurance. Jim'd become a liability on the community. It would be traumatic not to let him stay at the Centre. Most unkind. Most inhumane."

"See what I'm doing?" Wilson said during the recess. "I'm piling on the evidence that the Centre is in the best interests of the kid and so on, and then whenever Osler, Hoskin gets us into court on appeal, I've got everything in my favour on the record. The crown doesn't like what's happening, though. They're mad at me for taking the whole afternoon."

Wilson called more witnesses: the principal of the Centre, Mrs. Oliver, and Jim.

For Jim's testimony, Wilson moved out from behind the counsel table where he'd stood to question the other witnesses and took up a position, almost intimately close, beside the witness-box. He leaned in towards Jim. Almost everyone in the courtroom, Jim's teachers and his mother, Mrs. Underwood and the Clarke Institute psychologist, strained in their seats, willing that the boy would perform, that he'd come up with the right answers, *impressive* answers.

Wilson: "Jim, you try and speak up loud enough so that everybody in the room, right down to the back seats there, can hear you. Okay? Now, Jim, what's good about the Toronto Learning Centre?"
Jim: "Get more teaching there."
Wilson: "What about the teachers?"
Jim: "They're nice."
Wilson: "Do you want to go back?"
Jim: "I need an education."
Wilson: "Why is that, Jim?"
Jim: "I want to learn to drive. I want to read good enough so I can drive a truck."
Wilson: "What's that in your hand there, Jim, your report card?"
Jim: "Report card, yeah."
Judge Durham: "May I see it, Jim?"

The judge looked at the report card. Jim let his head hang down, studying the floor of the witness-box. The courtroom fell utterly silent.

Judge Durham: "A very good report, Jim. Good for you."
Wilson: "What about this offence, Jim, the bicycle generator that you took from the store? Do you have any idea why you took it?"
Jim: "No."
Judge Durham: "Why did you do it, Jim?"
Jim: "I don't know. I wanted it."
Judge Durham: "Will you do it again?"
Jim: "No. I know I won't."

For the first time, with his last words, Jim's voice lost the monotone he'd used to answer the other questions. His voice rang through clearly. He was almost animated. He was also scared.

Wilson: "No more questions, Your Honour."
Judge Durham: "All right, Jim, you go back to your seat."

The judge held out his hand to stop Jim.
"Jim," he said, "I've always liked and respected you."
The teachers from the Centre, sitting in a group at the back of the courtroom, murmured to one another. They smiled. The kid, they told themselves, had done all right.
Wilson's address to Judge Durham, twenty-five minutes long, covered familiar territory. The Learning Centre, he said, was the place for Jim. "The municipality, Peel, has had plenty of time to come up with another plan," Wilson said. "But it hasn't thought of any real alternative to the Centre." Section 20 of the Juvenile Delinquents Act, he went on, gave the judge enough power to act in Jim's best interests. He cited the cases and authorities. He avoided mention of the Supreme Court of Canada's oral judgment of the day before in the Viking case. "With Jim," Wilson finished, "he's just seeking a fair deal under the Juvenile Delinquents Act."
As before, Judge Durham dictated his judgment. As before, it was thorough and labyrinthine and heavy on digressions. Ritalin took him up one path. "A lot of thought has gone into the treatment, but in the case of Ritalin, I wish there was another way. Maybe the people at the Centre will find it." He took another detour to slap down the government's tendency to tuck kids with learning disabilities into provincial training-schools. "A training-school costs $93 a day. That's staggering. And the point is that the children go into these places and come out no better than they were before. But if they're properly educated, then they stay in society and turn into productive people."
The judge joined in the silent conspiracy with Wilson to avoid the Supreme Court's Viking decision. Not relevant, he implied, not in Jim's case anyway. But, again as before, he went over each witness's testimony. "There's even more

evidence than there was last time, back in November, that the only way Jim's going to get on a good course in life is for him to stay at the Centre. I'm not going to put him in one of those invisible agencies that the government runs. It'll be my order that Jim stays at the Toronto Learning Centre. Since the parents can't afford it, I direct the municipality to pay the fees. That's $7,400 in four instalments."

It was almost 5:30. Sergeant Crossin stood up. "Your Honour," he said, "I've got baseball. There are fifteen boys waiting for their coach. Me."

"Okay, sergeant," Judge Durham said. "Good luck with the game."

He looked down at Jim. "On the theft from the Canadian Tire store, Jim, I'm fining you ten dollars."

Jim held the judge's gaze.

"That's your own money, remember," Judge Durham said. "Not anybody else's."

Jim nodded.

"All right," the judge went on, "we'll adjourn now till a year from now, June 26, at 9:30 a.m., and we'll see how we've all made out."

He banged his gavel.

In the corridor outside the courtroom, Jim offered a display of dimples. The people from the Learning Centre took turns shaking his hand. They congratulated him on the day. Then they congratulated themselves.

In his chambers, Judge Durham contemplated a puzzle. "Jim's the first kid I've sent to that place, the TLC. Funny, I keep thinking it stands for Tender Loving Care. Anyway," he said, his judge's robe hung on a hook, his shirt undone at the top button, "he's the first, and it's working for him, and Peel's paying the shot. So I wonder how come other lawyers haven't come into my court and asked me to give their kids the same treatment? I thought there'd be a line-up to follow Jeffery Wilson's example. Aren't there any more lawyers out there thinking like him? Beats me why not."

The next day Wilson wrote letters of thanks to each of his

witnesses. He wrote to Jim reminding him to pay the ten-dollar fine and to hold on to the receipt. He added a short paragraph to the end of the letter: "I do not have to say anything about a repeat performance with respect to taking things which are not yours. That will only get in the way of your desire to get an education."

At Osler, Hoskin and Harcourt, J. Edgar Sexton waited for instructions from Peel. Wilson waited, too. On July 25 he received word from Osler, Hoskin that they'd be bringing a motion in the Supreme Court to quash both orders of Judge Durham, the one of November 8, 1978, and the other of June 29, 1979, and to ask for leave to appeal the orders. Then silence set in, months of it. Jim went back to the Toronto Learning Centre in the fall, Peel continued to pay his tuition fees, and Osler, Hoskin made no move to pursue the case into higher court, no motion to quash, no motion for leave to appeal.

"It's just temporarily stuck in the works somewhere at Peel or Osler, Hoskin," Wilson said in his office one afternoon late in the autumn. "The day of reckoning is inevitable, the day when we'll get up in court and argue all these points about what a judge can or can't do under the Juvenile Delinquents Act. We'll thrash at everything. We'll go at the Supreme Court's decision in the Viking case. Nothing gets ignored in this business. All the chickens come home to roost eventually."

Wilson was sitting at his desk under the photographs of the laughing children, the *Annotated Alice*, and *Jacob Two-Two Meets The Hooded Fang*. He talked quickly and he was, as always, all energy and tension.

"None of this really matters as far as Jim's concerned," he said. "He's the winner because while the rest of us are sitting around waiting to go back to court, he's at the TLC and he'll get enough education to become what he wants to be in life. A truck driver."

Wilson smiled, a swift smile that came and went, a beatific smile, lighting up his face for just an instant.

"That's my job — right? — getting Jim an education."

Wilson stood up. He had other things to get on with. He was taking part in a public panel discussion that night at the St. Lawrence Hall. The subject was "The Children of Divorced Parents".

Epilogue

Igor Kaplan, a tall, elegant, droll gentleman in his early fifties, may have been the end of my search. I hadn't been looking for the *perfect* lawyer. It was enough that I found myself enlightened by so many lawyers in so many fields who showed me the skill and decency and wit they brought to their practices. But I held on to the faint expectation that somewhere among all those Canadian practitioners there was one who might fairly be labelled the "all-round lawyer". The notion reached back to the impossible image I'd formed years earlier for myself as "an all-round practitioner, a little criminal work, some dabbling at the higher reaches of corporate negotiations, a few more humble services along the lines of assisting old ladies to redraw their wills and young couples to arrange their first house purchase". Igor Kaplan, it turned out, was close to the dream.

By the time I met him, Kaplan's reputation was secure as "Conrad Black's lawyer". Black was, in turn, "the Boy Wonder of Canadian Business", to borrow *Fortune* magazine's title, the young controlling wizard behind a dazzling group of Canadian corporations that centred on Hollinger Argus Limited and included such heavyweights as Massey-Ferguson, Standard Broadcasting, and Dominion Stores. And it was Kaplan who offered whatever lawyerly advice the Boy Wonder called for. But before he arrived at Black's right hand—by a bizarre circumstance which we'll come to —Kaplan had been a criminal lawyer, a general practitioner, a one-man operation. He had dabbled in every sort of law. He was authentically an all-rounder. Kaplan was special. He was irreverent, funny, generous, and canny.

Irreverent?

"Most people in corporate law take themselves very, very seriously," he told me one morning sitting in his office at the Aird and Berlis firm on King Street West in Toronto. "The theory is that the big-buck work has to go to them in their big firms because they're the only lawyers who have the brains to handle the business. I disagree. There's no magic in corporate work. The guy sitting down with two immigrant butchers to hammer out a partnership agreement is doing the same thing as the guy who makes out an agreement between Massey-Ferguson and Hollinger. I should know. I've done both."

Funny?

"To John Turner I was a nobody at first. I'd begun to attend meetings with Conrad, gatherings of the big movers and shakers in the corporate world, and Turner would nod at me as if I was a puzzle to him in those surroundings. Probably I was. Then he learned the reason why I was at the meetings. I was 'Conrad Black's lawyer'. I was a somebody. All of a sudden John Turner's arm was around my shoulder and I'd become 'Igor'.

" 'Well, Igor,' he said to me one day, 'why don't you think about coming over to our firm? There's always room for you at McMillan, Binch.'

" 'But John,' I said, 'I didn't know McMillan, Binch took in Jews.' "

Telling the story, Kaplan was wearing the deadpan expression, the George Burns look, that he saves for funny stories.

"I have to hand it to Turner," Kaplan finished. "He told

me McMillan, Binch did hire minority groups and they'd have to improve their public relations."

Generous?

Brian Greenspan, a specialist in criminal appeal work, tells a story about Kaplan. "Samuel Ciglen was a big commercial lawyer in Toronto in his day, a Q.C. before most of us were born. He got himself into a bunch of deals, most of them shady. He went to jail. He came out and got into more trouble. By then he was in his seventies and down to his pension and not much more. He lived with his wife, who had the townhouse and whatever money was left, and in 1977 or so he was about to go on trial for fraud. He came to the Legal Aid Committee to ask for a lawyer to defend him for free.

"I was one of the five guys on the panel hearing the application, and it was Igor who walked in to argue it on behalf of Ciglen. He was appearing without fee. He wanted to establish the precedent that when a man is bust and his wife has a bit of money, there's no reason to refuse him a legal-aid certificate. I thought it was a good argument. But Igor lost, four to one. He appealed our decision to the Supreme Court. Again without fee. Again he lost.

"The point is that Igor had no self-interest in the case. When Ciglen went to trial, Igor wasn't going to defend the man and collect the legal-aid fee. There was only one reason why he took the time and trouble to argue the application and the appeal. Once, way back when Igor was starting up in practice, Ciglen did him a favour.

"Igor didn't forget."

Canny?

To demonstrate Kaplan's creative turn of mind, it's necessary first to grasp the intricacies of the first and possibly most crucial step in the building of Conrad Black's corporate empire. This goes back to March 15, 1978, the day on which Bud McDougald died at his winter home in Palm Beach, Florida. At the time of his death, McDougald was president of Argus Corporation, the mighty holding company that was founded in 1945 by E. P. Taylor and two other Canadian businessmen. Argus thrived over the years — the value of an original share climbed from ten dollars in 1945 to over ten times that much, including a preferred-share distribution, in 1978 — and from the time he assumed the presidency on Taylor's retirement in 1971, Bud McDougald was Argus's guiding genius.

McDougald was also central to another holding company called Ravelston Corporation. It was set up in 1969 by the owners of Argus to bind themselves more closely together, and Ravelston in effect controlled Argus. When McDougald died, Ravelston broke down into five owner-ship shares. Two blocks of 23.6 per cent each were owned by McDougald's widow, Maude, and by her sister, Doris Phillips, the widow of yet another old Argus hand, Eric Phillips. A further 26.5 per cent was held by Maxwell Meighen, a financier and the son of former Prime Minister Arthur Meighen. Argus's executive vice-president, General Bruce Matthews, owned 3.9 per cent, and the Black brothers — Conrad and his older and equally brainy sibling, Montagu — held the remaining 22.4 per cent, a slice they had purchased from their father, who was once a Taylor associate and had been an Argus board member for sixteen years.

Bud McDougald had always been close to Conrad, the wily old baron dropping bits of wisdom to the emerging young tycoon, and he no doubt expected Black eventually to succeed him at Argus. But Maxwell Meighen didn't par-ticularly share McDougald's admiration, and at the first Argus board meeting after the death of McDougald, Meighen led the way in freezing Conrad and Montagu out of posts of authority in the company. Conrad fought back, and the principal weapon of his fight was a curious provi-sion in the 1969 Ravelston shareholders' agreement that allowed a majority of shareholders, for any reason they wanted, to force a minority to sell out to them.

"The purpose of the provision," Kaplan explained, "was

231

in case one of the bunch got senile or died and left his share to heirs that the rest thought were lightweights."

On May 15, 1978, the Blacks entered into an agreement with the two widows, Mrs. McDougald and Mrs. Phillips, under which the three groups would vote as a block in Ravelston over the following ten years. The move gave Conrad control over nearly 70 per cent of Ravelston's shares.

"Part of the *quid pro quo* to the ladies on the deal," Kaplan further explained, "was that until the death of old General Matthews, whom the ladies liked, Conrad and Montagu would leave his shares alone. That surprised me because Matthews' 4 per cent could kill them under certain circumstances."

Two days after the agreement with the widows, the Blacks served notice on Meighen pursuant to the 1969 provision that they wished to buy his 26.5 per cent of Ravelston. All seemed secure for the Blacks until late June, when the widows pulled a swift manoeuvre. Repudiating the May 15 agreement with the Blacks, they set out unilaterally to purchase General Matthews' 4 per cent, the very emergency that Kaplan had feared. If the widows succeeded, they would have control of slightly over 51 per cent of Ravelston, which would put them in a position, alas, to shaft Conrad and Montagu. The move came as a shock to Conrad. Only a week earlier, the widows, knowing that Conrad was an admirer of Napoleon, had sent him as a gift a bust of Bonaparte. Still, it appeared that the ladies, prodded on by a third sister, Cecil Hedstrom, a topnotch real-estate saleswoman, and by another real-estate developer named John Prusac, meant business. Bad business for the Blacks. At that point Kaplan began to make moves like a lawyer.

"On the day that Conrad heard about the ladies' ploy," Kaplan recalled, "he phoned me at home to tell me, eleven o'clock at night. I stayed awake thinking the thing through and went into the office at four in the morning. More lawyers gathered, five of us maybe, and we began to talk through the options. I mean, that was when you felt the responsibility of corporate law."

Kaplan had a scheme.

"This turned out to be my one big contribution to the whole enterprise. I took it on myself to sign an agreement on behalf of the two ladies to sell their shares in Ravelston to the Blacks. I decided I could sign the agreement for them. I don't know to this day whether I was right or wrong. I don't have to know any more. But I took the position I was their attorney-in-law. We had the agreement with them from May 15 that they'd join in with us. So, okay, it was unique in law in that I could get a court to give me specific perform-ance of that agreement. I had what's called an equitable right. If I had that, why not go all the way and sign their names to an agreement to sell to us."

There was more.

"We also drafted a writ suing the ladies for piles of money. That was a very carefully drawn writ. I consulted Peter Atkinson, the head of litigation at Aird and Berlis, and he put plenty of thought into it. Then I phoned up the ladies' lawyers and told them, if it came to the crisis, we'd issue it."

The squeeze play aided the Black cause. The ladies backed off, and in the early summer they sold their Ravelston interest to the Blacks for $18.4 million. In due course Conrad and Montagu bought out Meighen's 26.5 per cent and went about the business of streamlining Argus, which they now controlled through Ravelston. Over the following couple of years they carried out a complex shift that converted Argus from a holding to an operating company, made Hollinger Argus the parent outfit in the stockpile of corporations, rescued one of its failing sub-sidiaries, Massey-Ferguson (taking it from a $250 million loss in 1978 to a $30 million profit in '79), and generally behaved like high-class entrepreneurs. And Igor Kaplan was along for more than the ride.

Kaplan's credentials, going back to the roots, were hardly

the stuff of Bay Street boardrooms. He came from Windsor, Ontario, took a B.A. at Assumption College (now the University of Windsor), proceeded to Osgoode Hall, and articled at the Windsor firm of Yuffy and Yuffy. After his call in 1955 he went looking for clients in Toronto, *any* clients. He handled general work, but he relished criminal cases. He liked digging into the pits of magistrates' court and provincial court. He slugged it out with crown attorneys. And he kept a sense of idealism about his battles.

"One time I was at a party talking in a group to a Supreme Court judge," he said, reminiscing in his office. "This judge said he was sorry he wasn't going to be able to hear a rape case he was scheduled to sit on the next day. He had to attend a funeral. He was sorry, he said, because he knew the case was good. How did he know? He wasn't supposed to have a clue about the case until evidence was presented before him in court. Well, he knew because he'd already got a report on the facts from the Attorney General's office. It seems it was a practice that'd been going on for a long time, getting AG's reports. But judges didn't receive similar reports from defence counsel. I was shocked. I talked about it to other criminal lawyers, and we wrote to the Lord Chancellor in England and asked if that was the custom over there. The Lord Chancellor fired back a letter, certainly it was *not* the custom. Eventually word about all this spread, and not long after, the habit, those AG's reports, was cut out."

Kaplan swung along, practising law. He had partners. He went on his own. He shifted offices. He ran into trouble; some non-legal investments turned sour and he was forced to declare personal bankruptcy. He took in strange and exciting clients; for one lengthy period he hustled around Ontario fending off prosecutions for a sporting gent who was pioneering off-track betting in the province. Kaplan practised to the hilt.

Then one day Conrad Black got himself nailed by a traffic cop on an improper-change-of-lane charge, and

Kaplan's life and career began to undergo a radical shift. Black himself, a man with a blocky build, a deceptively offhand air, and a surprisingly candid way of expressing himself, tells the story best.

"It was 1974 and I was moving down from Montreal to Toronto," he says. "My parents had already been living here for years, of course, and on the drive down, I'd reached a point about half a mile from my parents' house, still on the 401, when some ignoramus stormed into the highway and rammed me. The police got their signals crossed and ended up charging me. It was completely spurious. But I told a friend of mine about it, David Smith, the fellow who once ran for mayor of Toronto, and he got Igor on it. I don't know what happened — I think perhaps the cop didn't show up in court and the charge was dismissed — but Igor took care of it. I liked him. My brother and I were in Draper, Dobie then, the brokerage firm, and Igor tended to the legalities over there for us. When my parents both died in June 1976, Igor looked after the estates. And he came along with us as we got busier in corporate work."

But why Kaplan? Why him rather than an established Bay Street firm?

"Most lawyers are as dry as parsley," Black says. "They lack humanity. Igor isn't like that. He's enjoyed the benefit of not having led the sheltered life that the rest of corporate lawyers are burdened with. Once, I know, when Igor was much younger, he worked as a clerk at the Lasalle Hotel in Montreal, a place where the manager regularly parcelled out gifts to the police for reasons I needn't go into. Igor's different. Most corporate lawyers, you see, represent themselves as uncommitted dispensers of opinion. They take refuge in judge-like impartiality, so that if anything goes wrong, it's the fault of the witless client. Igor, on the contrary, identifies with his clients. He fights for them, and as one of those clients I appreciate his partisanship."

Kaplan prepared himself for the responsibilities of the

Black empire by hurrying up to York University to earn a Master of Laws degree. (He also took time to proof-read the galleys of Black's massive 743-page biography of Quebec's former premier, Maurice Duplessis.) But the big crunch came when Black suggested Kaplan cast around for a large firm to attach himself to. As a single-lawyer operation, he lacked the manpower and the hardware to turn out the paperwork that Black demanded, all those corporate documents. Which explains how the Jewish grad from Assumption, steeped in the tradition of Yuffy and Yuffy, ended up in an office down the carpeted corridor from John Aird, Scots and blunt, grandson of a president of the Bank of Commerce, recruited by C. D. Howe as a Liberal party bagman, director of more than thirty significant corporations, and senior partner in Aird and Berlis, which is as Establishment as a corporate firm can get.

"Guys like John Aird are at the very top," Kaplan explained in his office. "They negotiate and wheel and deal, and I don't mean that in the pejorative sense. The senator" — although Aird resigned his senatorship in 1974 to avoid conflict with his new role as head of the Institute for Research on Public Policy, he's still referred to by one and all as "the senator"— "doesn't have to do anything except sit on boards. He practises his negotiation skills at their meetings and brings business into the office. He knows everybody. Suppose I wanted to see a deputy minister in Ottawa. I'd phone him and he'd see me all right, but it'd be for ten minutes three weeks from Friday. If the senator phoned the same deputy minister for me, it's an appointment tomorrow at eleven o'clock."

And how did Kaplan, the distinct outsider, go about relating to the old guard at Aird and Berlis?

"I'm a great believer in asking people for help who aren't corporate lawyers," Kaplan said. "They'll see things in a way that isn't the usual. That's how it is with me in this firm. I have a different eye because I arrived here from a general practice. We have meetings, discuss office matters, and it

236

always seems to be me alone on one side against the rest. But that's good. Good for everybody."

Kaplan settled into a fresh career at Aird and Berlis. His life assumed a new rhythm, three parts serendipity to one part razzle-dazzle. He lived in a luxury apartment on Lake Ontario, played plenty of tennis, and, divorced, dated a selection of gorgeous and bright women. He developed the habit of arriving early at Aird and Berlis, 6:30 a.m., after a sweet stroll from his apartment. He made himself a cup of coffee, lit a cigarette—one of many—and gave thought to the plots Conrad Black was hatching for that day.

"The stuff I do for Conrad," Kaplan said to me, "might surprise you."

Such as?

"Lunches. I make appointments for him to have lunch with people I think might interest him. I arranged a luncheon date with Arthur Maloney just because Arthur is one of the great courtroom advocates this country has ever known. A guy came through from New York City who is the number one advisor to the Murchison family, the Texas billionaires. He was on his way to Ottawa to see the Minister of Consumer and Corporate Affairs, and I thought Conrad should take a lunch to see him. I set up another lunch with a woman who was a pensions expert and couldn't sell the message about the things that were wrong with pensions at Massey-Ferguson to the people under Conrad. These lunches, they're not things I bill Conrad for or docket as time spent on the Black account. They're not within a corporate lawyer's real capacity."

In the traditional line of work, a corporate lawyer's more usual function, Kaplan discovered that his duties fell into two general categories.

"Black will think of something, some takeover or merger or other corporate deal," Kaplan said. "He'll phone me, explain it, and say, will it fly? I'll answer yes or no or I don't know. Usually it's I don't know. I check it out. I sit down and read. The Corporations Act. The Securities Act. When I have an answer—faster preferably to slower—I phone him back. That's called legal advice. Then there's another kind of advice."

The other kind is called political advice.

"If you've worked with people over a number of years, especially when the people have a personal stake, a family interest, in their businesses—the Black brothers, the Eaton family, the Bronfmans—then you fall into the habit of offering advice that nobody's really asked you for."

Kaplan had an example.

"Nelson Davis was on the Argus board from 1977. He was a great Canadian businessman, put together his own consortium of companies over many years, and he was seen as a source of respectability behind Argus. His presence, so the thinking went, gave the young whippersnappers who ran Argus, the Blacks and their friends, some credibility. Well, in March 1979 Nelson Davis died in the swimming-pool of his monster estate north of Phoenix, Arizona, and his death made some people figure something might go wrong at Argus. As it happened, the week after Davis died he was scheduled to be re-elected to the board of directors at Crown Trust, a company that the Blacks have a big share of. I phoned Conrad and Monty and said, 'Why don't you ask Nelson's son, Glen, to stand in his father's place?' Glen accepted. He was delighted. He went on the board, and by being there he showed that the Davis power was still behind Argus. That wasn't a lawyer's conventional role, making the suggestion, but it was servicing the client."

At Aird and Berlis, Kaplan continued to tend to a number of clients apart from the Blacks. "Just to keep my hand in," he said. He drew wills for ladies who'd been coming to him since his days in slightly less grand quarters. And he wouldn't turn down a nice fraud case, something that would put him, the old defence lawyer, back in the criminal pits. But principally his time was devoted to the Black interests.

"It's only powerful men who run large corporations, not Mr. Milquetoasts," Kaplan said, "and the more powerful they become, the more satraps and kowtowers they attract. Conrad once said that only ten people in the world tell him the truth, the rest tell him what they think he wants to hear. A lawyer can't be a yes-man. It's the legal advisor's job to be among Conrad's ten truth-speakers."

Some corporate lawyers judged Kaplan's methods to be perhaps a trifle unorthodox. "I admire what he's done for the Blacks," Jim Tory told me. "I once had lunch with Igor and he said he didn't know anything. He admitted it. He said a problem came along and he retired to the library until he came away with an answer. I've no doubt that system is good for a fresh flavour to any problem.

"But," Tory went on in his gently reluctant style, "I don't know if it's enough in the long run. You need so many pieces of advice, so much knowledge, you need to be so *large* to do corporate work."

Kaplan appreciated such views of his approach. He rejoiced in them. But he was too busy at his work and fun to pause and question himself.

"It's been a fascinating experience for me from the time I met Conrad," Kaplan said. "There are one hundred people who run this city. They do it in the back boardrooms and over lunch at the Toronto Club, which is the last bastion of Old Toronto. That's where it's decided who's going to get the money from the banks to do whatever it is they have in mind. And there I came from out of left field, taking a hand in the process, even when it's just as an observer.

"I remember the first time I was elected to a board of directors. It was Crown Trust, and Conrad suggested I should go on the board. After the meeting, after my election, a Crown Trust functionary came over to me.

" 'Congratulations, Mr. Kaplan,' he said. 'Another directorship for your string.'

" 'Yeah,' I told him. 'A string of one.' "

239

Still, for all the joy and laughs he found in the heady reaches of the corporate world, Kaplan never forgot where he came from.

"From a social standpoint, it's the general practitioner who's number one," he summed up. "He acts on impaired-driving charges, divorces, house deals, draws your will, settles your estate. He has to read like a maniac to keep up with everything, criminal reports, civil reports. That man renders a legal service to a very large segment of the community, and for the most part he does it very well. I consider the general practitioner to be the most noble lawyer of them all."

When he delivered homilies like that, speaking of what he knew from long and close and occasionally painful experience, Kaplan made my dream of dazzling myself and the legal world as "an all-round practitioner, a little criminal work, some dabbling at the higher reaches of corporate negotiations..." seem a possibility. Almost a reality. But it was an old dream, a personal dream, that had faded long ago and died a death that I mourned just barely.

I admired all the lawyers I spoke to in the course of the odyssey that began so incidentally in the courtroom where I'd testified on Keith Richards' behalf. "Poke around in the profession," Richards' lawyer, Austin Cooper, had suggested to me. I poked and I listened.

"It's a game," Shelly Altman told me, speaking of his criminal-law practice. "But seriously played." I believed him. I believed Paul Moore of Tory, Tory when he talked of feeling "socially useful, a productive member of society" in arranging corporate takeovers and mergers, and I believed Jack Major, the Calgary counsel, when he claimed, partly in earnest, partly in jest, that the way the law often works is "so goddamned ludicrous". They'd told me stories that went with their views, Altman and Moore and Major and the others, and I'd found in the stories enlightenment and laughs and even significance.

Epilogue

Maybe, I recognized, I'd confined my conversations with the legal profession to lawyers who were both savvy and honest. Maybe I'd ignored the shysters among them, the lawyers who look only for their own edge and don't bring any sense of service to their hapless clients. Maybe. But that wasn't the point. I'd set out deliberately to hunt down lawyers who stirred my respect, to find out what separated me, the indifferent lawyer of years ago, from the guys who had such grand talents for the profession. I found the lawyers. I found enough answers.

And I found Igor Kaplan, the one lawyer who, more than the others, had lived the old dream I'd had, the dream of the all-round practitioner. I felt satisfied.